JN250730

Existential Sentences from
the Diachronic and Synchronic Perspectives:
A Descriptive Approach

To Hiroshi

Existential Sentences from the Diachronic and Synchronic Perspectives:
A Descriptive Approach

Michiko Yaguchi

KAITAKUSHA

Kaitakusha Co., Ltd.
5-2, Mukogaoka 1-chome
Bunkyo-ku, Tokyo 113-0023
Japan

Existential Sentences from the Diachronic and Synchronic Perspectives: A Descriptive Approach

Published in Japan
by Kaitakusha Co., Ltd., Tokyo

First published 2017

Printed and bound in Japan
by ARM Corporation

Cover design by Shihoko Nakamura

Preface

The objective of this work is to investigate both the diachronic development and the contemporary states of existential sentences and to offer a descriptive account for them. This work originated as my Ph.D. dissertation submitted to Kobe City University of Foreign Studies, and the publication in its present form reflects my desire to impart this data, which was compiled for the elucidation of superficially enigmatic existential sentences, to a wide range of readers.

It is thanks to numerous people that I have been able to finalize my endeavor. First and foremost, I greatly thank Prof. Yoko Iyeiri for showing me what research should be like. Her research papers and my conversations with her, about private or professional matters, have always put my work and my life into perspective. I'm very grateful to Prof. Michiyasu Shishido for providing me with tremendous support and encouragement, emotionally and mentally, to pursue my interest in this linguistic field. His determination to pursue a new career as a lawyer has inspired me. My thanks also go to Prof. Mitsunori Imai, who has given me so many things, literally. He is the person who convinced me to write a dissertation, an idea which I had never thought of. Without his words of advice, I wouldn't have attempted this venture of researching the *OED*'s ample data. Prof. Kensei Sugayama has been my mentor for a long period of time. His encouragement often saved me from giving up my academic career. I thank Prof. Shiro Wada for teaching me the joy of studying linguistics and the late Prof. Masatomo Ukaji for offering me invaluable advice. Both of these scholars gave me important and accurate evaluation. I would also like to thank Prof. Makoto Sumiyoshi, one of my classmates at my graduate school and now a colleague at my workplace, for his presence in my life. He has been both a friendly rival and a role model for me as a scholar and as a teacher. I am very grateful to Prof. Kaneaki Arimura, Prof. Haruhiko Yamaguchi, Prof. Akira Honda, and Prof. Norio Nasu for offering helpful suggestions for this work. The homework they gave me was of great value. I also thank Prof. Takako Fujii for helping me parse quotation texts in the *OED* and Professors Breivik and Martínez-Insua for generously sending me their publications.

I am also indebted to Mr. Masaru Kawata and his colleagues at Kaitaku-sha for their encouragement and patience as well as their celerity in editing and publishing this work. I must also express my gratitude to the Japan Society for the Promotion of Science, which kindly offered me a Grant-in-Aid for Publication of Scientific Research Results (No. 17HP5066).

Lastly, I would like to thank my late father Osamu and my late mother Masako for the precious time we spent together. And this work is dedicated to my husband Hiroshi, who stands by me at all times. Without him, my life would be very boring.

Michiko Yaguchi
Kobe 2017

Contents

List of tables and figures

Figures

Abbreviations

BNC	British National Corpus
Brown	Brown University Standard Corpus of Present-Day American English
CED	Corpus of English Dialogue
CEECS	Corpus of Early English Correspondence Sampler
CLMETEV	Corpus of Late Modern English Texts (extended version)
COCA	Corpus of Contemporary American English
COHA	Corpus of Historical American English
FLOB	Freiburg-LOB Corpus
Frown	Freiburg-Brown Corpus
LLC	London-Lund Corpus
LOB	Lancaster-Oslo-Bergen Corpus
Non-*be* construction	*there* + VP (non-*be* verb) construction
OED	*Oxford English Dictionary*
SBCSAE	Santa Barbara Corpus of Spoken American English
SOAP	Corpus of American Soap Operas
T*been* construction	*there* + *be* + NP + *been* construction
T*havebeen* construction	*there* + *have* + NP + *been* construction
T*have*P construction	*there* + *have* + NP + past participle (intransitive verb) construction
TP construction	*there* + *be* + NP + past participle (intransitive verb) construction
Tpp construction	*there* + *be* + NP + past participle (transitive verb) construction
TV construction	*there* + *be* + NP + VP construction
UKspoken	UKspoken subcorpus of Collins WordBanks Online

Introduction

The construction *there* + *be* is a puzzle in the grammatical system of present-day English. It is often said to be the sixth sentence pattern, because it does not fall into any of the basic five sentence patterns (Subject + Verb, Subject + Verb + Complement, Subject + Verb + Object, Subject + Verb + Object + Complement, Subject + Verb + Object + Object). Indeed, the grammatical category of *there* is difficult to determine, since it is inherently ambiguous between a noun and an adverb. According to Milsark (1974: 154–155, 1977), there are four types of *there* existential sentences in present-day English:

(1)   A Ontological Existential Sentences
      a.   There are no ghosts.
      b.   There is little sense to his remarks.
   B Locational Existential Sentences
      a.   There is a fly in the mustard.
      b.   There are a lot of pretentious people in Cambridge.
   C Periphrastic Existential Sentences
      a.   There is a lot going on.
      b.   There are peasants murdered every day.
      c.   There were many people sick.
   D Verbal Existential Sentences
      a.   There arose many trivial objections during the meeting.
      b.   There walked into the room a fierce-looking tomcat.

(Milsark 1974: 154-155)

In the *there* + *be* examples in (1A, B, C), it is generally maintained in linguistic circles that syntactically *there* functions as the subject of the sentences, but it is rare to find anyone brave enough to assert that it is a noun. On the other hand, it can be categorized as an adverb if one regards these sentences as inverted, but it is rarely asserted as an adverb either, perhaps because existential *there* takes the raising structure.

In addition, existential sentences exhibit a number of interesting phenomena for contemporary linguists. A well-known example is that the number between *be* verbs and notional subjects often disagrees as in (2):

(2) a.   There's two women in the waiting room.
    b.   *There is two women in the waiting room.

(Ando 1986: 47)

Although he considers the *there* + *is* + plural notional subject in (2b) to be an infelicitous, non-concord combination, Ando (1986: 47) accepts the use of *there's* for the plural notional subject in (2a). Ando (1986: 47) proposed that *there's* functions as a "particle" expressing existence.[1] Indeed, his judgment confirms that of other contemporary linguists. For instance, Svartvik & Leech (2006: 196) maintain that "since *There's* + plural is such an everyday usage, especially in speech, there is no reason to regard" it as unacceptable in informal standard English. Biber et al. (1999: 186) and Crawford (2005) claim that this apparent lack of agreement is caused by the speaker's conceptualization of the same item as an unanalyzed chunk. Furthermore, Breivik & Martínez-Insua (2008) discuss in depth the grammaticalization and subjectification of the combined sequence *there* + *be*, *there's* in particular, concluding that the fusion of *there* and *be* in the historical development of existential sentences resulted in the inseparability of *there's*. This phenomenon often stands in the way of theoretical approaches to elucidate existential sentences as counter evidence.

To cite another example, there is a construction which is difficult to parse as in (3):

(3) a.   There is a parcel come for you.

---

[1] Ando (1986: 47) uses the term "particle" without defining it. In Section 1.3 of Chapter 1, I will provide my own definition, which is different from what he means in this particular account. In Chapter 6, I will make a detailed argument that *there's* occasionally functions as an adverb-like particle in present-day English.

b.   There's a book gone from my desk.

(Quirk et al. 1985: 1404)

According to Quirk et al. (1985: 1404), the above sentences in (3a) and (3b) are informal usages. Their structure is inconsistent with present-day English grammar. I will attempt to provide an account for them in Chapter 6, showing that these sentences contain perfective features of earlier English's grammatical system. In fact, there are numerous puzzling constructions in existential sentences, which need elucidation. This study aims to show that such multifaceted aspects of existential sentences have often been derived from their diachronic developmental transition.

Thanks to the development of corpus linguistics and the growing availability of various corpora in recent years, a number of linguistic phenomena, details of which were unknown, have come to be uncovered. Furthermore, employment of tools equipped with computer technology has made it possible to retrieve data from even large-scale corpora. Thus, it has become possible to conduct qualitative and quantitative research with ease.

The present study will adopt a descriptive approach using the method of quantitative analysis to address a wide range of issues on existential sentences throughout the history of English. While the scope of almost all previous quantitative studies was limited to certain periods of time or to only the contracted form *there's* from the perspective of synchronic contexts, the present study will attempt a comprehensive examination of the longitudinal development of existential sentences using quotation text data from the *Oxford English Dictionary* (*OED*) to clarify the superficially inconsistent behaviors of existential sentences in present-day English. Simultaneously, I will analyze various other corpora, both large- and small-scale, to supplement the extensive but shallow distribution of quotation texts in the *OED*. The resulting descriptions will show that existential sentences underwent gradual changes until the end of Modern English, and are still evolving in contemporary English.

There are other features to distinguish this study from previous ones. First, it analyzes the five verbal forms (i.e. *there's*, *there is*, *there are*, *there was*, and *there were*). As mentioned above, previous studies often focused only on *there's*, but this study will deal with the other forms as well. Identifying the pragmatic use of each verbal form will clarify the functions of existential sentences even more accurately. Second, it will advance the status of *there's* as not only a single phrase, but also as an adverbial-like particle, whose syntactic role is hard to determine. No previous studies have separated the grammaticalized stage of *there's* into two. Third, the presentative function of existential sentences will be focalized. Although existential sentences are said to operate a number of functions, previous diachronic and synchronic studies have often failed to focus on this basic function. It will be shown that syntactic structures are closely related with the presentative function. Fourth, the diachronic transition of *there's* as a contracted form of *there* + *has* and that of lexically definite form of notional subjects, both of which have been described insufficiently in the literature, will be revealed. This study will take on the challenge of quantitatively analyzing over 46,000 quotation texts the *OED* as the basis data to uncover these issues.

This study is structured as follows. Chapter 1 will introduce the definitions of the terms used in this study, as well as the key concepts I assume for existential sentences. Chapter 2 will introduce the corpora used for the analysis and discuss their strengths and shortcomings. Concise explanations of general methodology of data collection will also be given. In Chapter 3, previous studies relevant to the diachronic development of Old English and Middle English will be summarized. Chapter 4 will demonstrate the diachronic development of existential sentences in frequency and syntactic variation via the analysis of the *OED* and review of previous studies. In Chapter 5, the connection between *there* and *be* in the diachronic context will be examined in terms of the five verbal forms (*there's, there is, there are, there was*, and *there were*). The behaviors of *there's* and *there was* will be the focus of this discussion. Chapter 6 will present an analysis of three peripheral existential constructions and prove that *there's* occasionally functions as a particle in present-day English. Chapter 7 will attempt to elucidate the *there* + VP + NP and *there* + *be* + past participle + NP constructions to examine the transition of their functions. These structures will be contrasted with ordinary existential sentences. In Chapter 8, existential sentences in British English and American English will be compared to explore how they are currently changing. The last chapter will conclude this study.

Chapter 1

Terminology and Linguistic Facts

This chapter introduces the terms and concepts relevant to existential sentences and when needed, provides the definitions assumed in the rest of this study.

1.1 Existential sentences with and without *there* in present-day English

Bolinger (1977: 91) asserts that sentences expressing the existence of a referent without *there* such as (1a) and *there* existential sentences such as (1b) represent different meanings, although both serve a presentative function. Note his examples:

(1) a. Across the street is a grocery.
    b. Across the street there's a grocery.

(Bolinger 1977: 93)

The conceptualization of (1a) is based on "the immediate stage (bring something literally or figuratively BEFORE OUR PRESENCE)" whereas that of (1b) "presents something to our minds (bring a piece of knowledge into consciousness)." The following pair given by Bolinger (1977: 94) clearly shows how existential *there* creates a sense of objectivity in the conceptualization:

(2) a. *As I recall, across the street is a grocery.
    b. As I recall, across the street there's a grocery.

(Bolinger 1977: 94)

Sentences without *there* were prevalent in Middle English. (In Chapter 3, we will see the diachronic transition of existential sentences without *there* such as (1a).) They still exist in present-day English to express deixis in the form of the PP(AdvP) + *be* + NP such as (1a). The analysis of the PP(AdvP) + *be* + NP construction, however, is beyond the scope of this study, although it presents a number of interesting phenomena. From here on, the term "existential sentences" will exclusively refer to constructions containing existential *there*, specifically, *there* + *be* and the derivative constructions such as *there* + *be* + pp + NP, *there* + *be* + NP + VP, and *there* + *be* + NP + pp. The sequence of *there* + VP will be also considered an existential sentence.

Bolinger (1977: 94) contrasts the deictic *there* with *here* and with existential *there*, claiming that the speaker's vantage point in existential sentences is conceptualized as outside the immediate, deictic scene. In other words, the original sense of deictic *there* pointing at something distant from the speech participants, different from that of *here* pointing at something close to them, still functions to distance the speaker from the immediate scene, which is why (2b) is well-formed. Likewise, Bolinger (1972) insists that the role of demonstrative deictic *that* as distancing the speaker from the immediate scene (in contrast with the deictic *this*) is preserved in the conjunctive and relative pronoun *that*, which both express objectiveness and anaphoricity. Yaguchi (2001) elaborates this notion on the framework of cognitive linguistics. It is quite interesting that in both cases, the distant demonstrative pronouns *there* and *that* developed into function words to represent an existential marker and conjunction and relative pronoun respectively.

1.2   Grammaticalization and subjectification

In this study, the term grammaticalization is defined, to follow Traugott (1995: 32), as "the process whereby lexical items or phrases come through frequent use in certain highly constrained local contexts to be reanalyzed as having syntactic and morphological functions, and once grammaticalized, continue to develop new grammatical functions." In the same token, subjectification is defined as "the development of a grammatically identifiable expression of speaker belief or speaker attitude" toward the proposition, according to Traugott (1995: 32).

Bybee (2011: 71–8) describes the process of grammaticalization, citing the example *in spite of*. The use of a high-frequency targeted item leads to its chunking and phonetic reduction, which propels an increase in autonomy "from the words and morphemes that compose them" and downgrades "the contribution of meaning from the components," assigning "pragmatic functions and meaning to the whole unit." In other words, she suggests that grammaticalization entails phonetic reduction, a loss of analyzability, pragmatic inference, an increase in autonomy, and decategorization. She shows that the sense of *spite*, i.e. a feeling of wanting to hurt or upset people, is lost in the phrase *in spite of*, which operates as a chunk and exercises a new pragmatic function. All these phenomena are applicable to existential *there*. In fact, this study will explore these phenomena to elucidate the grammaticalized process of not only *there* but also the sequence *there + be*.

Here, the phonetic situation should be explained in brief, since the rest of this study will focus on the syntactic, semantic, and pragmatic aspects. The phonetic reduction of *there + be* in present-day English is attested. It is generally agreed that deictic or locative *there* is pronounced [ðéɚ], [ðɛr], or [ðéə], while existential *there* is pronounced [ðɚ] or [ðə]. The latter is phonetically reduced. In addition, the shortened form *there's* is pronounced as [ðɚz], [ðɛɚz], [ðəz], or [ðɛəz]. Certainly, although it is almost impossible to exactly trace how the change of *there's* pronunciation took place over time, we can witness the grammaticalized status of existential *there* through phonetic reduction in present-day English. It would be very interesting to explore the pronunciations of the five verbal forms targeted in this study (i.e. *there's, there is, there are, there was,* and *there were*) synchronically as well as diachronically, but such phonetic investigation is beyond the scope of this study. Further research is necessary to confirm the synchronic and diachronic trend.

1.3   Particle

Crystal (1980: 258) defines a particle as "an INVARIABLE ITEM with grammatical FUNCTION, especially one which does not readily fit into a standard description of PART OF SPEECH." Generally, in the English linguistics circle, it is defined as a function word that is always associated with another word or phrase but has no lexical meaning of its own. In a rigid sense, clitics such as *n't* and *'ll*, are categorized as particles, while in a broad sense, discourse markers such as *well*, *like*, and *um* are categorized as particles. The latter have no direct semantic meaning but serve a pragmatic function: they indicate the speaker's attitude, or the need to organize her/his interactions with other conversation participants. Another type of particle is the aspectual particle, which often appears in phrasal verbs such as *climb up*. As Bolinger (1971) indicates, particles of this type are connected with the verb, rather than form a constituent with a following NP (e.g. *He raised up his hand*). Because this type is not relevant to this study, we use the term "particle" only in reference to something similar to discourse particle.

An example of a particle pertinent to this study is the particle usage of *let's*. Hopper & Traugott (2003: 10–13) explain the grammmaticalization of *let's*: after a long process of the grammaticalization and the subjectification of *let* + *us*, it now works as a particle in some sentences. Note the following examples:

(3) a. Let's <u>you and I</u> take 'em on for a set.

> (Hopper & Traugott 2003: 10)
> [1929, W. Faulkner *Sartoris* III. 186, *OED*]

  b. Lets <u>you</u> go first, then if we have any money left I'll go.

> (Hopper & Traugott 2003: 11)[1]

  c. Let's <u>us</u> try it out.   (Ando 2005: 882)
  d. Let's wash <u>your</u> hands.   (Cole 1975: 268)

The examples above would be ungrammatical, if we presumed that *let's* is composed of *let* + *us*, because of the unnecessary presence of *us* in *let's* in (3a) and (3b) and the redundancy of *us* in (3c). In (3d) where the speaker's condescending encouragement to a child is expressed, *us* in *let's* hardly includes the speaker. Clearly it is unanalyzable in that *us* in *let's* lacks its lexical meaning and semantic function, so that the syntactic category of *let's* is almost impossible to identify. It is obvious that *let's* works as a particle to serve hortatively and structure the speaker's interactions with her/his addressee. In Chapter 6, I will demonstrate that the shortened form *there's* occasionally functions as a particle, and, broadly speaking, in a very similar manner to *let's*.

1.4   Presentative function

It is widely assumed that the main function of existential *there* followed by

---

[1] Hopper & Traugott use the form *lets* (apostrophe is missing) when the subject is other than the first-person plural.

be is to introduce a new referent into the discourse. Meanwhile, the term "presentative" is also extensively used in the literature to refer to the function of existential *there*. Indeed, for the purpose of this particular study, it is significant to define the term "presentative function," distinguishing it from the basic function to introduce a new referent into the discourse.

Biber et al. (1999: 951) identify a presentative type of existential *there*, which focuses on the existence or occurrence of something rather than just introducing a new referent into the discourse. They cite the following example:

(4)   A man goes in the pub. There's a bear sitting in the corner. He goes up, he goes up to the bartender. He says, why is there a bear sitting over there?   (Biber et al. 1999: 951)

In (4), existential *there* is used not for the first new referent, *a man*, despite the fact that it appears at the beginning of the discourse, but for the other new referent, *a bear*, which is introduced in an existential sentence. *There* draws the listener's/reader's attention to the referent's (*a bear*, the main character in the story) existence. We define this usage as the presentative focusing function, following Quirk et al. (1985: 1408).[2] In contrast, some existential sentences do not perform such a function, as in (5):

(5)   Few people have jobs. There is no one to work for. No government, no schools, no police force, fire brigade, ambulance service.
                                                             (BNC Newspaper)

In (5), because the preceding sentence, *few people have jobs*, already explains the situation, the existential sentence that follows, *There is no one to work for*, is a mere restating of the same situation. Additionally, the presence of a negative element, i.e. *no*, indicates that there is no specific referent to present. Thus, this particular existential sentence does not play a presentative role. Indeed, as will be thoroughly discussed in Chapters 6 and 7, the presentative function is syntactically realized affirmatively in the main clause indicative form as an expression of the speaker's categorical assertion. To my knowledge at least, few previous attempts have been made to elucidate presentative function of existential sentences, so this will be a focus of the present study.

---

[2] Bressnan (1994) and Aissen (1975) use presentational to refer to the same function. Pfenninger (2009) defines ontological existential sentences such as (1A) in the Introduction as presentational, though the usage is not presentative.

1.5   Present-day English, contemporary English, and current English

In linguistics, present-day English refers to English after 1900. In this study, I will follow this convention, while interchangeably using contemporary English and current English to specifically refer to English after 1950.

1.6   *there's*[3]

According to most contemporary English dictionaries, *there's* is generally described as follows:

(6)   contraction of *there is*
      contraction of *there has*

It is obvious that *there's* marks present tense, whether *'s* represents a contraction of *is* or *has*. However, it is possible that some dialects employ or previously employed *there's* as the contraction of *there was*. For instance, Hay & Schreier (2004) report that the use of *there's* as past tense is observable in speech of New Zealand English.[4] Scrutiny of their data, however, reveals that the ratio of preterit *there's* (9 tokens) to the total use of *there was* (790 tokens) is so low that the inclusion of preterit *there's* into present *there's* is affected to only a minimal degree. I also examined all the 1,745 tokens of *there's* in the Helsinki Corpus and the Corpus of Late Modern English Texts (extended version) (CLMETEV) whose contexts are relatively more recoverable than those in the *OED*, and found no tell-tale cases of *there's* as a contraction of *there was*.[5] Therefore, while the data may include tokens of *there's* as a contraction of *there was* synchronically as well as diachronically, even in writing, the present study will not take this possibility into further consideration.

A more complicated issue to be addressed is whether *there's* is a shortened form of *there is* or *there has* in the *there + be + NP + past participle (pp)* construction such as *There's a parcel come for you*, which will be called TP construction in this study. Although the TP construction will

---

[3] Part of this section appears as Yaguchi (2009).

[4] Montgomery & Chapman (1992) also report the use of *there's* as preterit sense in Appalachian English, a dialect spoken in the U.S.A., which is said to contain similar features to English used by Chaucer, Spenser, and Shakespeare.

[5] The three corpora will be described in depth in Chapter 2.

be discussed at full length in comparison with what are called *there*-contact clauses, namely the *there* + *be* + NP + VP construction (TV construction) such as *There's a man wants to see you*, in Chapter 6, it is necessary to ascertain that *there's* in these periphrastic constructions, both of which were employed since Middle English, almost always represents a contraction of *there is*, not *there has* in the diachronic context. First, note the examples of the TP construction as follows:

(7) a.   There was newes come to London, that the Devill …

[1563, W. Fulke *Meteors* (1640) 10b, *OED*]

    b.   'Look! there's a pretty little lady come to see you,' said Polly
      …   [1848, Dickens *Dombey and Son*, Chap.6]

    c.   There's a few shingles gone off the roof, but that's normal.

(COCA, spoken)

If these sentences above constituted the TV structure, *come* in (7a, b) would be *came* and *comes* or *will come* respectively. Apparently, the TP construction is totally different from the TV construction in syntactic structure. Before examining *there's* in the TP construction, it is worthwhile to conduct an in-depth discussion on *be* + pp perfective. In (7) *be* in the existential part and *come* form a perfective complex, and the use of *be*, instead of *have*, in perfective sentences was common in earlier English when intransitive verbs were employed, as in (8):

(8) a.   The Dutch … were fallen on our fleet at Chatham.

[1667, Evelyn *Mem.* (1857) I. 26, *OED*]

    b.   Blindness in part is happened to Israel.

[1611, Bible *Rom.* xi. 25, *OED*]

In colloquial present-day English, *be* + pp is also used to express present perfective as follows:

(9) a.   Is she gone now?   (COCA, news)

    b.   It was been going for two years.   (BNC, spoken)

    c.   And when they were come, and settled into conference with him
      …   (BNC, fiction)

    d.   Having said that, three hundred are been forced to leave, three hundred are being sacked, as we've heard before. (BNC, spoken)

    e.   The military is been very aggressive running after the Abu Sayyaf.   (COCA, spoken)

The examples in (9) are considered ungrammatical in present-day English grammar. However, perfective *be* + pp, as in (9), is often used in some dialects such as the Shetland Islands in Scotland, according to Smith & Durham (2012). Furthermore, *be* + *gone* as in (9a) is acceptable even in present-day standard English.

Quirk et al. (1985: 170) define *be* + pp as a "pseudo-passive" construction, stating that "with most intransitive verbs, this construction has been superseded" by *have* + pp at present, and add that it survived with certain types of verbs as follows:

(10) a. Why are those cars stopped at the corner?
     b. By the time she got there, her friends were gone.
     c. I'll soon be finished with this joy.

(Quirk et al. 1985: 170)

Curiously enough, some combination of *be* + pp can be interpreted both as passive and perfective. Observe (11):

(11) a. Once we are done pre-boarding, we will start boarding all our First Class and Business Class passengers, Marco Polo Club members, and ...   (COCA, fiction)
     b. The thing with electrical currents is, once they are done and gone, there's no trace level.   (COCA, news)
     c. Later, when her son was finished with his learning, she and he might make their way to Corporation Park, ...   (BNC, fiction)
     d. The whole building is finished now and we take our first patient in on April 13 ...   (BNC, news)

Example (11a) is parsed as present perfective. Example (11b) is an interesting case in that *they* (i.e. *electrical currents*) *are done* is parsed as passive, though (*they are*) *gone* expresses present perfective. The subject's (in)animacy seems to influence on the construal. Example (11c) constitutes a perfective construction due to the subject being human, but when the subject is an inanimate as in (11d), it can be construed as a passive construction.

This pseudo-passive perfective can be traced back to perfective usage of *be* + pp in earlier English, as mentioned in connection with (8). It has been generally understood that in Early Modern English, perfective *be* + pp with intransitive verbs was replaced by the perfective auxiliary *have*, which was formerly employed only with transitive verbs in earlier English. However, Rydén & Broström (1987) clearly demonstrate in their quantitative research that *have* was used about 10% of the time up to 1600, 20% in 1700, 40% in 1800, and 90% to 95% in 1900, with 50% reached around 1810–1820, thus defying the common assumption that *be* + pp disappeared by 1800. In addition, they claim that some types of verbs were more prone to be associated with *be* even in the nineteenth century; for instance, 22.3% of usages with *come* appeared with *be* even in nineteenth-century English. Thus, the pseudo-passive construction and the TP construction are both vestiges of the *be* + *pp* perfective in earlier English, because the TP construction has been observed since Middle English in the *OED* as mentioned above (see Section 6.3 in Chapter 6). In this sense, we can reasonably conclude that *'s* in *there's* in TP sentences represents a clitic form of *is*, not *has*.

Having said that, we should contemplate the possibility of *have* appearing in the TP construction. First of all, it is important to examine the diachronic development of existential sentences containing perfective *have*. The *there* + *have* + *been* sequence appeared in Middle English as in (12):

(12)   With him ther hath been many a sundry leeche ...

[1400s, Hoccleve *Min. Poems* xxiv. 514, *OED*]

Observe the following table for raw occurrences of *there* + *have* + *been* tokens in the *OED*:

Table 1-1: Raw occurrences of *there* + *have* + *been* in *OED*

period	−1499	1500–1599	1600–1699	1700–1799	1800–1849	1850–1899	1900–1949	1950–
there's been	0	0	0	0	2	8	6	20
there has been	7	5	20	33	40	110	106	176
there have been	1	1	28	21	17	52	41	101
there had been	0	5	26	20	21	73	52	78

Clearly, it is not until the early 1800s (viz. 1815) that the contracted form *there's* of *there has* emerged in the *OED*, while in the Corpus of Historical American English (COHA) and the CLMETEV, it made its first appearance in 1830 and in 1796 respectively. Therefore, it is a fair conjecture that *there's* in all TP tokens before 1796 constituted a contracted form of *there is*, not *there has* in writing.

Conversely, there is a possibility that tokens after 1800 may contain *there has*, replacing *there is*. I would like to offer two pieces of evidence to suggest that these forms are still comprised of *there* + *be* + NP + pp. First, the structure *there* + *have* + NP + pp itself was rare in the longitudinal development of existential sentences and thus, is unlikely to have survived in English grammar. In fact, there are only seven tokens of *there* + *have* +

NP + pp, including transitive usages as in (13a, d, e, f, and g) in the *OED*'s quotation texts:[6]

(13) a. There had you seen many a gowne torne and broken.
[c1489, Caxton *Sonnes of Aymon* i. 37, *OED*]

b. There had men of warre fallen out of Syria, and caried awaye a little damsel.   [1535, Coverdale *2 Kings* v. 2, *OED*]

c. Whereas sinne hath abounded, there hath grace overabounded.
[1577, *St. Aug. Manual* (Longman) 68, *OED*]

d. There hath he made Walkes, hedges, and Arbours, of all manner of most delicate fruit Trees.
[1623, J. Taylor (Water P.) *New Discov. by Sea* C2b, *OED*]

e. For there hath he ... vsed such a deale of intricate Setting, Grafting, Planting ... turning, winding, and returning circular [etc.].
[1623, J. Taylor (Water P.) *New Discov. by Sea* C2b, *OED*]

f. There has no sooner any one done me good service, but ... he cancels his interest in me by some deep injury.
[1825, Scott *Talism.* xxi, *OED*]

g. Wherever a pole-boat had made its way, there had the name of Jack Bannister found repeated echoes.
[1841, *Kinsmen* I. xiv. 163, *OED*]

Apparently, among the seven tokens, there are only two tokens appearing in the early 1800s and there are no instances after 1900, which indicates that the *there* + *have* + NP + pp structure is sparse in present-day English. (Among the seven tokens, only two tokens (13b, c) form the *there* + *have* + NP + pp (intransitive verb) structure (henceforth, the T*have*P construction.)

Here, in order to validate the distribution of the *there* + *have* + NP + pp (intransitive verb) sequence, it is important to investigate the data in the COHA, which contains more abundant data from Late Modern English than the *OED*. The following table shows all the tokens of *there* + *have* + NP + pp in the COHA by applying the pattern "*there* [vh*] * * * * * [v?n*]" to a wild card search and by setting 200 types for each search. 37 tokens were retrieved from the COHA:

---

[6] To be more precise, there are eight instances in this construction, because (13a) appears twice in the *OED*.

Table 1-2: Tokens of *there* + *have* + NP + pp in COHA[7]

Year	Genre	
1819	Fiction	There have I lingered, for two long years and upwards.
1822*	Fiction	There has One taken you up who will not leave you, nor forsake you, …
1822	Fiction	There hath he been ever since the sun went down.
1823	Fiction	There have I enshrined the woman that I love.
1825*	Fiction	There has One' taken you up who will not leave you, nor forsake you, …
1827	Fiction	Alas! there has he touched me to the quick (aloud)
1830	Fiction	There had immense rains fallen, and the passes were all but impassable.
1831	Magazine	Wherever poetry has been found, there has music been found also, her inseparable companion.
1833	Fiction	Yes, there has she stood beckoning me when the sun beat upon it;
1844	Fiction	… there have I sat ever since by her side, with our poor boy in my bosom.
1847	Fiction	There has a great deal of that gone out of fashion.
1847	Fiction	… there has the game been lately—hold hard, bold cavaliers— …
1847	Fiction	there has no harm befallen any one, …
1849	Fiction	… there hath Love spread his wing, …
1852	Fiction	There has a chillness crept into the air Since forth we walked?
1853	Fiction	… Why, there has a bird come on board," replied the surgeon …
1853	Mystery	There has an idea been advanced, that candied honey is injurious to bees, …
1857	Fiction	… there have two ships lately arrived from England, bringing, …
1863	Fiction	There have a great many gone from Oneida—
1866	Fiction	There have I travelled, —there, transported, seen Blue inland oceans …
1868	Magazine	There has no one been found to live there for years past; for they say …
1877	Magazine	… there has a coolness grown up between them …
1880	Fiction	… there hath some slanderous report Gone forth against my sister …
1889	Fiction	There have I prayed.
1889	Fiction	There have I sent up thanksgivings.
1891	Fiction	There have I wept bitter tears.
1896	Fiction	There has one already gone, whoer he be!
1896	Fiction	… there have aye been daughters o'Heth to plague honest houses wi'.
1902	Fiction	And there have I beheld the Wordlings buy Their Paris Gowns …
1905	Fiction	There has man learned how the Fates may be cheated
1907	Fiction	There hath no trouble taken you but is common to all men.

---

[7] Accessed in February, 2013.

The COHA occasionally contained the same texts in two different years as of February, 2013.

1910	Fiction	There has nothing occurred between us, I am sure, which requires explanation.
1912	Fiction	… although there haven't many of 'em showed up yet this season.
1920	Fiction	Since morning until now there has not a cloud been seen.
1922	Fiction	… and there has a letter come from overseas which I must read
1934	Fiction	But there has no letter come a long time to this hamlet …
1953	Fiction	There have great things been done to mitigate the worst human sights …

One cannot deny that *there* + *have* + NP + pp was a feasible construction, at least in American English, until the middle of the 1950s, as investigation with a larger-sized corpus can reveal items that smaller-scale corpora such as the *OED* cannot retrieve. Nevertheless, it is my view that the construction under discussion did not become entrenched in English, because only 28 tokens appeared in Late Modern English and only nine tokens between 1900 and 1953. Since then, it has disappeared. In addition, among the 37 instances in Table 1-2, 24 tokens do not exactly conform to the T*have*P construction using intransitive verbs' pp: 16 tokens represent transitive usages of *have* + pp (e.g. *Alas! there has he touched me to the quick*) or eight tokens show locative usages of *there* (e.g. *There have I prayed*). In other words, there are only 13 true T*have*P tokens with *have* in lieu of *be* (e.g. *There has no letter come a long time*) in the COHA.

In the British National Corpus (BNC), I found only one token in conversation: *I know there have attempts made to find someone to replace him.* However, this particular token is ungrammatical; *have* is most likely mistakenly used in the place of *are*, *were*, or *have been*. In the examination into the Corpus of Contemporary American English (COCA),[8] I found only three instances in speech, out of which only one token forms the T*have*P construction (*There has no link been made that …*) Thus, the contemporary corpora displays that there is almost no instance of the *there* + *have* + NP + pp (intransitive verb) sequence in current English. Hence, because of rarity of this pattern since 1800, it is difficult to support the hypothesis that *has* superseded *is* in *there's* after 1800 in *there's* in TP sentences.[9] Indeed, as the second evidence, the following TP example from 1848 clearly points to the fact for *there's* to comprise of *there is*, as *is* is derived in the tag question:

---

[8] I extracted 200 types at most for each pattern "*there* [vh*] * * * * * [v?n*]".

[9] Jespersen (1927: 111–112) recognizes the pattern of *there* + *have* + NP + pp through his examples cited from English dating around 1800:

    there has scarce a day passed but he has visited him. (Keats 4. 184)

    Since the year 1614, there have no States-General met in France. (Carlyle FR 106)

(14)   "There's a change comed over him ... is there not?"

[1848, Mrs. Gaskell *Mary Barton* vi, *OED*]

Thus, it is reasonable to conclude that *there* + *have* + NP + pp did not take root in English, despite its occasional appearance. Furthermore, against the backdrop of the eclipsing tendency of the TP construction in contemporary English, it is possible to infer that *have* could not intrude in those obsolescent sentences.

The argument so far also shows that *there's* in TV sentences with non-disagreeing tense can also be parsed as shortened forms of *there is*, not *there has*. Note the following example of the TV construction:

(15)   ... there's a girl g̲o̲t̲ a room two above me.

[1949, Kanin Garson *The Rat Race*, COHA]

In this example, it is possible to assume that *there's* constitutes a shortened form of *there has*, rather than *there is*, in order to form perfective linking with *got*. However, the above discussion arrives at the conclusion that *there's* in the TV construction comprises *there* + *is*, since *there* + *has* + NP + pp failed to make inroads in the English language. As a matter of fact, this particular example can be parsed as the structure of *have* being omitted between *a girl* and *got*. A detailed discussion will be provided in Section 6.5 in Chapter 6.

Hence, it should be emphasized that the present discussion yields *evidence* proving that *there's* in the TV construction also derived historically from *there is*. This study, therefore, assumes that *there's* in the TP construction and the TV construction stems from the longitudinal contraction of *there is*.

However, we have contradictory data of a similar construction to the TP construction using *been* + (pp/v-*ing*) in the part of pp in the TP construction (we will call it T*been* construction), as in (16a). It is worth noting the constituents of *there's* in this particular construction. Contemporary English speakers generally do not accept the use of *have* in existential sentences involving *been* as follows (e.g. Quirk et al. 1985: 1409, Lakoff 1987: 562–5):

(16) a.   There's a visitor been waiting to see you.

(Quirk et al. 1985: 1409)

   b.   *There has a visitor been waiting.   (ibid)

   c.   There are three visitors (?been) waiting to see you.   (ibid)

   d.   There was a new grammar (*been) published recently.   (ibid)

   e.   *There is a man been shot.   (Lakoff 1987: 563)

    f. *There has a man been shot.   (ibid)

    g. *There's a man been shot, isn't there?   (ibid)

    h. There's a man been shot, hasn't there?   (ibid)

    i. *There've many people been killed this week. (ibid)

As seen in (16b, f, i), the intuition shared by the contemporary grammarians clearly suggests that the TP construction avoids the use of *has/have* in present-day English. Furthermore, it is that they deny the use of *are*, *was*, and even *is*, as in (16c, d, e). However, Lakoff's acceptance of the tag question *hasn't there?*, as in (16h), is contradictory data against the conclusion that *there's* constitutes *there is*. What kind of account can we provide? I will conduct an in-depth discussion to prove *there's* in the T*been* construction is also made up of *there is* in Section 6.5 of Chapter 6.

1.7   Locative vs. existential

Kuno (1971), Bolinger (1977: 91), Lyons (1977: 723), and Breivik & Swan (2000) provide accounts in which the existential sense of *there* developed through the grammaticalization of its original locative sense. Note the developmental course from an adverb denoting deictic location (17a) to an existential marker (17b), as Breivik (1981) shows:

(17) a.   There's an elephant. Over <u>there</u>. Look!

       b.   <u>There</u> are elephants in North America.

                                    (Breivik 1981)

As in (17), the forms of locative and existential constructions are often superficially almost identical, which eventually triggers the question of the accuracy of the collection of data. Indeed, Breivik (1981) argues that it is occasionally very difficult to distinguish between the locative and the existential senses of *there*. Additionally, quotation texts from the *OED* in particular lack sufficient contexts, making it impossible to retrieve only existential constructions. Therefore, the quantitative data in this study may contain locative tokens, which brings a certain imprecision in the results. Nonetheless, I would like to insist that some existential sentences imply a locative sense to a certain degree. For instance, one often comes across *there* + VP tokens that may denote both locative and existential senses. The typical case is as follows:

(18)   Joe looked at his mother and <u>there came</u> into his mind a thought
that wasn't new: his mother didn't like Martin; she liked Harry but
not Martin; and Martin didn't like her.   (BNC, fiction)

There in (18) works as a presentative existential sentence, expressing abstract
locative or/and temporal sense as a setting-provider, although *there* in (18) is
not deictic. In fact, *there* signaling a presentative feature seems to connote a
locative sense. The following example, which appears as (4), will be shown
here again as (19):

(19)   A man goes in the pub. <u>There's a bear sitting in the corner.</u> He
goes up, he goes up to the bartender. He says, why is there a bear
sitting over there?   (Biber et al. 1999: 951)

Obviously, it is possible to interpret *there* in the second sentence as a set-
ting-maker designating *in the pub* or temporal-maker. It is indeed ambiguous between locative and existential denotations.

Thus, even when *there* + *be* tokens look like full-fledged existential
sentences, some cases occur with locative and/or temporal elements in expletive *there*. In fact, Breivik & Swan (2000) argue that existential *there* "has
not undergone complete desemanticization; it retains a vestige of spatiality"
in present-day English. In addition, assuming Hopper's (1991) Principle
of Persistence, which stipulates that "the original semantics of the grammaticalizing element determine and remain visible in its grammaticalized
meaning," Pfenninger (2009: 247) argues that the "slight locative flavor can
be understood as a continuation of its original lexical meaning" in the grammaticalization of *there*. As touched upon in Section 1.1, Bolinger (1972)
also discusses the vestiges of the locative sense of *there* in terms of objectivity and anaphoricity. Hence, unless *there* clearly manifests a case of deictic
sense as in (17a), *there* + *be* tokens are counted as existentials' instances in
this study.

Furthermore, the *here* + *be* sequence expressing locative and deictic
senses discussed in Sections 5.5 and 6.8 shows very distinctive characteristics from its *there* + *be* counterpart.

1.8   Dialects

Since existential sentences are commonly used in speech as well as in
writing, differences in dialect may have some impact on quantitative
data. Chapter 8 will focus on contemporary British English and American

English. Of course, I recognize that the use of existential sentences differs from dialect to dialect, but research into the two standard English varieties reveals their general tendency. For the diachronic data, this study will mainly analyze longitudinal data in the *OED*, which is a collection of British English, Scottish English, Irish English, American English, Canadian English, Australian English, and other texts. While Late Modern English and present-day English data include world-wide English, earlier English data contain regional dialects centering on the London area. It is therefore assumed that the analysis of the *OED* would reveal the general tendencies of English, rather than accurate features of a particular dialect. To supplement the *OED*'s data, other corpora, which will be listed in Chapter 2, are also examined in this study.

Chapter 2

Database and Data Collection

2.1 Database[1]

This study used the dataset of quotation texts in the *OED*, second edition (version 3.1) on CO-ROM as the primary data for diachronic research. The *OED* is considered to be the world's most comprehensive English dictionary, containing over 2.4 million quotations selected from a wide range of literary and other sources, some of which are dated as recent as 2003 and as early as 525. It provides abundant diachronic data for linguistic research. The *OED*, however, poses several concerns for the analysis of existential sentences, as a number of scholars have pointed out (e.g. Sinclair 1996, Hoffmann 2004, 2005: 9–16, Iyeiri 2010: 197–198).

The first concern is that the *OED* is an imbalanced representation of the English language. As Hoffmann (2004, 2005: 9–16) notes, certain authors' works are over-featured, while texts in some genres, such as working-class newspapers of the nineteenth century, are scarcely quoted. As a result, the variety of the data may not be consistent throughout all the periods. Nevertheless, the *OED* furnishes extensive longitudinal data with 2.4 million quoted texts, as mentioned above, which should be sufficient for conducting reliable research, particularly because *there + be* is used in informal speech as well as in formal writing. Other sources fail to cover such a wide range of texts or compile such a large amount of data.

---

[1] An earlier version of part of this section appeared as part of Yaguchi (2010a).

Secondly, because of technical limitations, version 3.1 of the *OED* makes generation of normalized statistical data difficult. Information on occurrences per 10,000 words, for instance, is unavailable. Because the CD-ROM allows only partial data exporting, moving the texts as a whole to a spreadsheet for further statistical analysis is impossible. Another problem, as Hoffmann (2004, 2005: 9–16) notes, is that the number of quotation texts varies significantly by period: the number of quotations per year increased gradually until the seventeenth century (approximately 4,000), then decreased sharply until the end of the eighteenth century (about 2,500) and again peaked around the year 1900 (about 10,500), followed by a sharp decline. Hoffmann (2004, 2005: 9–16) also showed that the average length of quotations also varies: it increased from approximately 13 words per quotation on the average between 1450 and 1900 to more than 16 words per quotation in twentieth-century English. The present study, therefore, basically calculates rates, such as how many target forms appear per 100 quotations in order to obviate the disadvantages caused by the CD-ROM's restricted technical capabilities and inconsistent data collection of quotation texts.

Finally, omission of some sequences of quotation texts and repeated appearances of certain texts may affect the reliability of the data. I encountered a number of repeated uses of the same quotation texts under different entry words by manually investigating all tokens including *there* in the *OED* (more than 70,000 tokens in total). Hoffmann (2004, 2005: 9–16) reports that 20% of the quotation texts contain omissions of subordinate clauses or other elements, posing some questions as to the accuracy of analysis. As he suggests that the large majority of these deletions are unlikely to distort the results, the impact of the deletion is constrained to a minimum level, thanks to the tendency for existential sentences to appear at the initial position of a clause. I counted the same two tokens separately and logged them as two, since the total number of quotation texts itself includes these repeated quotation texts. This study primarily focuses on occurrences per 100 quotation texts, so counting the same token only once would result in inaccurate data. Again, as far as the ratio is calculated, the presence of the same tokens hardly affects the reliability.

Despite these concerns, the use of the *OED*'s dataset can be justified.[2] It offers significantly abundant and comprehensive data, and allows

---

[2] In addition, version 3.1 features the wild card function. While it only works with certain search forms, this function makes it possible to conduct a detailed investigation into some features.

developmental trends over time to be expressed quantitatively, as Hoffmann (2004, 2005: 9–16) insists. Iyeiri (2010: 197–198) is also "fully convinced of its usefulness" as a historical corpus, although she admits its shortcomings. It should be kept in mind that since any corpus will have a certain level of imprecision, the aim of utilizing the *OED* is to grasp the general picture, not a perfect statistical representation, of a targeted linguistic item.

Equally important, this study also used the British National Corpus (BNC, 100 million words, 1980s–1993),[3] the Corpus of Contemporary American English (COCA, 450 million words, 1990–2012)[4] and the Corpus of Historical American English (COHA, 400 million words, 1810–2009). The online versions of all of these databases were developed by Professor Mark Davies at Brigham Young University (BYU), and they have a useful wild card search feature, which compensates for their limit (as of March, 2013) of 1,000 tokens for retrieval.[5] Although several versions of BNC dataset are available online and on CD-ROM, I chose the BYU-BNC produced by Davies. In this version, the BNC comprises seven genres of spoken, fiction, magazine, newspaper, non-academic, academic, and miscellaneous.

The COCA provides a large proportion of spoken and written contemporary American English texts from speech, fiction, magazine, and academic genres, recorded between 1990 and 2012. This corpus has some shortcomings: as of January, 2015, the same text is sometimes cited twice in the same year in two different instances. This redundancy could potentially lead to inaccurate analysis. As I did with the *OED* data, I counted identical tokens as two instances in my analysis to accurately calculate occurrences per 10,000 words. Since such errors decrease accuracy, corrections will have to be made.[6] Nevertheless, as in the case of the *OED*, the COCA's ample-sized dataset should mitigate such minor inaccuracies.

The COHA (a compilation of four genres: fiction, popular magazines, newspapers, and non-fiction between 1810 and 2009) was an invaluable dataset for the present study. Its abundant word count made it possible to investigate data from every ten years of Late Modern American English and present-day American English. However, the corpus used, as of February,

---

[3] As of February, 2015, the spoken sample can be heard online at the BNC web (QP Edition) through Lancaster University, UK. (cf. http://bncweb.lancs.ac.uk)

[4] As of September, 2017, the COCA contains 520 million words between 1990 and 2015.

[5] As of February, 2015, this limit is removed.

[6] The online data is not as stable as in the data compiled in the CD. If a removal of overlapped data mentioned above is made for correction, the figures calculated will change.

2013, also has several drawbacks. First, the distribution of word counts varies over different time periods. The word counts in the 1810s and 1820s data, for instance, are extremely low, compared with counts after the 1880s, so tendencies observed in these periods may not be as representative as in those of other periods. Second, newspapers do not appear in the corpus until the 1860s, which may cause an imbalanced representation of the data up to the 1860s. Third, some sentences occasionally appear twice in the same year or in two different years in the early data of the 1800s. (As of January, 2015, such redundancy has been corrected.) In summary, the data from the 1800s, particularly up to the 1880s, may have some inaccuracies. Again, despite these insufficiencies, the COHA's large dataset can provide an adequate reflection of actual tendencies in language use during the time it covers.

For contemporary speech data, I used three subcorpora and three corpora. British English data came from two subcorpora and one corpus: the speech data in the BNC (recorded between 1980s and 1993) and Collins WordBanks (550 million words) offer contemporary British English spoken data. I accessed WordBanks Online (recorded between 1985 and 1998[7]) through the Shogakukan Corpus Network to cull 3,000 tokens in each search. The BNC's speech data contain both formal and informal speech with 11.7 million words, while WordBanks' UKspoken data include 7.92 million words of informal speech. The London-Lund Corpus (LLC) was also used. The corpus consists of 500,000 words of spoken British English recorded in the 1960s and 1970s. It contains educated speakers' conversation. Also, I have analyzed three American English datasets: COCA's spoken subcorpus (95.6 million words between 1990 and 2012), the Santa Barbara Corpus of Spoken American English (SBCSAE, 249,000 words recorded between 1988 and 1996) and the Corpus of American Soap Operas (SOAP, 100 million words of transcripts of 22,000 soap operas broadcast between 2001 and 2012 in the U.S.A.). First, the COCA's spoken data are very useful. However, one caution should be given: the COCA's subcorpus of spoken language is transcription of TV talk shows, so the speech compiled is considered to be rather formal.[8] The Santa Barbara corpus is based

---

[7] As of October, 2014, Collins WordBanks Online (http://www.collins.co.uk/page/Wordbanks+Online) compiles more update informal speech data uttered between 2001 and 2005. The Shogakukan's dataset offers an older version as of January, 2015.

[8] An informant makes a comment that the language used on US talk shows is rarely formal: one would encounter formal register of language in such shows only in prepared statements or formal debate. As discussed in Chapter 8, however, my findings concerning the COCA's data show that it is rather formal.

on naturally occurring spontaneous speech. It is a relatively small-scale corpus, but its dataset includes face-to-face interactive conversation in every-day situations, which is a useful supplement to the formal public speech in the COCA. Also, the SOAP was analyzed when a vernacular type of data was needed.

Also, to collect additional diachronic data in Old English, Middle English, Early Modern English, and Late Modern English, the Helsinki Corpus (1.5 million words) and the Corpus of Late Modern English Texts (extended version) (CLMETEV, 15 million words), A Corpus of English Dialogue (CED, 1.2 million words), and Corpus of Early English Correspondence Sampler (CEECS, 450,000 words) were used to supplement the data of the *OED* and the COHA. The Helsinki Corpus consists of a selection of texts covering the Old, Middle, and Early Modern English periods (c.730–1710), obtainable on the CD-ROM from the ICAME, while the CLMETEV is a collection of British writers' work written between 1710 and 1920, obtainable online.[9] CED is a collection of speech related texts between 1560 and 1760 available online,[10] and CEECS is a compilation of letters written between 1418 and 1680 available on the ICAME CD-ROM.

To compare written American English and written British English in the 1990s, I used the Freiburg-LOB Corpus (FLOB) and the Freiburg-Brown Corpus (Frown), both compilations of 1,000,000-word written texts covering 15 categories in standard British English and standard American English respectively.[11] In addition, to investigate changes in contemporary English, I used the Lancaster-Oslo-Bergen Corpus (LOB) and the Brown University Standard Corpus of present-day American English (Brown), both of which contain the same 15 writing categories with one million words written in the 1960s. These corpora were valuable for understanding the evolving usage of target items and comparing the two varieties of English because of the sizes of their subcorpora with the same 15 categories.[12] The FLOB, Frown, LOB,

---

[9] For more information, see http://perswww.kuleuven.be/~u0044428/.

[10] https://cqpweb.lancs.ac.uk/engdia/

[11] The 15 categories: reportage; editorial; reviews; religion; skills, trades and hobbies; popular lore; belles letters, biography, essays; miscellaneous (government documents, reports, industry reports, college catalogue, industry house organ); learned and scientific writings; general fiction; mystery and detective fiction; science fiction; adventure and western fiction; romance and love story; and humor.

[12] There are small differences in the word count (4,000 words at most) in three genres (religion, skills, trade and hobbies, and popular lore) between the British corpora (FLOB and LOB) and the American corpora (Frown and Brown). Within each variety of corpora,

Brown, and LLC are all available on the CD-ROM from the ICAME.

2.2   Data collection

Since this study uses quantitative methods to determine the characteristics of existential sentences and related linguistic phenomena, I conducted an analysis of written data and transcriptions of speech by searching for targeted items in the abovementioned corpora. While detailed caveats on the data collection methods will be presented when needed, the general principles followed will be summarized here.

This study addressed number disagreement between the form of the verb accompanied by *there* and the notional subject in existential sentences. A number of studies have investigated the same feature concerning number non-concord of existential sentences (e.g. DeWolf 1992, Meechan & Foley 1994, Carter 1999, Cheshire 1999, Martinez Insua & Martinez 2003, Martínez-Insua 2004, Crawford 2005, Breivik & Martínez-Insua 2008, *inter alia*). Although there are no established criteria for the judging number disagreement in literature, this study adopts the following rules:

1) *none*
For *none*, no distinction is made in terms of number. This study recognizes neither *there* + singular *be* + *none* as in (1a) nor *there* + plural *be* + *none* as in (1b), both of which are observed relatively frequently in the *OED* throughout the history of English, as number disagreement:

(1) a.   Only Thou art holy, <u>there is none</u> beside Thee, Perfect in power, in love, and purity.   [1827, Bp. Heber *Hymn*, *OED*]

   b.   I tried to see the arms on the carriage, but <u>there were none</u>; so that cock wouldn't fight.

                    [1850, Kingsley, *Alt. Locke* xxiv. (1874) 179, *OED*]

2) ambiguity
When the singular/plural status of a token is difficult to judge, I generally judged it to agree in number. For example, the following two cases were treated in this study as instances of number concord:

---

consistency is maintained. These variations are not problematic, because a maximum of 4,000 words is considered to be an insignificant level.

(2) a.   There is a new sort of Oats, or Groats growing like unto whole
          Oatmeal, without any Hulls ...

                              [1669, Worlidge *Syst. Agric.* (1681) 41. *OED*]

    b.   But there is many a youth Now crescent, ...

                              [1859, Tennyson *Elaine* 448, *OED*]

In the particular case of (2a), it is difficult to determine which constitutes the
head, *a new sort* or *Oats* (This issue is an interesting research theme). If
the head of the notional subject is *Oats*, the sentence is considered to be a
token of number disagreement. In such ambiguous cases, I always judge
them as number agreement tokens. Conversely, (2b) is an interesting case
in that despite the presence of *many*, noun phrases including *many a* are
conceptualized as singular not only in present-day English but also in earlier
English. None of the tokens containing *many a* in the *OED* showed plural
features.

    In addition, uncountable mass nouns were counted as instances of num-
ber agreement even when two notional subjects linked by *and* are used as in
(3):

(3)   There is meat and wine in the pantry.   (COCA, fiction)

3) repetition
As Biber et al. (1999: 952) note, the sequence *there* + *be* is occasionally
used to organize the discourse through repeated use (see a more detailed
discussion in connection with Section 4.3 of Chapter 4 and Section 8.1 of
Chapter 8). For instance, some quotation texts in the *OED* include more
than one *there* + *be* sentence:

(4)   There are things that are certainly utterly outrageous.... Then, there
       is dirty tricks, then there is political hardball, then there is pranks.
                    [1973, P.J Buchanan in *Black Panther* 6 Oct. 17/3, *OED*]

In the analysis of the *OED*, such repeated instances of *there* are counted as
a single instance of *there* in this study. Because the *OED* only yields occurrences per 100 quotation texts, counting all instances, instead of just one,
would distort the real situation. Owing to the low frequency of such tokens
(336 occurrences out of over 43,000 *there* + *be* tokens in the *OED*), the general tendencies found by this study can be considered quite accurate. Meanwhile, in the analysis of other corpora, each token including repetitions is
counted, because they form part of their occurrences per 10,000 words.

This study will analyze the definiteness of notional subjects. Proper nouns, demonstratives, and definite articles are categorized as definite notional subjects. Exceptional cases are as follows:

1) superlatives

When notional subjects are superlative as in (5), such tokens are not counted as definite notional subjects, even though the syntactic form represents a definite noun phrase.

(5)   I believe, there is <u>the best</u> opportunity here for lasting peace, by which I mean a total cessation of violence ...   (BNC, spoken)

2) *the same*

By basing her argument on Prince (1992), Abbot (2006) maintains that there are definite reading and indefinite reading in existential sentences when notional subjects containing *the same* are used. Consider the following examples:

(6) a.   There were <u>the same</u> nominees on both ballots
     b.   The Executive Committee came up with a list of nominees, and it happened that the Nominating Committee chose <u>the same</u> nominees.

(Abbot 2006)

Prince (1992) provides an account that (6a) is an example of indefinite reading, meaning that the two *ballots* had the same choices, while *the same nominees* in (6b) refers to the *Executive Committee*'s *list* and thus renders definite reading. Since it is often difficult to draw the line between definite and indefinite reading especially in the *OED*, all instances of notional subjects with *the same* are included as definite notional subjects.

3) *all*

Notional subjects including *all* as in (7a) are considered indefinite notional subjects, while those containing definite elements like *this* as in (7b) are considered definite:

(7) a.   ... what happened was it was a hell of a stink in dock, because there was <u>all</u> different workers for different jobs, ...

(BNC, speech)

     b.   But it was a pity that there was <u>all this</u> emphasis on blood.

(BNC, fiction)

Thus, this study considers *all* without definite elements indefinite and *all* with definite elements as definite.

Finally, transcription of speech often poses difficulties for this analysis. For example, notional subjects are missing in a number of cases as in the following example:

(8) a. … there were, there were reasons why there were a lot of women working in the studios …   (WordBanks, UKspoken)
     b. Yes. In the national agreement, there is.   (COCA, spoken)
     c. But er there there were I couldn't see none.   (BNC, spoken)

(8a) is a case of repetition of *there + be*; and the first token of *there were* is excluded from the analysis (so only one token is added to the count for (8a)). Example (8b), despite an omitted notional subject, forms an existential sentence when the notional subject is retrievable from the context. Furthermore, *there were* in (8c) lacks the notional subject, and this particular token may not comprise an existential sentence. Therefore, I have included tokens such as (8b) in the count of ordinary existential sentences because the information in respect to the notional subject is available from the context, but excluded (8c) because the existential sentence is incomplete.

2.3 Summary

This chapter summarized the strengths and shortcomings of the *OED*, the main dataset in this study as a data source. Along with previous studies, I argued that it offers invaluable data to elucidate diachronic changes of any linguistic item, since its strengths offset its shortcomings. Some shortcomings of the COHA and the COCA, both of which are important datasets, were also outlined. Some of these problems are correctable, (and some were in fact corrected). The features of the other corpora were also summarized. In addition, the general rules in the data collection were outlined. The results of this study cannot be directly compared with those of other studies, since criteria for including tokens (such as cases of number disagreement, lexically definite notional subjects, repeated appearances of *there + be* sequences) vary from study to study. However, I argued that general trends can still be identified by this study.

Chapter 3

The Diachronic Development of Existential Sentences in Old and Middle English

This chapter will provide a general introduction of how existential sense was realized in Old English and Middle English, based on findings from previous studies. There were three basic types of syntactic structures for expressing existentials in earlier English: *there*-existential sentences, *it*-existential sentences, and zero-existential sentences. Breivik (1989: 38) provides different structures in different manuscripts of line 2210 of *Cursor Mundi* as follows:

(1) a. Þat tim *it* was bot a language (Cotton).
'At that time there was only one language'
b. Þat time was bot an language (Fairfax).
c. Þat time *it* was bot a language (Göttingen).
d. Þat tyme was þer but o language (Trinity).

(Breivik 1989: 38)

Examples (1a, c) are *it*-existential sentences, (1b) is a zero-existential sentence, and (1d) is a *there*-existential sentence. Breivik (1989) observes that "existential *it* lingered on after Early Modern English in archaic ballad style," but the existential construction using *it* was very rare in early English. Thus, since previous studies tended to ignore *it*-existential sentences, he does as well. The following three patterns were prevalent in Old English:

Type A: Topic + verb + (Loc)
(2) a. Micel yfelnyss wæs in iudeiscum mannum
'There was great evilness in Jewish men'   (Ælfric 1 XI: 317)

    b.   7 gyt ma wœs þe þœt don ne wolde
        'but there were yet more who would not do so'   (Bede 48: 21)
        (Breivik 1991: 35)

Type B: (Loc) + verb + NP
(3) a.   On ðam ylcan dæge com sum bisceop helenus gehaten
        'On that same day came a bishop who was called Helenus'
        (Ælfric 1 II: 57–58)
    b.   Nis nan leahter swa healic þœt man ne mœg gebtan
        'There is no sin so great that a man may not atone for it'
        (Ælfric 1 XII: 157–158)
        (Breivik 1991: 35)

Type C: *there* construction
(4) a.   Gif ðær beoð fiftig wera wunigende on þam earde
        'If there are fifty en living in the place'   (Ælfric 1 XIII: 196)
    b.   Þær bið swyðe mycel gewinn betweonan him
        'There is very much strife between them.   (Orosius 20: 17–18)
        (Breivik 1991: 36)

Types A and B constitute a zero-existential, parallel with (1b), while Type C exhibits the same construction as the prototypcial *there* existential sentence of today. According to Breivik (1977, 1981, 1983, 1984, 1989, 1990) and Breivik & Swan (2000), Type B above is governed by the Old English verb-second construction rule, as it is generally agreed that Old English was a verb-second language. Type A is a case in which the NP precedes the verb. Breivik (1977, 1981, 1983, 1984, 1989, 1990) offers the following data of when and how *there*-existential sentences began to outnumber their zero-existential counterparts:

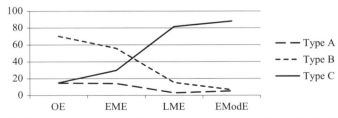

Figure 3-1: Percentage change in the various types of existential sentence in Old English (OE), Early Middle English (EME), Late Middle English (LME), and Early Modern English (EModE)
(From Breivik 1977, 1981, 1983, 1984, 1989, 1990)

In the Old English period, Type B prevailed, but yielded its place to the *there*-existential structure of Type C in Late Middle English, while Type A showed consistently low occurrence. This pattern is well in accordance with the widely shared view that *there*-existential sentences were established by the end of Middle English. According to Breivik (1977, 1981, 1983, 1984, 1989, 1990), by the beginning of Early Modern English, the zero-existential construction of Types A and B was governed by the same syntactic and semantic rules that operate in contemporary English as discussed in Section 1.1: it expresses the immediate scene of the speaker/writer. In contrast, the speaker's vantage point is distant from the referent in *there*-existential sentences. Thus, the use or non-use of *there* at the beginning of Modern English already reflected the semantic and functional distinctions in force today. Further syntactic development had yet to advance further during the Modern English period, as will be elucidated in Chapter 4, but expletive *there* already played a major role in expressing the objective existence of a referent in Late Middle English, as Figure 3-1 shows.

Breivik & Swan (2000) maintain that existential *there* evolved into its present form as follows: the separation of existential *there* from locative *there* occurred in Old English, in the very local context in which *there* was coreferential with a locative phrase in the same sentence. As English shifted typologically from verb-second (TVX, T=topic) to verb-medial (SVX) order, the Old English topic-marker *there* was syntactically reanalyzed as a subject. The reanalysis from a locative adverb to an empty topic-marker thus led to its grammaticalization and subjectification.

The idea is supported by empirical data on the grammaticalization of locatives into existential adverbs in Scandinavian languages such as Danish, Norwegian, and Swedish, which are related to English. According to Breivik (1977, 1981, 1983, 1984, 1989, 1990), Breivik & Martínez-Insua (2008), and Breivik & Swan (2000), these languages have existential expletive markers identical to their locative adverbs: Danish and Norwegian *der/der* and (Southern) Swedish *där/där*. These previous studies cite Western (1921), who states that the presence of the co-referential locative adverb in (5b) led to the generation of the existential adverb in (5c) from the fully stressed locative adverb in (5a) in Norwegian:

(5) a.   Der$_{loc}$ bor en gammel mann.
         'There$_{loc}$ lives an old man'
    b.   Der$_{loc}$ bor en gammel mann, i det huset.
         'There$_{loc}$ lives an old man, in that house'

    c.   Der_{exis} bor en gammel mann i det huset.

Der$_{exis}$ bor en gammel mann i det huset.
    'There$_{exis}$ lives an old man in that house'

                    (Breivik & Martínez-Insua 2008)

Breivik (1977, 1981, 1983, 1984, 1989, 1990), Breivik & Martínez-Insua (2008), and Breivik & Swan (2000) conjecture that these Scandinavian languages, as well as English, followed the same development, noting that in early English, the distinction between locative *there* and existential *there* was so slight that it is possible to assume that existential *there* functioned more or less as adverb.

The following chapters will elaborate on the diachronic development of *there* and the *there* + *be* sequence as well as the *there* + VP construction in the English language. It would be interesting to compare their developmental paths in English.

Chapter 4

The Diachronic Development and Current Situations of *there* and *there* + *be*[1]

Quite a few studies have investigated the development of existential sentences from a diachronic perspective in the literature, but their scope is either limited to a fixed period of time, or they are based upon small-scale corpora. An extensive study spanning the whole of English history is certainly required. As mentioned in Chapter 2, the *OED* offers abundant, comprehensive diachronic data from throughout the history of English, so it can facilitate identification of the time when a target item first appeared in English. Thus, the investigation into the *OED* provides a profound insight into the course existential sentences in English have taken.

This chapter will focus on the prototypical form *there* + *be*. In present-day English, the sequence of *there* + *be* accounts for 99.1% of the data in the FLOB and 97.8% of the data in the Frown (conversely, 0.9% and 2.2% of the tokens form *there* + VP in the FLOB and Frown respectively). We will examine how it diachronically developed into what it is in terms of frequency and syntactic configuration and how it semantically and pragmatically functions in present-day English. As a matter of fact, a very long time was needed for *there* + *be* to come to function in many ways.

---

[1] Earlier versions of part of the present chapter appeared as Yaguchi (2010a), Yaguchi (2013) and Yaguchi (2016b).

4.1   The syntactic development of *there + be*

This section will overview how existential *there + be* prevailed in number and expanded its syntactic variations. As noted in Chapter 3, there are general agreements in the literature that existential *there* originated from the adverb of locative *there* and that *there + be* became established by the end of Middle English. We will conduct an examination into how the original adverbial nature was attenuated in existential *there*. According to a number of previous studies (e.g. Breivik 1977, 1981, 1983, 1989, 1990, 1997, Nagashima 1992, Hosaka 1999, Breivik & Swan 2000, Breivik & Martínez-Insua 2008, Pfenninger 2009, *inter alia*), its sense of existence was already attested in Old English, where full-fledged existential sentences with expletive uses of *there* already occurred as in (1):

(1) a.   Þær is sum beladung on ðær sægne. [Ælfric's *Lives of Saints*]
(by Breivik and Martínez-Insua 2008: 353)

  b.   forÞi Þe Þær syndon IX hus innan Þær helle and …
[Homily 4, l.42, *Eleven Old English Rogationtide Homilies*]
(by Ukaji personal communication)

  c.   & Þær wæs micel ungeÞuærnes Þære Þeode betweox him selfum.
[*Anglo-Saxon Chronicle* MS A Early]
(by Hosaka 1999: 10)

The three examples in (1) all use prepositional phrases to designate location along with the presence of *there*, which strongly suggests that *there* in these cases is expletive and does not denote any location.

Now we are in a position to examine how *there + be* sentences diachronically developed into the present system by analyzing quotation texts in the *OED*. All the tokens of *there + be* were counted, and the frequencies of *there's*, *there is*, *there are*, *there was*, and *there were* were calculated. The shortened form *there're* was excluded from the analysis, because of its scarcity of the data in the *OED* (viz. only two tokens). Furthermore, tokens with elements between *there* and *be* or inversions of *there* and *be* were excluded from the analysis. Since only a few tokens of these kinds occur, their exclusion will have little effect on the result. Other syntactic sequences containing auxiliaries, such as *there + will + be*, *there + be + going + to*, *there + have + been*, *there + be* and *there + being*, were also excluded from the analysis, partly because of their low frequencies in present-day English as will be referred to in Chapter 8 (16.4% for FLOB and 15.9% for Frown), but mainly because of the great differences in their first appearance dates in the *OED*. As discussed in Chapter 2, since the locative and the existential senses are occasionally difficult to distinguish, the present analysis may include ambiguous tokens. There are several other caveats in the data collection. Observe (2) through (4):

(2)   Whan the dwellers <u>there were</u> aware of hit.

[1489, Caxton, *Faytes of A.* II. iii. 94, *OED*]

(3)   In the mountains of Sudnos in Bohemia <u>there was</u> some years ago <u>found</u> a metal, by them called Bismuto.

[1674, *Phil. Trans.* IX. 189, *OED*]

(4)   Feole thinges <u>ther beth</u> ynne Craftilich ymad with gynne.

[c1410, *Chron, Eng.* 180 in Ritson *Metr Rom.* (1802) II, *OED*]

Cases such as (2) were excluded from the count, since *there* is used as a locative adverb. Passive tokens such as (3) are included in the data. Sentences with verbal forms like *beo, ben, beth, beoth, byeth, beon, bi, bio, sind, syd, siondon, sindon, syndon, synde, sende, sunde, sonde, seondeð,* etc. as in (4) were excluded from the analysis even though they are fully considered to be *there + be.* Since they had become obsolescent by Modern English, their exclusion will hardly affect the results of the present research, which highlights Modern English and present-day English. In addition, when the dates of some quotation texts span several years (such as 1470–85 and 1620–55), the first year is adopted as date for the purposes of this study. While it may be true that the data includes locative *there + be* sentences and excludes genuine *there + be* sentences containing an adverbial phrase between *there* and *be* or archaic forms of *be*, possible errors of those kinds are considered to be minor, partly because the amount of data as a whole is sufficiently ample, and partly because the present analysis focuses on Modern English and present-day English. All the tokens that include *there's, there is, there are, there was,* and *there were* are collected (over 43,400 tokens in total) by verbal form for each 50-year period. After exporting some of the quotation texts with their quotation dates (since the *OED*'s version 3.1 disallows full exporting of searched data, missing dates and texts were manually retrieved) to an Excel spreadsheet, quantitative analysis was conducted to identify quoted dates accurately. The figure below illustrates the numbers of quotation texts with *there + be* sentences out of a hundred quotation texts in the *OED* every 50 years (note Yaguchi (2010a)) and the table below exhibits the raw occurrences:

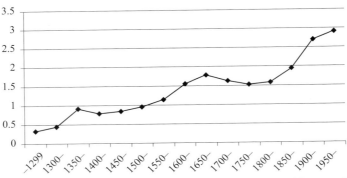

occurrences per 100 quotation texts

Figure 4-1: Frequency of *there* + *be* sentences in *OED*

Table 4-1: Raw occurrences of existential sentences in *OED*

	-1299	1300-	1350-	1400-	1450-	1500-	1550-	1600-	1650-	1700-	1750-	1800-	1850-	1900-	1950-
sum	186	178	475	467	444	805	1,855	3,192	3,139	2,139	2,164	4,441	9,336	6,126	8,496

Apparently, after its usage increased gradually until the end of Modern English, the *there* + *be* construction showed a sharp increase in the twentieth century. It is true that this pattern may have resulted from longer quotation texts in present-day English (more than 16 words per quotation in twentieth century English vs. approximately 13 words per quotation in Modern English), as noted in Chapter 2. However, *there* + *be* sentences are used more frequently in present-day English than in earlier periods (about 38% more abundantly in the period from 1900 to 1949 than in the period from 1850 to 1899), apart from the lengthening of each quotation text (23% longer in word count than in the 1850–1899 period). Thus, it is attested that existential *there* + *be* made a substantial increase in the twentieth century.

In line with their rise in frequency, *there* + *be* sentences expanded their syntactic variation over time as well. In present-day English, the following five syntactic structures are available, in addition to the affirmative form:

(5) a.   Was there an accident in the town?   [Questions]

    b.   There appears to be an accident in the town.   [Subject Raising]

    c.   He expected there to be an accident in the town.

                [Object Raising (for Epistemic Verb)]

    d.   It is possible for there to be an accident in the town.

                [Object Raising (for Preposition)]

e.   There was an accident in the town, wasn't there?

[Tag Questions]

As mentioned in Chapter 3, Breivik & Swan (2000) and Breivik (1990: 38) state that during the shift of English from verb-second (TVX) to verb medial (SVX) word order, English word order rules underwent extensive changes, and the Old English topic-marker *there* came to be syntactically reanalyzed as an empty subject.[2] Breivik (1981, 1989) insists that as a result of this reanalysis, the five structures in (5) came to be available in present-day English, because *there* now acts as a subject NP. Quirk et al. (1985: 1408) also maintain that existential *there* behaves like the subject of a clause in present-day English and is thereby allowed to appear in the five structures exemplified as in (5). Additionally, many other linguists have noted the subject-like behavior of existential *there* (e.g. Ross 1973, Greenbaum & Quirk 1990: 426, Biber et al. 1999: 944, Downing & Locke 2002: 138, Huddleston & Pullum 2002: 1390, *inter alia*). Whereas the status of *there* concerning whether it is an NP and/or a subject is worth examining, this study focuses instead on providing descriptive data.

Here, it is worthwhile to examine in depth the dates each of the structures in (5) emerged, scrutinizing the *OED*, COHA, CLMETEV, CED, CEECS, and the Helsinki Corpus as well as previous studies. Let us first examine the question form. The first token in the *OED* appears in around 1305 as in (6):

(6)   Question
       What is Þer in paradis, Bot grasse and flure and grene ris?

[c1305, *Land Cokayne* 8, *OED*]

Hosaka (1999), whose research used data from the Helsinki Corpus, found that the first tokens emerged between 1350 and 1420:

(7) a.   "Is ther any thing thane," quod sche, …
               [1350–1420, BOETHCH, 435, C1, Helsinki, by Hosaka]
      b.   "And, fader, es Þar na noÞer wan?"
               [1350–1420, CURSOR, 222, Helsinki, by Hosaka]

Nagashima (1992: 58) identified the first question token in the second half of the thirteen century. Therefore, this token in (8) using *beo* is the earliest

---

[2] Breivik (1991: 38) states that by 1550, the use or non-use of *there* is virtually governed by the same syntactic operative in present-day English, as mentioned in Chapter 3.

one detected by my literature survey.

(8) Ʒef hire lauerd is forwurde, / An unorne at bedde & at borde, /
Hu miʒte þar beo eni luue / Wanne a swuch cheorles buc hire ley
buue? / Hu mai þar eni luue beo / Þar swuch man gropeʒ hire
þeo? (1491–96)[3] [*The Owl and the Nightingale*, by Nagashima]

The present investigation into the *OED* did not include any tokens containing *beo* type verbs.

Second, subject raising shows an interesting development. According
to my knowledge, no comprehensive diachronic research seems to exist on
the raising of existential *there* in English. Thus, a descriptive record of this
linguistic structure is required. Since there were not as many functional differences between *there + be* and *there + VP* sentences up to 1750, as will
be discussed in Chapter 7, the data here include raising tokens of *there +
VP*. In addition, I would like to adopt the broadest possible definition of
raising constructions. The available literature generally applies Denison's
(1993: 219) definition: "In Present-day English the verbs which are generally given a Raising analysis are SEEM, CHANCE and their synonyms,
aspectual verbs like START, CEASE when used with non-agentive subjects
… plus a number of predicates like BE *certain*, BE *likely*, etc." This study
also includes deontic type of existential sentences following the rationale that
even deontic sentences, such as *There is required to be a ceremony*,[4] can be
parsed as raising because of the empty nature of *there*, as subject raising is a
structure in which "surface subjects … are not 'really' subject of the higher
verb" (Denison 1993: 218). Interestingly enough, deontic modals such as *to
be* can occasionally be interpreted as epistemic. For example, the following
is likely to evoke an epistemic sense:

(9) … the higher you ascend in the social scale among boys, the less of
bullying there is to be found. (1862, COHA)

Thus, the present analysis encompasses raising structures that use 'seem',
'happen', 'begin', '*be* + adjective', and deontic type predicates.

The first token of subject raising of *there + be* in the *OED* appears in

---

[3] Translated by British Library London as follows (http://www.southampton.ac.uk/~wpwt
/trans/owl/owltrans.htm#1400):
  If her lord is inadequate, and has little to offer in bed and at the table, how could
  there be any love when such a churl's carcase was lying on top of her? How can
  there be any love when a man like that is pawing her thigh?
[4] This is not a grammatically correct sentence in current English.

1511 as shown in (10):

(10)   There is required to be therein [in their hearts] moche cautele and sobrenesse.[5]   [1511, Elyot *Gov.* l. iv, *OED*]

Earlier tokens of (11), which appear in *Paston Letters*, written in 1465 and 1478, are given by Breivik (1991) and Breivik & Martínez (2008):

(11) a.   … ther is like to be troble in the maner of Oxenhed …
         [1478, *Paston Letters*, by Breivik (1991: 47) and Breivik & Martínez (2008)]

     b.   … that ther wer leek to be do gret harme on bothe ouyr pertyes.[6]
                                 [1465, *Paston Letters*, by Breivik (1991: 47)]

Hosaka (1999) cites the earliest token appearing in the Helsinki Corpus from 1531:

(12)   For sone after the begynniyng of the citie there hapned to be a great earth quaue, …   [1531, ELYOT 153, by Hosaka (1999)]

While the above texts are all manifestations of the *there + be* construction, an even earlier token found in this present research is a *there + VP* construction from the *OED*:

(13)   And by discente Þer is not like to ffalle gretter heritage to any man than to Þe kyng.
       [c1460, Fortescue *Absol. & Lim. Mon.* x. 134, *OED*, by Yaguchi (2016b)]

I will provide a detailed discussion of this particular token in Chapter 7, in connection with the *there + VP* construction. Despite its *there + VP* status, however, as a raising case, (13) is the earliest token in the *OED* in the present search. We can confirm that subject raising of existential sentences started to appear in writing as early as around the middle of the fifteenth century. From this point, raising tokens of *there + VP* will also be included in the discussion and the data in this chapter.

A close examination of the quotation texts in the *OED* reveals the chronological development of syntactic configurations. The earliest subject raising took the form *there + be + like(ly) + to* in the mid-1400s, as seen in

---

[5] As noted in Footnote 4, deontic raising of this kind is considered ill-formed according to the grammatical system in present-day English.

[6] The *OED* (s.v. *do* verb., 8 γ) explains that *do* was used as *done* in earlier English.

(11a, b) and (13). In other words, the employment of *there* + *be* + adjective + *to* led the development of subject raising. Subsequently, the earliest raising token of *there* + *be* of (10), assuming the form of *be* + past participle (pp) + *to*, emerged in the *OED* (dating from 1511). Thus, the first two syntactic configurations share the employment of an adjectival component.

It is not until the early 1530s that raising verbs began to appear; an example of *happen* was identified in the Helsinki Corpus by Hosaka (1999), as shown in (12). The *OED*'s oldest example of *there* + verb + *to*-type raising appeared in association with the verb *chance* in the mid-1500s, as shown in (14). The *OED* contains six tokens that use *happen* or *chance* between 1553 and 1649. (Note that (14) is a case using *come* instead of *be*. Out of the six tokens, three are instances of *there* + VP.) In contrast, *seem*, the most common raising verb in the *OED* (accounting for 64.0% of all verb-type subject raising tokens and 37.4% of all subject raising tokens), first appeared in the *OED* as late as 1603, as seen in (15):[7]

(14)   There chaunsed ... to come to my hands, a shiete of printed paper.[8]
         [1553, Eden *Treat. New Ind.* (Arb.) 5, *OED*, by Denison (1993; 233)]

(15)   In Philosophie, where at the first there seemeth ... to be some strangenesse, obscuritie, and ....
                                    [1603, Holland *Plutarch's Mor.* 62, *OED*]

Thus, verb-based raising originated with a 'happen' type semantic function, followed by an epistemic 'seem' type.[9] Aspectual raising of the 'begin' type was established much later, around the middle of the nineteenth century:[10]

(16)   When, after so much talking and tampering, there began to be re-crimination among the leaguers.
                                    [1860, Motley *Netherl.* iv. I. 117, *OED*]

Along with the appearance of verbal raising sentences, the passive complex *there* + *be* + *to* + *be* + pp + NP emerged in the latter half of the 1500s:

---

[7] Hosaka (1999) reports a *seem* token from 1612.

[8] As discussed in 7.1 of Chapter 7, *there* + *chance to* + verb is not allowed in the grammatical system of present-day English.

[9] The *there* + *appear* + *to* + *be* sequence appeared for the first time only in 1713. It seems that the frequent use of *there* + *seem* + *to* induced the emergence of *there* + *appear* + *to*.

Visser (1969: 1369–1371) reports the first 'happen' type and 'seem' type raising tokens of non-*there* subjects appeared in c.1205 and c.1380 respectively.

[10] In COHA, the first token appears in 1839.

(17) a.   There are also to bee founde and seene in armes Crosses double partited, semyed, quartered of the fielde wherein they stande.

[1572, J. Bosselwell *Armorie* 26, *OED*]

   b.   There is to be found a M. Hagbuts within youre house to ruinate this Realme.

[1574, Hellowes *Gueuara's Fam. Ep.* (1584) 243, *OED*]

   c.   There were to be imploied five or six hundred courts about a wall of small bredth.

[1587, Fleming *Contn. Holinshed* III. 1542/1, *OED*]

It should be noted that in this stage any element between *there* + *be* and *to* was no longer required to form the raising construction. The passive structure in (17) was followed in the middle of the next century by *there* + *be* + *to* + *be* + NP, as in (18):

(18) a.   There are to be peculiar elective plaisters to heale these wounds, because these wounds are often differing.

[1643, T. Goodwin *Child of Light* 117, *OED*]

   b.   This day there is to be a Carousel, viz. Running at the Quintain and the Ring.   [1693, *Lond. Gaz.* No. 2845/2, *OED*]

Tokens (17) and (18) represent similar meanings, to the extent that the presence of pp such as *founde*, *seene* and *imploied* in (17) is not necessarily required in present-day English grammar. One can conjecture that what was expressed by the passive element in the late 1500s came to be omitted by pragmatic inference and reinforcement, resulting in the formation of the *there* + *be* + *to* + *be* + NP structure. In other words, this configuration is considered to be a reduced version of the more semantically rich structure in (17). Of course, it can be argued that these two are distinct structures in that the structure shown in (17a) was independently available to express a locative phrase before NP; in fact, no *there* + *be* + *to* + *be* + NP tokens in the *OED* contain a locative phrase before NP. Nevertheless, out of the *OED*'s nineteen instances of *there* + *be* + *to* + *be* + pp + (Locative) + NP + (Locative) that appear between 1571 and 1670, only six comprise the placement of locative before NP.[11] Therefore, our hypothesis that the *there* + *be* + *to* + *be* + NP structure emerged through pragmatic inference and reinforcement is maintained. In fact, the following table shows that in the early stage of the construction's development, up to 1670, the use of pp was semanti-

---

[11] Of the thirty tokens in the *OED*, nine contain locative before NP.

cally required in the formation of *there* + *be* + *to* + *be*-type raising: about 30 years later, after the emergence of the pp-less simple form in 1643, it became the major form.

Table 4-2: The ratio of *there* + *be* + *to* + *be* tokens to the total use of *there* + *be* + *to* + *be* + pp and *there* + *be* + *to* + *be* in *OED*

1571–1670[12]	1671–1770	1771–1870	1871–1970
5.3% (1/19)	85.7% (6/7)	88.9% (24/27)	78.6% (44/56)

The above discussion is summarized in the following diagram:

1460s	1510s	1550s	1570s	1600s	1640s		1860s
→*there* + *be* + adj + *to*							
	→*there* + *be* + pp + *to*						
		→*there* + verb + *to*					
		(happen)		(seem)			(begin)
			→*there* + *be* + *to* + *be* + pp				
				→*there* + *be* + *to* + *be*			

Figure 4-2: The chronological order of subject raising development in *OED*

Note that subject raising originated from *be* + adjective + *to* components, then adopted the use of verbal predicates, and subsequently developed into simpler adjective-less or verb-less forms in its final stages. Based on the fact that syntactic configurations of non-*there* subject raising, namely, Subject + *be* + adj + *to*; Subject + *be* + pp + *to*; Subject + verb + *to*; and Subject + *be* + *to* + *be* + pp, were all available in the 1400s (cf. Denison 1993: Chapter 4 and Fischer 1991: 147) and that Subject + *be* + *to* was already operative in Old English (cf. Visser 1969: 1445–1474), this observed order may indicate that Subject + *be* + adjective + *to* was the most explicit syntactic configuration and/or the most available configuration at that time to realize an epistemic sense by using the subject of the expletive *there* and that the simplest form of *there* + *be* + *to* offers insufficient clues to be parsed as raising. The late appearance of *there* + *begin* + *to* may be attributed to the difference in aspect between *begin to* and existential sentences in early English. Further research to identify the relationship between the above discussed order and these factors is greatly required. In Section 4.2, the dia-

---

[12] The year 1571 was set as the first year because the first token of *there* + *be* + *to* + *be* + pp appeared in 1572.

chronic change in frequencies of subject raising tokens will be shown.

The next structure that we will consider is, of course, object raising for epistemic verbs. It is, however, unfortunate that there is not much data to show the date when the structure concerned made frequent appearances in the *OED*. In addition, none of the previous diachronic studies that I have researched referred to object raising. The present search can only provide the following token from the *OED* in Early Modern English.

(19)   And this boke made swepestake of the blessed sacrament, declaring there to be nothing els but bare bread and wine.

[1557, R. Edgeworth *Serm*.314, *OED*]

It is hoped that further research concerning object raising will be conducted more extensively.

The other type of object raising involving the object of preposition *for*, as in (5d), is also scarce in terms of frequency in any corpus. My research result shows that it needed more than 250 years to emerge since object raising was first observed in 1557 as in (19). In addition to the earliest token of a quotation text from 1933 in the *OED* as in (20a), I have found a token from 1839 in the COHA as in (20b) and a token from 1884 in the CLMETEV as in (20c).

(20) a.   The strength of American parties is, as a rule, too sectional, too much divorced from any current national controversies, for there to be anything like our 'swing of the pendulum'.
                [1933, D. W. Brogan *Amer. Polit. Sytem* x. iv. 368, *OED*]
       b.   It is not usual for there to be two Moderators of the Assembly at the same time.
            [1839, Samuel Miller *Report of the Presbyterian church case*, COHA]
       c.   ... but it is too late now for there to be any chance of the Queen's sending for me tonight.
                [1884, Webster *Daffodil and the Croäxaxicans*, CLMETEV]

In fact, the frequency of occurrences is low, and therefore, caution should be taken in the process of determining the date of the first appearance. As far as the present search is concerned, the year 1839 is considered to be the first year for *there* to emerge as the object of the preposition *for*.

In the same vein, we witness several, not many, tokens of tag question in our references in earlier English. Only two tokens were retrieved in Early Modern English from the *OED*, the Helsinki Corpus, the CLMETEV, CED, and CEECS:

(21) a.   ... take the Hand-basket, and heere, there's ten shillings is there not?   [1595, Warner William *Menaecmi*, CED]
     b.   I beleeve there is some such doings, is there not?
                                   [1648, unknown *Woman Will Have*, CED]

It should be mentioned that both tag questions take the form of *is there not*, not *is not there*. According to Ukaji (1977), the tag question, in general, had developed by Early Modern English times, taking several different syntactic forms. In spite of the extensive coverage of a wide variety of genres by the *OED*, the only token I have retrieved from Middle and Early Modern English is the following example:

(22)   Here's a most sweet Gudgeon swallowed, is there not?
             [1606, *Sir G. Goosecappe* I. iii. in Bullen *O.Pl.* III 21, *OED*]

Example (22) is a token in which *there* in the tag question refers to the pronominal form of *here*.[13] Ukaji (1977) also provides the same type of tag question as follows:

(23)   Here's goodly 'parrell, is there not?
             [1589–1590, Christopher Marlowe, *The Jew of Malta* 1830–31, by Ukaji (1977)]

Certainly, tag questions for existential sentences as well as *here* + *be* sentences were used in Early Modern English, but perhaps because of their low occurrences in writing, no instances were retrieved from data of Middle English. Further research into Middle and Early Modern English texts is strongly desired. However, since the early 1800s, quite a few tokens appeared in the corpora. Note (24):

---

[13] In present-day English, it is impossible to employ tag questions with *here* + *be* sentences. For instance, the following sentence is ungrammatical:
     *Here's your coat, isn't there?
Since *here* + *be* sentences function presentatively, the speaker's categorical attitude is expressed, which is inconsistent with her/his expression of uncertainty by employing a question.

(24) a.   There is nothing degrading in helping, is there?

     [1815, David Humphreys *The Yankey in England*, COHA]

 b.   "There is not enough, is there?" asked St. George.

     [1826, Benjamin Disraeli *Vivian Grey*, CLMETEV]

 c.   "What brings you away out here? there is a poor chance for you in the country, isn't there ?"

     [1835, Thomas Frederick W. *Clinton Bradshaw*, COHA]

The negative tag question form appeared in two configurations, namely *be* + *there* + *not* and *be* + *not* + *there*, in Late Modern English. Note the following texts:

(25) a.   ... surely, there is something of levity in this impatience. Is there not? [1822, Neal John *Logan: A Family History* 1, COHA]

 b.   There's a change comed over him ... is there not?

     [1848, Mrs. Gaskell *Mary Barton* vi, OED]

 c.   There were two twenties, were there not?

     [1850, *Househ. Words* 21 Sept. 620/1, OED]

 d.   Then, Lottie, there is some comfort in being sick, is not there?
   [1836, Sedgwick, Catharine Maria *The Poor Rich Man and the Rich Poor Man*, COHA]

 e.   I think there is a ladies' vestry somewhere isn't there?

     [1891, G. Gissing *New Grub Street* I. 198, OED]

Examples (25a, b, c) are *be* + *there* + *not*, while examples (24c, 25d, e) are *be* + *not* + *there*. In the COHA's dataset, there is one instance of *is there not* in 1946 as in (26):

(26)   There is the makings of saintliness in all that, is there not?

     [1946, Russell Janney *Miracle of the Bells*, COHA]

It appears that it is not until present-day English that the form of tag question was established as the present order *be* + *not* + *there*.

  Thus, the discussion has so far demonstrated that the process for *there* to be reanalyzed as the subject of a clause taking the above five patterns did not occur overnight; in fact, it took a very long period of 1,000 years. The following figure is a graphical presentation of the diachronic development of the five variations in addition to affirmative form:

	1000	1100	1200	1300	1400	1500	1600	1700	1800	1900	2000
Affirmative											
Question											
Subject Raising											
Object Raising											
for there to											
Tag Question											

Figure 4-3: Historical development of syntactic forms of existential sentences

If the chronological order demonstrated in Figure 4-3 makes a manifestation of how existential *there* developed into a subject, it is possible to hypothesize that the grammatical subject was expanded in the order of question, subject raising, object raising, tag question, and *for there to*.

Here, though sidetracking the discussion, it is quite interesting to consider whether or not adverbial phrases can be used as subjects in the structures into which existential *there* can fit. As a matter of fact, Matsubara (2009a, 2009b) introduces the prepositional phrase subject (henceforth PP subject) exhibiting the following behaviors:

(27) a.   [Under the chair] is a nice place for the cat to sleep.

(Stowell 1981)

    b.   [Under the bed] and [in the fireplace] are not the best places to leave your toys.   (Levine 1989)

    c.   Is [under the bed] a good place to hide?   (Bresnan 1994)

    d.   [Under the chair] seems to be a good hiding place.

(Chametzky1985)

    e.   They consider [after the holidays] to be too late for a family gathering.   (Jaworska 1986)

    f.   For [after lunch] to suit everyone is remarkable.

(Haegeman & Guéron 1999: 153)

(From Matsubara 2009a, 2009b)

In (27a), *under the chair* is a PP subject, which constitutes an adverbial phrase form and functions as the subject in this particular sentence, like existential *there*. It is significant to point out that the PP subject takes similar syntactic structures such as negation (27b), question (27c), subject raising (27d), object raising for epistemic verbs (27e), and object raising for the preposition *for* (27f).[14] In addition, the number between the subject and the verb agrees as example (27b) shows.

Certainly, it is worth trying to see if functional adverbs, *here*, locative *there*, and *now* can be used as the subject in present-day English. I asked six native speakers of English for grammaticality of the following sentences as in (28) to (30):[15]

(28) a.   Here is the best place to hold our conference.
     b.   Is here the best place to hold our conference?
     c. (?)Here is not a very good place to hold our conference.
     d. (?)Here seems to be the best place to hold our conference.
     e. (?)I consider here to be the best place to hold our conference.
     f.   *It makes sense for here to be the best place to hold our conference.

(29) a. (?)There is the best place to hold our conference.
     b.   ? Is there the best place to hold our conference?
     c.   ? There is not a very good place to hold our conference.
     d. ?? There seems to be the best place to hold our conference.
     e. ?? I consider there to be the best place to hold our conference.
     f.   *It makes sense for there to be the best place to hold our conference.

(30) a.   Now is the time to have a really good clear up in the greenhouse.   (BNC)
     b.   Is now the time for change?   (BNC)
     c.   I think now is not the time to give a detailed reply to this. (BNC)
     d.   Certainly, for hard pressed property developers, now seems to be the time to sell.   (Google)
     e.   God wanted now to be the time for me to get major exposure and major success.   (Google)
     f.   … it makes sense for now to be the time to announce the new Austin Powers.   (Google)

---

[14] Additionally, in the same way as *there* + VP sentences have some semantic restrictions for the verb (e.g. transitive verbs are not allowed to be used: ??*There sold books the man in the market*) in present-day English as mentioned in Chapter 7, PP subjects also require only certain types of verbs or predicates (for details, note Matsubara (2009a, 2009b)).

[15] Judgment of acceptability varies according to the native speakers (four American English speakers and two Canadian English speakers). Table 4-3 reflects the average acceptability.

The following table summarizes the acceptability rates of each structure:

Table 4-3: How the adverbial phrase fits into grammatical structures as subject

	there (existential)	PP subject	*there* (locative)	*here*	*now*
Affirmative	OK	OK	OK(?)	OK	OK
Question	OK	OK	OK?	OK	OK
Negation	OK	OK	OK?	OK(?)	OK
Subject raising	OK	OK	??	OK(?)	OK
Object raising	OK	OK	??	OK(?)	OK
for _ to	OK	OK	*	*	OK

Obviously locative *there* is the least inclined to function as subject, whereas *now* can appear in all the slots. It is quite interesting that the degree of how much an adverb or prepositional phrase is conceptualized as subject corresponds with the order of the syntactic development seen in Figure 4-3. The slot in *for _ to* is the most difficult to fit in. Conversely, the resistance of locative *there* to function as a subject can be attributed to its necessity to be distinguishable from existential *there*. It is perhaps reasonable to infer the above criteria (question, negation, subject raising, object raising, *for_to*) is an indicator to determine the syntactic and semantic property a linguistic item possesses regarding subjectness. These features will be further elaborated upon in Chapter 7.

4.2   Subject raising

In the prior section, we have seen how raising crept into existential sentences. In this section, the diachronic change in frequencies of subject raising will be focalized, because it has been used far more often than the other syntactic configurations in the *OED*. Some of the raising tokens of *there* + epistemic verbs (e.g. *there* + *seem* + *to* + *be*, *there* + *appear* + *to* + *be*) such as (31a, b), *there* + *be* + pp + *to* + *be* such as (31c, d), *there* + *be* + adj + *to* + *be* such as (31e), and *there* + *be* + *to* + *be* (31f) will be shown here:[16]

---

[16] *There* + *seem* + NP tokens as below were not included in the present research.
Some fifty years ago ... there seemed a general consensus of opinion that inventors were a nuisance.   [1883, *Law Times* 20 Oct. 409/1, *OED*]

(31) a. There seem to be certain bounds to the quickness and slowness of the succession of those ideas ...

[1690, Locke *Hum. Und.* II. xiv. §9, *OED*]

b. There appear to have been no further military outbreaks of Q fever until the Cyprus epidemic of 1974.

[1978, *Jrnl. R. Soc. Med.* LXXI. 765, *OED*]

c. There are reported to be in Venice ... twentie seven publique clocks.   [1611, Coryat *Crudities* 290, *OED*]

d. To found any harmonic theories on the synonymity of tones in any temperament, when there is known to be no synonymity in nature.

[1875, Ellis in *Helmholtz's Sensations of Tone* App. 659, *OED*]

e. So that now there is like to be a trouble in Triplex.

[1656, S. Holland *Zara* (1719) 71, *OED*]

f. There were to be three Anti-Christs, and ... the last should be born ... in the year 1790.

[1791, D'Israel *Cur. Lit.* (1834) VI. 247, *OED*]

The following graph shows how and when raising came to be entrenched in existential sentences by demonstrating the ratios of subject raising tokens of *there* + VP + *to*, *there* + be + pp/adj + *to*, and *there* + be + *to* and existential tokens to the total of all quotation texts in the *OED* (due to the scarcity of the data before 1500, this graph shows tokens after 1500) (also see Appendix 1):[17]

---

[17] The data include *there* + Raising Predicate + verb as follows:

There chaunsed ... to come to my handes, a shiete of printed paper.

[1553, Eden *Treat. New Ind.* (Arb.) 5, *OED*]

While subject raising of *there* + VP occurred rather frequently in earlier English, it rarely occurs in present-day English. Detailed discussion will be made in Chapter 7.

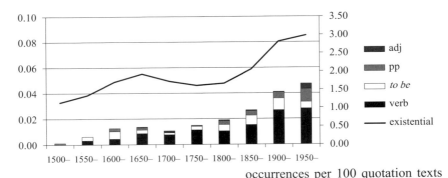

occurrences per 100 quotation texts

Figure 4-4: Ratio of raising tokens to total quotation texts in *OED*[18]

It is true that subject raising increased in frequency, but it can be said that this is the result of the augmentation of *there* + *be* existential sentences, as Figures 4-1 and 4-4 illustrate. Therefore, I will present another graph show-ing the ratio of subject raising to the total use of *there* + *be* and *there* + VP sequences in the *OED* (also note Appendix 1):

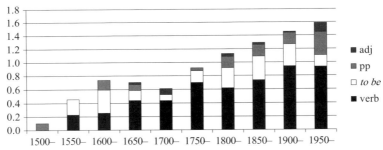

Figure 4-5: Ratio of subject raising of *there* + *be* + *to* + *be* (+ pp), *there* + *be* + adj + *to*, *there* + *be* + pp + *to*, and *there* + verb + *to* to total use of existential sentences *in OED* (%)   (percentage)

It is obvious that Figure 4-5 shows a steady increase of subject raising since 1750 after it exhibited a moderate decline between 1650 and 1749. The two figures above illustrate that after the first employment of *seem*, the major player in subject raising, was witnessed at the beginning of the 1600s, the frequency of *there* + verb + *to* tokens heightened, making a great contribu-tion to the increase of subject raising of existential sentences until now.

---

[18] In this graph, the total occurrences of the *there* + *be* sequence includes subject rais-ing tokens using verbs such as *appear, seem, chance, happen,* and *begin* as predicates.

4.3   The *there* + *be* construction in present-day English

This section will provide how and how often existential *there* is used in present-day English. First, a brief introduction will be made on how existential sentences are employed in contemporary English according to the register, since analysis will be conducted at full length in Chapter 8. Biber et al. (1999: 948) show the distributions in four registers:[19]

Table 4-4: Distribution of existential *there* across registers

Conversation	Fiction	News	Academics
■■■■■■	■■■■■■	■■■■	■■■■■

Each ■ represents 500 occurrences per million words

(From Biber et al. 1999: 948)

Table 4-4 indicates that existential sentences are used at 2,000 to 3,000 occurrences per one million words, in other words, 20 to 30 occurrences per 10,000 words, in four registers. Although the frequency is slightly higher in conversation and fiction than in news and academics, their ubiquitous presence in all the registers suggests their neutrality in nature in terms of formality. All in all, suffice it to say that existential sentences are an essential key element in present-day English.

Second, we should consider pragmatic use of existential *there*. Whereas it is often said that the basic function of existential sentences is to introduce a new referent into discourse, they have a wide variety of functions in actual language use. For instance, as mentioned in Section 1.4 of Chapter 1, it serves a presentative function. I will cite the example (4) of Chapter 1 by Biber et al. (1999: 951) again as (32):

(32)   A man goes in the pub. <u>There's a bear sitting in the corner.</u> He goes up, he goes up to the bartender. He says, why is there a bear sitting over there?   (Biber et al. 1999: 951)

---

[19] The data of Biber et al. (1999: 948), based upon Longman Spoken and Written English Corpus compiled in the late 1990s, is comprised of conversation (British English only), fiction (both American and British English), news (British English only) and academic prose (both American and British English). Biber et al. (1999: 18–25) state that the difference in register offsets the difference between dialects and thereby ignore the fact that the distribution of British English is dominant in their data. As will be discussed in-depth in Chapter 8, however, there are great differences in frequency of existential sentences between American English and British English after the 1990s, so the frequency should be treated with caution.

Biber et al. (1999: 951) state that existential *there* is occasionally employed to focus on the existence or occurrence of something rather than just to introduce it into the discourse. In (32), existential *there* is used to draw attention to the second new referent, *a bear*, the main character of this story. Obviously, the employment of *there* draws the listener's/reader's attention to the referent's existence. This presentative usage is considered a fundamental function of existential sentences, since the existence of a referent is focused on in the discourse.

Meanwhile, as Breivik & Martínez-Insua (2008) have noted, *there* + *be* sentences have a number of pragmatic, interpersonal, and speaker-based functions, such as making corrections or deductions, expressing personal opinions, or eliciting information. (33) and (34) below are examples of correction and repetition respectively, both from Martínez-Insua (2004), while (35) is an example of a "list" *there*-existential sentence, as provided by Breivik (1990: 153):

(33) <pause> Okay so we've got eleven and four is fifteen, and seventeen
      <pause> is thirty two. John577<pause> It says there were thirty pupils.
                                              (Martínez-Insua A. 2004: 138)

(34) A: ... There's only an extra...<unclear> so seven, eight...
      B: Fine.
      C: There's only an extra there!
      D: One, two, three, four, five, six, seven...
      B: We could leave literacy, numeracy...no?
      D: There's only an extra one there.
                                              (Martínez-Insua A. 2004: 145)

(35) A: Who's attending the meeting?
      B: Well, there's (*are) John, Michael, and Janet.
                                                  (Breivik 1990: 153)

The functions of *there* in the examples above, which are observed primarily in speech, are clearly not presentative, since *there* in (33), (34), and (35) neither highlights the existence of a particular referent nor draws the listener's attention to it. Rather, the sequence *there* + *be* in these examples works as a discourse organizer to prepare the listener for new information. *There's* in (35), in particular, is considered to function more or less as a particle, since *there's* is not necessarily required from a syntactic perspective (a thorough discussion of this will follow in Chapter 6). Breivik & Martínez-

Insua (2008) argue that these pragmatic functions have become available in present-day English, as a result of the long process of the grammaticalization and subjectification of *there* and the sequence *there + be*. Apparently, pragmatic, interpersonal, and speaker-based uses as in (33) to (35) have developed in speech: Biber et al. (1999: 953) maintain that these tokens agree with the loose syntactic organization of conversation.

In writing, existential sentences are often used for rhetorical purposes. Examples (36) and (37) show two rhetorical uses of existential sentences as examples:

(36)   There are two reasons for interpolating an insulating layer between a hot working lining and the 'outside.' These are: (a) to cool the back face, e.g., to preserve the mechanical integrity of an enclosing metal shell or for reasons of safety outside a wall or roof; and (b) to reduce the heat flux through the lining and hence improve process fuel economy. Both motives may apply at the same time, though the second usually predominates.   (Frown, science)

(37)   Later there would be time for the pain and pleasure lust lends to love. Time for body lines and angles that provoke the astounded primitive to leap delighted from the civilised skin, and tear the woman to him, There would be time for words obscene and dangerous. There would be time for cruel laughter to excite, and for ribbons colourfully to bind limbs to a sickening, thrilling subjugation. There would be time for flowers to put out the eyes, and for silken softness to close the ears. And time also in that dark and silent world for the howl of the lonely man, who had feared eternal exile.
                    (FLOB, general fiction)

(36) and (37) show the use of existential sentences as organizers of discourse. In (36), by presenting how many points the writer intends to bring up in the following discourse, she/he can get her/his message across clearly and effectively. Existential sentences are employed for this purpose, showing the number of points she/he will make in advance. On the other hand, the existential sentences in (37) serve rhetorically to organize the text through repetition of the same phrase. (See more discussion in Chapter 8.) Thus, in present-day English, we find a wide range of pragmatic functions both in speech and writing. As seen in connection with Figure 4-1, the boosted use of existential sentences in the twentieth century seems to reflect their expanded functions. At the same time, even though we cannot attest

the use in speech in olden times, it is possible to assume that the variety of pragmatic functions were developed from speech.

4.4   Summary

This chapter showed the diachronic development of *there* + *be* sentences in frequency and syntactic variation. Existential sentences have expanded in both aspects, making themselves an indispensable element in present-day English. The chronological order of the syntactic development assuming *there* as subject was identified. The diachronic development of subject raising was also focalized in terms of syntactic configurations and their frequencies. Existential *there* was compared with that of the functional adverbs, *here*, locative *there*, and *now* in present-day English. It was demonstrated that whether the register be formal or informal, in writing or in speech, existential sentences are used quite frequently in any register.

Chapter 5

The Diachronic Development
of *there* + singular *be* as a Phrase[1]

As mentioned in the Introduction, we have seen that one of the interesting phenomena concerning existential sentences is number disagreement between *be* and the notional subject, as in *There's two women in the waiting room*, which shows the status of *there's* as a single unit. This chapter will demonstrate that *there* and *be* have been diachronically becoming an inseparable phrase, causing the grammaticalization and subjectification of *there* + singular *be*, in particular. We will see when and how the grammaticalization and subjectification took place. Section 5.1 provides an overview of *there's* in present-day English, while Section 5.2 highlights the diachronic development of *there* + *be*. Section 5.3 focuses on the contracted form *there's*, and Section 5.4 discusses the characteristics of *there was*, which has rarely been the target of any previous research, to my knowledge. Section 5.5 reveals the present status of *here's*, in comparison with *there's*. A summary of this chapter will be offered in the last section.

5.1 An overview of the contracted form *there's*

It is widely acknowledged that the contracted form of *there* + *is*, i.e. *there's*, often disagrees with the notional subject in number in present-day English (e.g. Wolfram & Christian 1976, Feagin 1979, Woods 1979, Quirk et

---

[1] Early versions of part of Chapter 5 appeared as Yaguchi (2010a) and Yaguchi (2010b).

al. 1985: 1405, Eisikovits 1991, DeWolf 1992, Meechan & Foley 1994, Tagliamonte 1998, Biber et al. 1999: 186, Huddleston & Pullmam 2002: 242, Martinez Insua & Palacios Martinez 2003, Hay & Schreier 2004, Crawford 2005, *inter alia*). See (1) to (3):

(1) if there's a lot of people down the railway I go that way up there Yeah, to get out the way with the dogs 'cos the dogs tend to fight you know.   (WordBanks, UKspoken)

(2) I would run out of things to say and I know there is managers and coaches who do.   (WordBanks, UKspoken)

(3) I think there was loads of questions we had last year.
                                                    (WordBanks, UKspoken)

There are a number of previous studies in the literature which deal with number concord of existential sentences. For instance, the following table summarizes the situation in several spoken registers:[2]

Table 5-1: Percentage of non-concord according to register and variety in previous studies (%)

	Register	*there's*	*there is*
Woods (1979)	Ottawa English	13	
Crawford (2005)	American speech	12.4	8.5
	Academic lecture (U.S.A.)	15.3	3.4
Breivik & Martínez-Insua (2008)	BNC spoken	13.3	
	COLT (London teenage English)	21.3	
Yaguchi et al. (2007)	American professional speech	1.1 – 9.6	

Table 5-1 shows number disagreement ratios in Canadian English by Woods (1979), American speech and academic lecture in the U.S.A. by Crawford (2005), standard British English and teenage English in the London area by Breivik & Martínez-Insua (2008), and American professional people's conversation in public settings by Yaguchi et al. (2007). While it is important to bear in mind that the criteria for number disagreement differ in each study, number non-concord of *there's* is firmly entrenched in all registers. A plethora of previous studies have discussed the factors causing frequent number disagreement. There are two types of account widely shared. First, sociolinguistic factors play a pivotal role. As evidenced by the data in Table

---

[2] The scope of these previous studies is limited to the shortened form or present tense *there is*.

5-1, number disagreement rates are very high in vernacular such as teenagers' English as seen in the study by Breivik & Martínez-Insua (2008), while those in formal speech by American professionals in the study by Yaguchi et al. (2007) are quite low. Certainly, Meechan & Foley (1994) have found a correlation between the level of education of speakers and the frequency of concord occurrences in Canadian English. Hay & Schreier (2004) also report that New Zealand English professional speakers use number agreement tokens more often than their non-professional counterparts.

Second, syntactic factors induce non-concord in number. There are three often cited syntactic factors in the literature: (1) notional subjects with additional elements such as *There is a limited number of whales* ... (e.g. Meechan & Foley 1994, Martinez Insua & Palacios Martinez 2003, Hay & Schreier 2004); (2) coordination of notional subjects such as *There is a concord and a harmony* ... (e.g. Martinez Insua & Palacios Martinez 2003); and (3) intervening material between the existential part and the notional subject such as *There is generally four persons concerned* ... (e.g. Martinez Insua & Palacios Martinez 2003).

The previous studies above were carried out on a presupposition based on the prescriptive grammar that absence of number agreement is considered to be ungrammatical and associated with informality. As stated in the Introduction, however, Svartvik & Leech (2006: 969) maintain that number disagreement of this kind is no longer considered as ill-formed in the informal speech of standard English. Moreover, by investigating professors' speech in college lectures, Crawford (2005) argues that even a formal register of college lectures of American English shows frequent disagreement regarding the phrase *there's* when it is spontaneous speech. Apparently, from the latest linguists' point of view, the absence of agreement concerning *there's* is hardly associated with ungrammaticality in contemporary speech.

Many linguists point out the strong inclination to use *there's* as a formula for introducing both singular and plural notional subjects in spontaneous speech (e.g. Breivik 1981: 15, 1990: 153, 1999: 10, Hannay 1985: 15, Quirk et al. 1985: 756, Givón 1993: 207, *inter alia*). Quirk et al. (1985: 756) provide the following explanation:

(4) It is possible to generalize the rule of concord to 'A subject which is not clearly semantically plural requires a singular verb'; that is, to treat singular as the unmarked form, to be used in neutral circumstances, where no positive indication of plurality is present. This would explain, in addition to clausal subjects, the tendency in infor-

mal speech for *is/was* to follow the pseudo-subject *there* in existential sentences such as *There's hundreds of people on the waiting list.*

(Quirk et al. 1985: 756)

Thus, the singular form is recognized as a default formula to present a new referent and draw the listener's attention in speech. Grammaticalization of *there's* as a single phrase is also discussed in the literature. For instance, Biber et al. (1999: 186) and Crawford (2005) claim that number disagreement is induced by the speaker's conceptualization of the same item as an unanalyzed chunk. Additionally, Breivik & Martínez-Insua (2008) make an extensive discussion on the grammaticalization and subjectification of not only *there* but the combined sequence *there + be*, concluding that the fusion of *there* and *be* in the historical development of existential sentences resulted in the inseparability of *there's*; they also contend that '*there* + singular *be*', *there's* in particular, has acquired the status of a fixed pragmatic formula.

Number non-concord of existential sentences takes place mainly in the case of *there's*. Interestingly enough, however, lack of number agreement is observed synchronically as well as diachronically not only in *there's* but also in all the other verbal forms of *there is*, *there are*, *there was*, and *there were*. Observe (5) to (9):

(5) a. See now, there's a lot of people who will speak to you friendly out on the street ...   (BNC, academics)

   b. There's thirty hearts there that wad hae wanted bread ere ye had wanted sunkets.   [1815, Scott *Guy M.* viii, *OED*]

(6) a. ... I think there is two buses cos whenever I meet mum it's always a little blue bus ...   (BNC, spoken)

   b. There is also many wordes that haue dyverse vnderstondynges, ... and som tyme they may be taken in dyuerse wyse in one reson or clause.   [1450–1530, *Myrr. our Ladye* 7, *OED*]

(7) a. There are a lesson to learn.   (COCA, spoken)

(8) a. She then said that when there was a lot of Polish people in the school, they never practised any of their culture here

                    (BNC, academic)

   b. There was a proude patrico and a nosegent.

                    [1567, Harman *Caveat* 87, *OED*]

(9) a. "There were a young man at the door after church," Ellen said

                    (BNC, fiction)

    b.   <u>There were</u> more ease in a nest of Hornets, then under this one
        torture.   [1657, S. Purchas *Pol. Flying Ins.* 276, *OED*]

The examples above display that *there* + *be* sentences have rendered number
disagreement since olden times. Examination of *there* + *be* sentences in a
diachronic context will provide a clue to elucidate how the grammaticalization of *there* + *be* proceeded. The main purpose of this chapter is to clarify
when the grammaticalization of *there's* started, what kind of functions developed over time, and whether or not the verbal forms other than *there's* have
also been grammaticalized via analyzing quotation texts in the *OED*, and to
further explore the trend of *there* + *be* sentences in current English by examining spoken data in the BNC and UKspoken of WordBanks.

5.2　The diachronic development of *there* + *be*

This section will first conduct research into how *there* + *be* sentences diachronically developed into the present system through examining their frequencies in the *OED*. All the tokens of *there* + *be* are counted to compare
the frequencies of *there's*, *there is*, *there are*, *there was*, and *there were*, as
far as a sentence can be interpreted as a *there* + *be*. (See Section 2.2 in
Chapter 2 and Section 4.1 in Chapter 4 for more information.) After counting the occurrences of *there* + *be* tokens depending upon each verbal form,
they are divided by the number of quotation texts in each 50-year period.
The figure and the table below illustrate how many quotation texts include
there + *be* out of a hundred (also note Table 4-1 and Appendix 1):

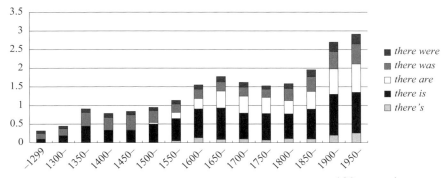

occurrences per 100 quotation texts

**Figure 5-1: Frequency of *there* + *be* sentences according to verbal forms
in *OED***

Table 5-2: Raw occurrences of *there* + *be* sentences according to verbal forms in *OED*

	-1299	1300-	1350-	1400-	1450-	1500-	1550-	1600-	1650-	1700-	1750-	1800-	1850-	1900-	1950-
there's							83	281	156	131	102	305	474	452	759
there is	57	73	231	195	172	422	971	1,584	1,491	918	1,011	1,865	3,828	2,491	3,176
there are		3	1	4	7	36	274	578	799	599	610	986	2,250	1,547	2,221
there was	90	76	193	203	213	271	361	512	441	320	313	914	1,899	1,067	1,581
there were	39	26	50	65	52	76	166	237	252	171	128	371	885	569	759
sum	186	178	475	467	444	805	1,855	3,192	3,139	2,139	2,164	4,441	9,336	6,126	8,496

As seen in Chapter 4, the overall frequency of *there* + *be* sentences increased gradually over time, (though it showed a slight decrease between 1700 and 1849,) to such an extent that in contemporary English, the construction under concern is used at the frequency of almost three occurrences per 100 quotation texts.

The present singular form *there is* appeared the most frequently in each period, while the present plural form *there are* has been the second most frequent since 1650. The preterit plural *there were* was the least frequently used since 1550, except for *there's*. Of course, it is taken for granted that the frequencies of each verbal form are determined by the nature of the genre, but a general transition is revealed: the contracted form and the preterit plural were employed infrequently. It should be heeded that the appearances of the singular verbal forms of *there is* and *there was* were predominant before Modern English, and it is only after the beginning of Early Modern English that the present plural form *there are* started to appear noticeably.

There's appeared for the first time in 1584 in the *OED*.[3] It should be mentioned that the contracted form without an apostrophe was observed as early as in 1562.[4] It is a rational conclusion, therefore, that *there's* as a

---

[3] The first token is as follows:
    We meet not now to brawl. *Faun.* There's no such matter, Pan.
                                    [1584, Peele, *Arraignm, Paris* I. i, *Pan, OED*]
[4] The contracted phrase without an apostrophe appeared as early as 1562 in the *OED*: *thers* appeared for the first time in 1562; *thars* in 1575; *theres* in 1592. The frequencies of those forms are low (only one occurrence, six occurrences and 27 occurrences in the *OED*, respectively). We may justifiably assume that the contracted form started to be used in written texts at the beginning of Modern English. In the present paper, the year 1584 is marked as the first year of its appearance. In the Helsinki Corpus, the first appearance is attested in 1570 in the form of *there's*.
Parkes (1992: 55) refers to the fact that the apostrophe was developed to indicate the elision of a vowel which no longer appeared in speech along with the advent of printers in the sixteenth century. He says as follows:

contraction of *there is* started to emerge in writing at the beginning of Modern English, and, in the present paper, the year 1584 is used to mark the first year of its appearance. Granted that the orthographical system was not fully established until the beginning of Modern English and that the same item was probably used in everyday speech earlier than that date, it is quite noteworthy that the first year that *there's* appeared coincides with the time when linguists claim existential sentences began to show full-fledged syntactic behaviors. As shown in Figure 5-1, the frequencies of *there's* were low throughout its history in the *OED*'s collection of written data. Indeed, the ratio of occurrences of *there's* to the total occurrences of *there* + *be* tokens is 6.3% (2,743 out of 43,443 tokens). For all that, the large amount of data in the *OED* will still yield valuable insight into the analysis of the syntactic, semantic, and pragmatic function of *there's*.

5.3   The historical features relevant to *there's*

The present section will examine the contracted form from a diachronic perspective. It will be proposed that *there's* was not just a contracted form of *there is* but was already a grammaticalized and subjectified unit with its own unique pragmatic functions at the time of its first appearance in the *OED*. Three pieces of evidence lend support to this proposal, and the next three subsections will provide a detailed discussion.

5.3.1   Non-concord in number

First, as discussed above, number disagreement between the verbal form and the notional subject exhibits interesting points. The rate of number disagreement of *there* + *be* sentences containing *there's*, compared with that of the other verbal forms, was high since its first appearance in the *OED*. The inclination for number disagreement was conspicuous not only in contemporary

---

It appears to have been promoted by Geoffroy Tory in *Champfleury* (Paris, 1529), ... In 1547 the apostrophe appears in the edition of *Marguerites de Marguerite* printed by J. de Tournes at Lyons. In England it appears in William Cunningham, *The cosmograhphical galsse*, printed by John Day in 1559; *A golden mirrour* [by R. Robinson of Alton], printed by Roger Ward for J. Proctor (London, 1589); *The phoenix nest*, 'set forth by R.S.' (London, J. Jackson 1593); and the 1596 edition of Spenser's *The faerie queene* printed by Field. In Shakespeare's *Loves labours lost* (1598) Holofernes refers to the *apostrophus* as a sign of omission.

(Parkes 1992: 55–56)

The year 1584 is well in accordance with the time of the emergence of the apostrophe.

English but also across time. The rates were calculated after counting non-concord tokens and dividing them by the number of *there + be* tokens with each verbal form for a 50-year period. Observe Figure 5-2 (also see Appendix 1), which shows the percentage of disagreement in each verbal form (*there's, there is, there are, there was,* and *there were*):

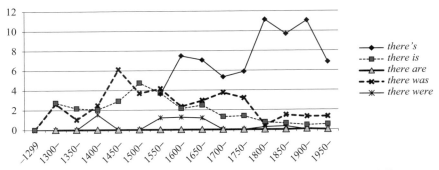

Figure 5-2: Number non-concord in each verbal form in *OED* (%)

Evidently, when *there's* made its first appearance in the *OED* in the 1550–1599 period, its disagreement rate was as high as that of *there is* and *there was*.[5] After that, its disagreement rate rose significantly: during the 1800–1849 period, for instance, it rose to as high as 11.1%. By comparison, the other verbal forms converged toward agreement over time after prescriptive grammar gained popularity in the eighteenth century. Conversely, even when prescriptive grammar affected the verbal forms in existential sentences to the extent that there was a remarkable decline in non-concord occurrences of *there is* and *there was*, writers of this era seem to have used *there's* as it was to represent the real language use of the time. Thus, existential sentences with *there's* displayed a completely different behavior from those with the

---

[5] There is a possibility that the writer used *there is* instead of *there's* though the writer may have meant it as *there's* in early days. In addition, in Middle English, number non-concord rate was high. For instance, the following example is explained as an omission of genitive case by grammarians who specialize in Middle English grammar:

þar was conuerted thusand fiue.   [a1300, *Cursor M.* 19134 (Cott.), *OED*]

Based upon Table 5-2, which shows that occurrences of *there are* were very low despite the relatively high number disagreement rates of *there is* and *there was* in Middle English, I gather that the notion of number agreement was scarce in Middle English. Indeed, as will be discussed in Section 5.4 of Chapter 5, Visser (1963: 73) and Franz (1986: 566) also surmise that speakers in Late Middle English were number insensitive in the use of existential sentences.

other verbal forms from 1600 to present-day English. If number non-con-cord is a phenomenon to reflect the grammaticalized situation of the phrase, it is reasonable to conclude that *there's* was grammaticalized and behaved as a unit at least in the year 1600 as even written texts reflected real language use to a great extent.

5.3.2   Passive structure

As will also be discussed in Chapter 7, in present-day English as well as in earlier English, existential sentences have five types of structures to express passives as follows:

(10) a.   There are reported to be in Venice ... twentie seven publique clocks.   [1611, Coryat *Crudities* 290, *OED*]

   b.   That ther sholde ... suche wrake be taken therof that hym myght growle that ever he sawe hym.

                              [1481, Caxton *Reynard* (Arb.) 78, *OED*]

   c.   In the second venter of a cow there is a round black tophus found, being of no weight.

                              [1607, Topsell *Four-f. Beasts* (1658) 65, *OED*]

   d.   ... wherein there are attributed to God such things as belong to manhood, ...   [1597, Hooker *Eccl. Pol.* v. §53, *OED*]

   e.   There are found ... goodly Marble pillars, with other hewne and carved stone in great aboundance among the Rubble.

                              [1614, Raleigh *Hist.World* II. 311, *OED*]

Example (10a) is a raising token. Due to the fact that raising fails to rep-resent passive voice in the *there* + *be* + NP structure, it is not targeted in the present analysis. (Full discussion concerning raising is made in Section 4.2 of Chapter 4). According to the research of Middle English by Yanagi (2011), four types of existential passive structures have been available since Middle English as *there* + (auxiliary) + NP + *be* + pp as in (10b), *there* + *be* + NP + pp as in (10c), *there* + *be* + pp + PP(AdP) + NP as in (10d), and (*there* + *be* + pp + NP + PP(AdP)) as in (10e). The latter two belong to the same structure, although there is a difference in the position of the prepositional phrase. Partly because *there* + (auxiliary) + NP + *be* + pp as seen in (10b) is an obsolescent type of passives in present-day English, and mainly because this analysis pays attention to the sequence *there* + *be* with-out modal elements between *there* and *be*, it excludes this type. In present-day English, Quirk et al. (1985: 1409) explain that the *there* + *be* + NP + pp structure as in (10c) is more common than the *there* + *be* + pp + NP structure as in (10d) and (10e). However, in order to examine the level of fusion between *there* and *'s*, only types (10d) and (10e) should be analyzed. Type (10c) cannot be an indication of the degree of the connection of *there* to *be* and, for this reason, an analysis of type (10c) is not carried out in the present analysis.

We are now in a position to highlight the passivized structure such as (10d) and (10e). If it is presumed that *there's* is a single invariable unit because of its grammaticalization and that it syntactically functions as an inseparable phrase, it is possible to predict that it does not call for pp to form passive voice. Because the presence of *is* would not be felt explicitly by the speaker, it is not likely to be connected with a pp in the speaker's conceptualization. The investigation is conducted through extracting all the passivized *there* + *be* + pp tokens including *there* + *be* + PP(AdvP) + pp sentences from quotation texts in the *OED* and dividing them by the total number of existential sentences occurrences according to the verbal form in each 50-year period. The result indicates that *there's* showed consistent resistance toward passivization throughout its longitudinal record. Note Figure 5-3, which is a graphical presentation of the ratio of passivized tokens to the total occurrences of *there* + *be* in each 50-year period according to the verbal forms (also see Appendix 1):

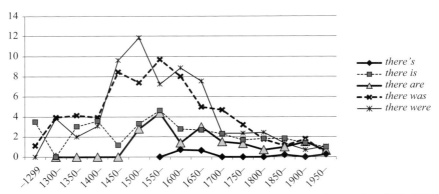

Figure 5-3: Passives of *there* + *be* according to verbal forms in *OED* (%)

As seen in Figure 5-3, *there's* was rarely used in passive voice, while the other verbal forms manifested a trend to converge toward non-passivization only after the 1700s. Evidently, this result indicates that the item under discussion was an inseparable phrase since the day it first appeared in 1584.

5.3.3   The definite referent of the notional subject

In present-day English as well as in Old English, the basic function of existential sentences is to introduce a new referent into the discourse as mentioned in Section 4.3 of Chapter 4 (e.g. Jenkins 1975, Milsark 1977, 1979, Lambrecht 1988, Nagashima 1992, Ward & Birner 1995, Breivik 1981, 1983, 1989, 1990, 1997, McNally 1997, Biber et al. 1999: 951, Breivik & Swan 2000, Breivik & Martínez-Insua 2008, *inter alia*). Biber et al. (1999: 943), for instance, offer an explanation about the basic function of *there* + *be* in order to show the characteristics of presentative existential sentences using example (11) (This particular token (11) is given as (4) in Chapter 1 to focus on the existence of a referent in the Introduction.):

(11)   A man goes in the pub. <u>There's a bear sitting in the corner.</u> He
       goes up, he goes up to the bartender. He says, <u>why is there a bear</u>
       <u>sitting over there?</u>   (Biber et al. 1999: 943)

They argue that it is most typical to expect that notional subjects contain an indefinite element as in (11). However, in contemporary English, definite referents as notional subjects are often observed, though such usage was long considered to be restricted according to some studies such as Baker (1973), Jenkins (1975), and Milsark (1979). Ward & Birner (1995), however, maintain that as far as the post-verbal NP carries hearer-new information, that is, the referent is previously evoked but judged by the speaker to be out of consciousness of the hearer at the time of utterances, the use of a lexically definite NP is allowed. Thus, the definite notional subject is not considered to be ungrammatical by contemporary scholars (e.g. Breivik 1990, Abbott 1993, Biber et al. 1999: 953, *inter alia*). For example, Biber et al. (1999: 953) insist that one of the effects of existential *there* followed by a definite notional subject is "to bring something already known back to mind, rather than asserting that it exists," as in (12):

(12)   "Do you know the town of Makara? Is there a medical station
       there?" But he said that Makara patients had always been brought
       to him at Kodowa. There wasn't even a trained nurse, only a
       couple of midwives. Then he brightened. "<u>There is the</u> cotton fac-
       tory," he said. (fiction)   (Biber et al. 1999: 953)

Evidently, the use of definite notional subjects has subsumed a pragmatic function, which connotes interaction between the speaker and the hearer, rather than presenting an objective fact of something being existent as in the case of (11). In (12), the speaker sends the hearer a message like "you know, they have a cotton factory in Makara, don't you remember? We both know it." Thus, the notional subject with a lexically definite element or without is interpreted differently.

Several features in respect to definite notional subjects should be addressed. First, what are called list *there*-sentences by Rando & Napoli (1978) are closely related to the use of definite notional subjects and the subjectified *there's*.[6] As existential sentences developed over time, *there's* has also acquired the function of a discourse marker. Note (13) to (15) ((4) in Chapter 4 is repeated as (14)):

(13)   <u>There's</u> always George. (We might ask him.)   (Breivik 1997)

(14)   A: Which of the Scandinavian capitals have you visited?
         B: Well, <u>there's</u> Oslo in Norway.
                                                                    (Breivik 1990: 153)

(15)   A: Who's attending the meeting?
         B: Well, <u>there's</u> (*are) John, Michael, and Janet.
                                                                    (Breivik 1997)

In the literature, especially in Breivik (1989: 33, 1990: 153, 1997), it is often suggested that *there's* co-occurring with lexically definite forms of notional subjects as in (13) to (15) functions as a 'presentative signal' to recall the referent into the focus of attention. meaning 'I could mention' or 'Don't let's forget' (e.g. Hannay 1985: 15, Lumsden 1988: 215, Breivik 1989: 33, 1990: 153, 1997, *inter alia*). Examples (14) and (15) above are characterized as list *there*-sentences. Syntactically, *there's* in (14) and (15) is not required to form a sentence, whilst semantically it does not express existence either. In other words, the contracted form is subjectified to express the speaker's point of view. Rando & Napoli (1978) and Breivik (1997) maintain that the use of the plural verbal form *are* is disallowed here, whereas *there is* can replace *there's*. According to my informants, *there's* is the default form in list *there*-sentences in speech, while the use of *there is* is considered grammatically appropriate but rarely employed. As will be extensively discussed in Chapter 6, the intolerance to use the plural form is convincing evidence to show that it functions as a particle, which also features further grammaticalization

---

[6] Rando & Napoli (1978) explain that notional subjects accept both definite and indefinite NPs in list existential sentences. McNally (1997: 193) also maintains that list *there*-sentences do not necessarily always require definite NPs.

of *there's*. At the same time, it should be noted that the pragmatic function as a 'presentative signal' meaning 'I could mention' or 'Don't let's forget' represents a subjectified aspect of the grammaticalized item. Returning to the point of notional subject, as seen in (14) and (15), list existentials often take definite NPs.

Furthermore, a definite NP sometimes evokes a cataphoric referent. Consider (16) and (17):

(16)   There is <u>the</u> possibility that she might go back to her country.

(17)   Plunkett ... used to say <u>there was this</u> difference between boy's kites and men's kites—that with boys the wind raised the kites, but with men the kites raised the wind.

[1859, Riddles & Jokes 98, OED]

Breivik (1983, 1990) and Breivik & Martínez-Insua (2008) state that definite notional subjects occasionally refer to a unit of discourse that follows. In the particular example of (16), *the possibility* refers to the clause that follows. On the other hand, as in (17), the opening line of conversational narratives often takes a demonstrative pronoun like *this* or *these*. In contemporary speech, we occasionally encounter the sequence of *there* + *was* + *this* + NP. This point will be discussed in depth in Section 5.4.

In a nutshell, existential sentences containing notional subjects realized as lexically definite NPs have some pragmatic, interpersonal, and speaker-oriented functions, rather than focusing on something existing as seen in (11): the interaction between the speaker and the hearer is implicitly entailed. It is true that the frequency of definite notional subjects may account for only part of the pragmatic tokens, since existential sentences with indefinite notional subjects also often express a wide variety of pragmatic functions, as referred to in connection with the study by Martínez-Insua (2004) in Section 4.3 of Chapter 4. However, the frequency of the definite notional subject use can be an indirect index of how often each verbal form expresses interactive mode in that it always subsumes what Traugott & Dasher (2002) call intersubjectivity.

It is quite surprising that throughout Middle English to present-day English, definite NPs were used rather frequently. Consider (18) to (20):

(18)   <u>Ther's Tom the Tapster</u> peerelesse for renowne, That drank three hundred drunken Dutch-men downe.

[1612, W. Parkes Curtaine-Dr. (1876) 26, OED]

(19)   Ther were the Cardinales of both collegis, both of Gregori and
        Benedict.   [1460, J. Capgrave *Chron.* 297, *OED*]

(20)   There was Marshall McLuhan receiving an honorary degree, pre-
        sumably in honor of gibberish he has flacked in the name of com-
        munications.   [1977, *Globe & Mail* (Toronto) 16 Mar. 8/1, *OED*]

Another intriguing fact is that a list *there*-existential sentence was already
used at the beginning of Early Modern English, as in (21):

(21)   ... there's your Parragon, Burragon, Phillipine, Cheny, Grogrum,
        Mow-hair.   [1668, Head *Eng. Rogue* II. xii. (1671) 112, *OED*]

The present analysis was conducted by counting notional subjects which
contain *the*, *this*, *that*, *these*, *those*, personal pronouns and proper nouns as
in (18) to (21). (Tokens including *those* (*who*) were excluded when *those*
means 'people'.) From a historical perspective, existential sentences with
definite referents show interesting characteristics as seen in Figure 5-4,
which represents the ratio of tokens that carry a definite notional subject to
the total tokens of *there + be* sentences depending upon the verbal form and
the period (also note Appendix 1):

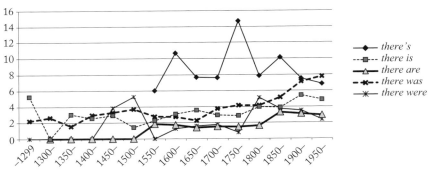

Figure 5-4: *There + be* **sentences with definite notional subjects in *OED*** (%)

Figure 5-4 illustrates that *there's* frequently introduced a definite notional
subject into the discourse throughout Modern English, although there was not
much difference in distribution among the three verbal forms with singular
be, i.e. *there's*, *there is* and *there was* in twentieth-century English. Breivik
& Martínez-Insua (2008) argue that grammaticalization "tends to be accompanied by an increase in pragmatic significance and subjective expres-
siveness," stating that the bleaching of the existential sense of *there* enabled

there + *be* sentences to "serve pragmatic, interpersonal, speaker-based functions" such as "making corrections or deductions, expressing personal opinions, or even eliciting information," as referred to in Section 4.3 of Chapter 4. For the same reason, the frequent co-occurrence with definite notional subjects seems to indicate that *there's* was more advanced in the level of subjectification than the other verbal forms at the beginning of Modern English. As seen in the example (21) of the year 1668, we can attest the subjectified feature of *there's* in the list existential sentence already in the same period. Admitted that the data in Figure 5-4 is not a direct piece of evidence to verify its grammaticalized status, *there's* showed a notable pragmatic tendency in Modern English at the time of its first appearance in the *OED*.

The diachronic data concerning *there's* in 5.3.1, 5.3.2, and 5.3.3 all demonstrate that *there's* already had a distinctive status at the beginning of Modern English. Considering writers' intention of employing the informal contracted version of *there is* in the period when the orthographical system of contraction and apostrophe *'s* began to be established in writing, it is valid to conclude that *there's* had a special function at the beginning of Modern English. Hence, the present study proposes that the phrase concerned was already grammaticalized at its first emergence in the *OED*. Conversely, it is a plausible hypothesis that by the end of Middle English, the special status of the item under discussion already prevailed at least in speech, since it is unlikely that grammaticalization occurred overnight. As the contracted form failed to evince itself in Middle English writing due to the absence of an established orthographical system, further research on the emergence and development of the shortened form is required.

5.4   *there was*

The diachronic investigation into *there* + *be* sentences in the previous section clarifies that the linguistic behaviors the contracted form *there's* showed were totally different from those of the other verbal forms at the time of its emergence. However, a closer look at the three figures in Section 5.3 reveals that *there was* also exhibited a very interesting behavior especially in twentieth-century English. Amongst the others, as seen in Figure 5-4, in contemporary English, the preterit singular form shows the highest co-occurrence rate with definite notional subjects, which certainly suggests its prominent pragmatic use. In Figure 5-3, the second strongest resistance of *there was* to be passivized, after *there's*, in contemporary English also hints at the status of *there was* as a single unit. Since the research in this chapter so far has been confined to the analysis of the *OED*, it is wise to examine speech data to detect the latest trend of existential sentences. In fact, it is speech, not prose, that triggers language change.

For the purpose of the present section, I have analyzed British English speech data mainly in Collins WordBanks' UKspoken (7.9 million words) via employing the Shogakukan Corpus Network. The network system can only retrieve at most 3,000 tokens during each search, so any linguistic item yielding over 3,000 tokens requires more than one standardization in the process of calculating rates. As the need arises, the spoken subcorpus (11.7 million words) in the BNC will be analyzed as supplemental data, since the BNC is considered to contain more formal English data than the UKspoken. The BNC spoken subcorpus contains both formal (e.g. business, educational and informative events) and informal (naturally spontaneous conversations) speech, while the UKspoken includes informal conversation such as telephone calls, service encounters, discussions, consultations, lectures, radio phone-ins, research interviews, and television discussion.[7] Thus, the analysis of this section will feature contemporary British English. (In Chapter 8, the COCA's spoken data will also be highlighted in comparison with the BNC and WordBanks.)

First of all, it is significant to extend our scope by examining the general trend of how existential sentences are employed in contemporary English speech. The following table shows the breakdown of the use of the five verbal forms in the quotation texts after 1950 in the *OED* and UKspoken:

Table 5-3: Breakdown of *there's, there is, there are, there was* and *there were* in the data after 1950 in *OED* and UKspoken[8]

	OED (%)	UKspoken (%)
there's	8.9 (759)	49.0 (13,825)
there is	37.4 (3,176)	12.9 (3,625)
there are	26.1 (1,581)	12.6 (3,559)
there was	18.6 (2,221)	19.0 (5,355)
there were	8.9 (759)	6.5 (1,827)
sum	100 (8,496)	100 (28,191)

(raw occurrences)

---

[7] As indicated in Chapter 8, the ratio of the use of *there's* to the total use of *there + be* sentences is higher in the UKspoken than the BNC's spoken.

[8] The data of the UKspoken are projected figures. After retrieving 3,000 tokens and discarding irrelevant tokens, the ratio was applied to the total number of each sequence.

It is very interesting that the breakdown of the five verbal forms is contrastive between writing and speech: the use of the contracted form is dominant in speech, while *there is* and *there are* play the leading role in writing. The ample use of *there's* is a feature of speech, while the abundant employment of the present non-contracted verbal forms characterizes written texts, admitted that the genre plays a pivotal role in determining the distribution of verbal forms, as will be shown in Chapter 8. *There was*, the targeted sequence in this section, is used almost at the same ratio in the two corpora.

As confirmed in the previous section, it is well acknowledged that *there's* presents a characteristic feature of number non-concord even in writing. It is, indeed, important to compare spoken data with written data. The data of all five verbal forms concerning number disagreement are shown in the following tables:

Table 5-4: Frequency of number non-concord *there* + *be* sentences in OED data after 1950[9]

	there's	*there is*	*there was*	*there are*	*there were*
Total tokens	759	3,176	1,581	2,221	759
Tokens with disagreement	52	17	21	0	0
Percentage	6.9%	0.5%	1.3%	0%	0%

Table 5-5: Frequency of number non-concord *there* + *be* sentences in UKspoken

	there's	*there is*	*there was*	*there are*	*there were*
Total tokens	2,730	2,735	2,780	2,811	1,827
Tokens with disagreement	582	94	347	28	54
Percentage	21.3%	3.4%	12.5%	1.0%	3.0%

Obviously, the non-concord rate of *there's* is the highest in both writing and speech, clearly demonstrating the status of *there's* as a single phrase. It is also noticeable that *there was* exhibits the second highest disagreement rate in speech as well as in writing (12.5% and 1.3%). (In fact, in the BNC's spoken subcorpus, which will be examined in Chapter 8, the number disagreement rate of *there was* (15.8%) is higher than *there's* (14.1%).) On the other hand, *there is* displays remarkably low percentages (3.4% and 0.5%), compared with *there was*. In speech, especially, the gap between these two

---

[9] The data in the *OED* include tokens of the TV and TP constructions.

(3.4% and 12.5%) is very large. Needless to say, the unity between *there* and the verb *be* is stronger in *there was* than in *there is*, which consequently leads to the conclusion that the grammaticalization of *there was* as a single phrase is currently in the process of formulation at least in speech. Meanwhile, the low occurrences of number disagreement concerning *there are* (0% and 1.0%) and *there were* (0% and 3.0%) both in writing and speech are in accordance with the contention by Breivik & Martínez-Insua (2008) that an absence of number agreement is likely to occur in the combination of singular *be* and plural notional subjects.

Based upon the results above, it is certainly reasonable to conclude that the connection between *there* and *be* is the tightest in *there's* and second closest in *there was*. Nonetheless, it is possible to argue that since *there was* represents two aspects, i.e. a grammaticalized variant and an ungrammaticalized variant, in other words, a casual version and a formal version, its ratios of number disagreement should naturally fall between *there's* and *there is*. *There is*, on the other hand, has the contracted form *there's* and thereby is likely to consistently imply formality, distinguishing itself from *there's*. Indeed, Imamichi & Ishikawa (2006) have found that in the BNC *there is* tends to co-occur with a notional subject having an abstract sense such as *room, evidence, need, danger, tendency, hope, possibility*, and *agreement*, while *there's* tends to call for a notional subject with a concrete sense such as *book, man, thing*, etc.[10] Apparently, the former connotes a far more formal sense in a more expository context than the latter. They argue that *there's* is not just a shortened version of *there is* but assumes an independent pragmatic-semantic role. The wide gap in number non-concord between *there's* (21.3%) and *there is* (3.4%) in speech, as observed in Tables 5-4 and 5-5, also supports their contention, at the same time verifying the argument that *there was* carries both expository and casual tokens because of the lack of a contracted form. Taking a different approach to the data by analyzing notional subjects, however, reveals that *there was* has its own unique characteristics.

Here, it is significant to consider the pragmatic use of lexically definite notional subjects. Note Tables 5-6 and 5-7, which show the ratio of notional subjects with definite lexical forms to the total number of existential sentences in the *OED*'s contemporary data and the UKspoken respectively:

---

[10] Imamichi & Ishikawa (2006) fail to specify what amount of speech data and written data in the BNC is analyzed.

Table 5-6: Ratio of definite notional subjects to total number of existential sentences in *OED*'s data after 1950

	there's	*there is*	*there was*	*there are*	*there were*
Total tokens	759	3,176	1,581	2,221	759
Tokens with definite NP	55	154	124	66	18
Percentage	7.2%	4.8%	7.8%	3.0%	2.4%

Table 5-7: Ratio of definite notional subjects to total number of existential sentences in UKspoken

	there's	*there is*	*there was*	*there are*	*there were*
Total tokens	2,730	2,735	2,780	2,811	1,827
Tokens with definite NP	240	208	270	55	75
Percentage	8.8%	7.6%	9.7%	2.0%	4.1%

Obviously, *there was* plays a leading part in pragmatic use in contemporary English. Both tables demonstrate that *there was* (7.8% and 9.7% for written and spoken data respectively) renders definite notional subjects more often than *there's* (7.2% and 8.8% for written and spoken data respectively). The percentages of *there is* (4.8% and 7.6%) are much higher than *there are* (3.0% and 2.0%) and *there were* (2.4% and 4.1%), but lower than *there's* and *there was*. These figures provide firm evidence that pragmatic, interpersonal functions tend to be realized by existential sentences with singular *be* forms, which is, again, consistent with the argument by Breivik & Martínez-Insua (2008). Furthermore, the breakdown of notional subjects exhibits the unique role of *there was*. In the *OED*'s contemporary data, notional subjects starting with *the* account for 87% of all the tokens including definite notional subjects (co-occurring with *the*, *this*, *that*, *these*, *those*, personal pronouns, and proper nouns), which is very high compared with 44% in the UKspoken. Certainly, this result confirms the contention by Akinnaso (1982) that the use of *the* is preferred in writing, while *this* and *that* are favored in speech. For instance, as mentioned in connection with (17), the opening line of conversational narratives or jokes often takes a demonstrative pronoun like *this* or *these*. Note (22). Although the referent *this car* appears for the first time in this particular discourse, *this*, not *a*, modifies the *car*. In fact, the first existential sentence with *this car* cataphorically opening a new conversation line vivifies this narrative, while the second existential sentence with *a car* expresses the existence of the car concerned. It certainly is impossible to use *the* instead of *this* in the first case:

(22)   Once when I was walking home from tai kwondo [sic], Mm, 'cos it's luckily I didn't live far so I came home on my own. Once *there was this car* like, Mm, behind me 'cos I was 'cos usually I was on the side which the car couldn't come behind me. And this time I came across and there was a car coming down and it started to slow up. I just started to walk because if I started running. And all of a sudden they just drove past.   (UKspoken)

Thus, the use of *this* combined with *there was* has the special function of forming a conversation opener. As seen in the list *there*-sentences of (13), (14), and (15), the use of proper nouns also characterizes the interactive mode. The following two tables demonstrate the use of *the* in each verbal form in contemporary writing and speech:

Table 5-8: Number of raw occurrences and ratio of *the* to total count of definite notional subjects in *OED*'s data after 1950

	there's	*there is*	*there was*	*there are*	*there were*
Tokens with definite NP	55	154	124	66	18
Tokens starting with *the*	34	148	100	64	17
Percentage	61.8%	96.1%	80.6%	97.0%	94.4%

Table 5-9: Number of raw occurrences and ratio of *the* to total count of definite notional subjects in UKspoken

	there's	*there is*	*there was*	*there are*	*there were*
Tokens with definite NP	240	208	270	55	75
Tokens starting with *the*	100	99	97	32	43
Percentage	41.7%	47.6%	35.9%	58.2%	57.3%

It is apparent that in the writing data of Table 5-8, *there was* pairing with *the* (80.6%) is higher than *there's* (61.8%) in percentage because, unlike *there was*, *there's* is most likely to appear in dialogues or letters even in written texts in the *OED*, as reported in Yaguchi (2009). However, in speech, *there was* appears with definite pronouns containing non-*the* elements, i.e. *this*, *that*, personal pronouns, and proper nouns more frequently than *there's* and *there is*. In other words, *there was* tends to co-occur with more dynamic, speech-specific referents than *there's* and *there is*. Thus, it is justifiable to conclude that at least in standard British English speech, *there was* is not just a phrase which can express both formality and casualness, but a pragmatic marker with a particular function.

Here, the characteristics of narratives in which *there was* often appears should be mentioned in connection with the functional distinction among the three singular forms. Biber (1988) presents the two most decisive factors which constitute texts, after examining 23 texts of both written and spoken data from very formal official documents to very informal telephone conversations, and then applying factor analysis: expository-vs.-involved (26.8% of shared variances) and narrative-vs.-non-narrative (8.1% of shared variances) distinctions significantly characterize the nature of language.[11] The first factor marks the differences between integrated, informational focus in detached contexts and involved, affective interaction in the immediate situation. The integrated, information-focused feature is a characteristic of *there is*, whereas the affective, immediate mode is realized by *there's*. The second factor signifies the differences between active, event-oriented discourse and static, descriptive or expository discourse. According to Biber (1988: 109), the narrative is represented in the past tense, featuring dynamism and active events, whilst the non-narrative is realized in the present tense with an expository and static style. It is noteworthy that narratives have a strong impact on the formation of texts and that the dynamism entailed in narratives is subtly different from casual mode. Naturally, while *there was*, the representative formula in narratives, may sometimes express a static, expository sense, it often connotes a dynamic, active mode. Again, I would like to suggest that the number non-concord frequency level of *there was* falls between *there's* and *there is*, not only because it can express both formal and casual mode depending on the context, but also because it often expresses dynamism in narrative texts.[12]

At this point, attention should be paid to *there was* from a diachronic perspective. We will examine the transition of number disagreement of the preterit singular form. For the sake of convenience, I will show Figure 5-2, a graphical representation of diachronic change in number disagreement rate, again as Figure 5-5:

---

[11] The impacts of the other seven factors are small. Factors 3, 4, 5, 6, 7, 8, 9, 10, 11 are 5.2%, 3.5%, 2.9%, 2.8%, 2.6%, 2.2%, 2.0%, 1.9%, 1.9%, respectively.

[12] *There was* may occasionally be pronounced with a reduced form, rather than with

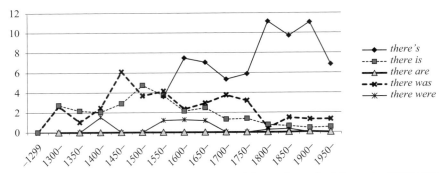

Figure 5-5: Ratio of number non-concord in each verbal form in *OED* (%)

Section 5.2 shows that *there's* already demonstrated grammaticalized features when it first appeared in the *OED* in 1584. The same phrase constantly showed a very high ratio of number disagreement throughout all the time periods. On the other hand, the other verbal forms also show relatively high occurrences of non-concord in Late Middle English and Early Modern English, as Visser (1963: 73) and Franz (1986: 566) assume that speakers in Late Middle English were not aware of the number of notional subjects when they used the existential *there* and *be*. In fact, the graph above may indicate that existential sentences were originally far from sensitive to number in Late Middle English. The concept of number agreement seems to have been promoted through Modern English to the extent that non-concord of the other verbal forms decreased sharply after 1800, owing to the prevalence of prescriptive grammar, as mentioned in Section 5.2. Because of the same discipline, written data in Late Modern English and present-day English may not reflect the real picture of number non-concord in the speech of the time. Indeed, the contemporary data in Tables 5-4 to 5-5 demonstrate that writing contains much lower occurrences of number non-concord than speech, because writers hone their work based upon prescriptive grammar in the process of writing and revision. However, the general trend in written data that the non-concord rate of *there is*, *there was*, and *there's* increases in this order is also detected in speech.

Between 1500 and 1699, the non-concord rates of *there is* and *there*

a strong form, as in the case of *there's* [ðəz]. In the case of Appalachian English, for instance, the contracted *there was* is pronounced like [ðeəz] and [ðez], according to Montgomery & Chapman (1992). Since the phonological approach is beyond the scope of this study, research into this topic is required.

was were on similar levels, and then until the 1750–1799 period, the dis-agreement rates of *there was* were quite high. Even after the convergence to the lowest level in the 1800–1899 period, the preterit singular form bounced back higher again after 1850. This provides a clue to surmise that *there was* constantly showed number disagreement more often than *there is* in everyday speech after 1700. In other words, *there was* signified mainly formality until around 1650 in the same way as *there is*, thereafter changing to a more ca-sual and/or dynamic mode.

The investigation into the historical use of notional subjects also shows evidence that *there was* changed in nature in Modern English. Observe Fig-ure 5-4 again as Figure 5-6:

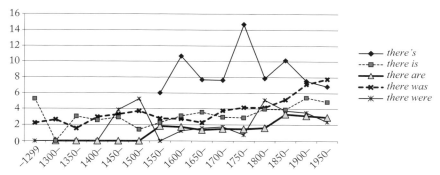

Figure 5-6: Percentage of existential sentences with definite notional sub-jects in *OED* (%)

As discussed in Subsection 5.3.3, *there's* predominantly co-occurred with def-inite notional subjects throughout the Modern English period, which clearly indicates that *there's* was already used as the primary interactive marker of the five verbal forms at this time. Whereas *there's* was employed the most frequently in interpersonal use in Modern English, *there was* gradually in-creased in percentage and topped in contemporary English. The function of *there was* as an interpersonal pragmatic marker seems to have emerged in writing around 1850 and firmly took root in present-day English. Here, it is important to discuss the relationship between number non-concord and the use of definite subjects in regard to *there was*. As stated above, it is a pos-sible inference that *there was* and *there is* shared the same kind of functions in writing during the Early Modern English period. Owing to the communi-cative need to express dynamism in narratives using the item under discus-sion, *there was* seems to have strengthened its pragmatic function around

1700, partially losing its formal feature due to its lack of a contracted form, and thus started to display number non-concord more noticeably in the middle of the Modern English period. It is at the end of Modern English that more explicit interactive use of *there was* started, which led to the abundant interactive use in present-day English. It is worth heeding that a more frequent number non-concord tendency set in first, followed by interactive use. Frequent informal use seems to have triggered more pragmatic use.

On the other hand, *there is*, retaining its formal sense, began to follow suit of its preterit counterpart in its pragmatic use after the beginning of the present-day English period. The present plural *there are* also displayed an upward tendency after 1850. Therefore, the major verbal forms' increased inclinations toward interactive use in present-day English suggest that existential sentences as a whole are used more interactively in present-day English than before. (However, a reversed trend is observed in contemporary English. See detailed discussion in Chapter 8.)

5.5　Grammaticalization of *here's*

It is a matter of course that the discussion of *there* + *be* invites an examination of *here* + *be*, the deictically proximal counterpart of the main item in study. Note the following examples:

> (23) a.　… we will be repeating them next week, but now here is the fi-
> nal question.　　　　　　　　　　　　　　　　　(BNC spoken)
>
> b.　… so I'm not prepared to carry on and here's my resignation.
> 　　　　　　　　　　　　　　　　　　　　　　(COCA written)

One wonders whether *here's* followed the same route as *there's* in terms of grammaticalization and subjectification. This section will explore features involved in the use of *here* + *be*.

Perhaps because of the deictic nature of *here*, the total number of tokens of *here* (67,296 occurrences) is much lower than those of *there* (316,902 occurrences) in the BNC, which renders a presumption that the frequency of *here* + *be* is also lower than *there* + *be*. Indeed, the projected occurrences of *here's*, *here is*, *here are*, *here was*, and *here were* in the spoken subcorpus of the BNC are only 541, 72, 25, 51, 3, respectively.[13] Taking

---

[13] After extracting 500 tokens of *here's*, 200 tokens of *here is*, 200 tokens of *here are*, 64 tokens of *here was*, and 21 tokens of *here were* and discarding the non-targeted tokens such as *everything here is perfect*, I calculated how many times each verbal form appears

into account that there are 16,976 tokens of *there's* alone appearing in the same subcorpus, *here* + *be* shows comparatively infrequent usage for all its similarity in form and function.

First, it is important to examine number non-concord. If grammatical-ization had taken place in the contracted form *here's*, it would be possible to observe a high level of number disagreement rates between the verbal form and the notional subject. Observe the following tables showing the number disagreement rate seen in the written and spoken data of the BNC and the written data of the COCA:[14, 15]

Table 5-10: Number disagreement between verbal form and notional subject (%)[16]   (raw occurrences)

	here's	*here is*	*here are*	*here was*	*here were*
BNC writing	1.0	0	0	1.8	2.1
	(1/100)	(0/22)	(0/55)	(1/56)	(1/47)
BNC spoken	7.4	0	0	1.9	0
	(35/473)	(0/37)	(0/18)	(1/51)	(0/3)
COCA writing	2.2	0	0	0	0
	(2/92)	(0/25)	(0/56)	(0/54)	(0/45)

The result is very striking in that number non-concord rates are low across the board, regardless of the differences of the verbal form or written/ spoken mode. It should be pointed out, however, that *here's* in speech shows a slightly higher rate of number disagreement than the other verbal

---

in the spoken subcorpus in the BNC. For the BNC's written data, 100 tokens of each verbal form were retrieved, out of which non-targeted instances were excluded from the analysis.

There would have been 56 tokens of *here are* rather than 25 tokens, if *here* + *are* + Name as below had been included in the count:

    Here are Kyle, here's your tea. Oh I like this song!   (BNC, spoken)

It seems that the sequence *here* + *are* + Name is a fixed phrase to draw the listener's at-tention.

[14] As mentioned above, the occurrences of *here is*, *here are*, *here was* and *here were* are very low in the spoken data of the BNC, so the data concerning these verbal forms can be inaccurate, because one token changes the percentage greatly.

[15] 100 tokens of each verbal form were retrieved from the COCA.

[16] *Here's what* (*how*, *where*, etc.) tokens as follows are excluded from the analysis:

    Here's how they smokers get their fingers burned …   (BNC, news)

For the analysis of BNC's spoken data, the tokens retrieved by the data collection men-tioned in Footnote 13 are investigated.

forms. Nevertheless, 7.4% is far below the high figures observed in regard to *there's* (21.3% as in the UKspoken of Table 5-5; 14.1% in spoken data of the BNC as shown in Chapter 8) and even lower than the levels of *there was* (12.5% as in UKspoken of Table 5-5; 15.8% in spoken data of the BNC as shown in Chapter 8). Thus, the present examination fails to manifest the fact that the phrase *here's* represents total grammaticalization, while showing signs of proceeding toward grammaticalization. The limited use of *here* as a deictic marker, which is reflected in the low occurrences compared with those of *there* existential sentences, may not have given it enough chance to be fully grammaticalized.

Next, the frequency of lexically definite notional subjects should be investigated. The main function of existential sentences is to introduce a new referent into the discourse, taking indefinite notional subject forms. As discussed in 5.3.3, interaction between the speaker and the listener often involves the use of definite notional subjects, when the speaker judges the referent to have previously been evoked in the discourse or she/he judges the listener to have forgotten it, lexically definite forms will be employed (e.g. Breivik 1990, Abbott 1993, Ward & Birner 1995, Biber et al. 1999: 953, *inter alia*). Otherwise, when the main function of existential sentences is set, notional subjects are usually realized by indefinite noun phrases. On the other hand, *here + be* is used on the immediate scene when the speaker tries to draw the listener's attention directly to a certain referent there. The referent does not have to be discourse-new or hearer-new. Note the following table to demonstrate the percentages of definite notional subjects according to the verbal form in written and spoken subcorpora of the BNC and written subcorpora of the COCA:[17]

Table 5-11: Use of definite notional subjects (%)   (raw occurrences)

	here's	*here is*	*here are*	*here was*	*here were*
BNC writing	27.0 (27/100)	40.1 (9/22)	14.5 (8/55)	14.3 (8/56)	36.2 (17/47)
BNC spoken	64.3 (304/473)	40.5 (15/37)	22.2 (4/18)	7.8 (4/51)	0 (0/3)
COCA writing	52.2 (48/92)	44.0 (11/25)	14.3 (8/56)	14.8 (8/54)	33.3 (15/45)

---

[17] Since there are only three tokens of *here were* in the spoken subcorpus of the BNC, the plural preterit form should be excluded from the analysis due to its inaccuracy.

It is manifested that *here* + *be* shows far higher ratios than *there* + *be* (in the UKspoken, *there was* showed the highest ratio of 9.7%, as seen in Table 5-7) across the board. In speech, *here's* (64.3%) is used the most frequently, followed by *here is* (40.5%), and in the writing of the BNC and the COCA, *here's* and *here is* show high ratios of 27.0% and 52.2% respectively as well.

These results clearly suggest that the function of existential sentences is different from that of *here* + *be*. It is possible to argue that the deictic *here* + *be* entails interaction between the speaker and the listener, provoking the use of definite notional subjects because the speaker is referring to something directly in the immediate scene, which can be seen in person and thereby are more likely to be realized as a definite form.

Thus, we have seen that *here's* is by no means fully grammaticalized as an inseparable phrase in a similar way to *there's*, although it is used interactively very often. Apparently, the investigation into *here* + *be* has shown the accentuation of the uniqueness of *there's* as a single chunk. In Section 6.8 of Chapter 6, *here's* will be extensively examined in respect of its use in an environment in which grammaticalization is prone to occur.

5.6   Summary

In this chapter, the diachronic development of the five verbal forms (*there's*, *there is*, *there are*, *there was*, and *there were*) were examined, with a special reference to *there's* and *there was*. The syntactic characteristics *there's* exhibits in present-day English were already detectable when it made its first appearance in the *OED* in 1584. It was concluded that the contracted form indicated grammaticalized and subjectified features at its onset in written texts. The singular preterit verbal form, *there was*, also started to strengthen its interactive function in Late Modern English, distinguishing itself as a single unit in speech. Even *there is*, the formal version of *there's*, showed signs of expansion of its pragmatic function. Thus, we saw that each verbal form demonstrated its own developmental course in the English language. On the other hand, the fully grammaticalized status of *here's* was not confirmed, although it displayed number disagreement to a certain extent. Its infrequent use as a deictic marker may have failed to completely induce its grammaticalization, compared with *there's*.

Thus, this chapter revealed how the sequence *there* + *be* has been fused in the history of English, resulting in the formation of the unique status of *there's*. The next chapter will present more advanced features of *there's* in present-day English.

Chapter 6

Peculiar Existential Constructions and *there's*[1]

This chapter will expand our discussion of the shortened form *there's* from the previous chapter and elaborate upon the grammaticalization and subjectification of *there's*, by clarifying the structures of peripheral existential sentences in colloquial English. Existential sentences in present-day English have many intrinsic patterns, as discussed in Chapter 4. Aside from the prototypical syntactic variations in formal English, Quirk et al. (1985: 1407–1409) introduced three kinds of structures restricted to use in informal vernaculars:

(1) There's a man lives in China.   (Quirk et al. 1985: 1407)

(2) There's a parcel come.   (Quirk et al. 1985: 1409)

(3) a. There's a visitor been waiting to see you.
    b. *There has a visitor been waiting.
    c. There's a new grammar been written.
    d. *There has a new grammar been written.

          (Quirk et al. 1985: 1409)

---

[1] Earlier versions of part of this chapter appeared as Yaguchi (2010a), Yaguchi (2015), Yaguchi (2016a), and Yaguchi (2017).

In this chapter, authors' names and titles of the COHA tokens will be described, although they are not explicitly shown in the other chapters. This chapter deals with texts of vernacular, so it is necessary to leave all the available data.

(1) has the structure *there* + *be* + NP + VP (TV construction), while (2) and (3) have the structure *there* + *be* + NP + pp (TP construction).[2] Although tokens with *been* as in (3) and those with other forms of the past participle as in (2) appear to be the same structure, this chapter will treat the two separately, calling the general pattern in (2) the TP construction and examples with *been* as in (3a, c) the T*been* construction, since they show totally different behaviors. After completing a detailed analysis of the three construction, I will show in Section 6.5 that the T*been* construction is a variant of the TV construction, rather than the TP construction.

As mentioned in Section 1.6 of Chapter 1, the TP construction in (2) can be traced back to the perfective usage of *be* + pp in earlier English, which is realized by *have* + pp in present-day English grammar. Perfective forms of intransitive verbs were primarily expressed with *be* until the beginning of Late Modern English, when it shifted to the perfective auxiliary *have*, which had previously been employed only with transitive verbs in earlier English. While it was generally acknowledged that *be* perfectives were superseded by *have* perfectives by the end of the eighteenth century and became obsolete in the first half of the nineteenth century, Rydén & Broström (1987) report that the disappearance of *be* + pp took place more slowly: the ratio of *be* + pp to the total use of perfective tokens with intransitive verbs gradually decreased (80% in 1700, 60% in 1800, and 5–10% in 1900, reaching 50% around 1810–1820). The TP construction is considered to have survived despite the progressive obsolescence of the *be* + *pp* perfective since the 1700s.

These three constructions have been attested since early times, as seen in (4):

(4) a.   There is no womans sides Can bide the beating of so strong a
passion.   [1601, Shakespeare *Twel. N.* II. iv. 304, *OED*]

---

[2] Curme (1931: 237) parses the TP construction in (2) as TV construction, providing an example "Well, Father, there's Rocket (name) [who has] come for you (Hugh Walpole, *the Green Mirror*, p. 29)." However, this study does not lend support to his interpretation partly because of the presence of inverted version as in (13b, c) and partly because of the behavioral difference in number disagreement rate between the TV and the TP constructions as shown in this chapter. His argument is untenable in any aspect. Lakoff (1987: 563–564) regards the T*been* construction such as (3a, c) as a strange existential construction. By adding a TV example (*There's a man robbed the drugstore down the street*) and a TP example (*There's someone fallen overboard*), he explains that *have* is not explicitly present, without specifying where *have* is supposed to be implicitly used.

    b.   There was newes come to London, that the Devill ...

                 [1563, W. Fulke *Meteors* (1640) 10b, *OED*]

    c.   There's mony waur been o' the race, And ...

                   [1786, Burns *A Dream* iii, *OED*]

The TV construction in (1) and (4a), otherwise known as the *there*-contact clause, has attracted significant attention in previous studies from diachronic and synchronic perspectives, although almost all of these have focused on certain limited periods, overlooking changes in the construction throughout the history of English (e.g. Jespersen 1927: 133, Erdmann 1976, 1980, Nagucka 1980, van der Auwera 1984, Harris & Vincent 1980, Lambrecht 1988, McNally 1997, Ukaji 2003, Nakazawa 2006, *inter alia*). By contrast, the TP and T*been* constructions as in (2), (3), and (4b, c) have hardly undergone in-depth examination either diachronically or synchronically in the literature, at least to my knowledge. Since the present chapter clarifies the diachronic shifts affecting these three peculiar constructions in detail, it will yield insight into the nature of existential sentences as a whole.

Along with the investigation into the historical development of the three constructions, this chapter will reveal how *there's* and the other verbal forms have been used in the three constructions. This analysis will propose and provide evidence that *there's* occasionally functions as a particle, which is a more advanced development of the blending of *there* and *is*. Quantitative analysis will be conducted using the *OED* and the COHA to determine the diachronic changes of the three constructions. Thus, while the data in Old English, Middle English, and Early Modern English will be extracted from the *OED*, discussion about the three constructions after the nineteenth century in this chapter will be based upon the American English data of the COHA. The COCA and the SOAP will be analyzed for additional data.

In Section 6.1, methodology on data collection will be presented. Section 6.2 will give detailed research results on the TV construction, while Sections 6.3 will focus on the TP and T*been* constructions. In Section 6.4, the status of *there's* will be discussed. Section 6.5 will offer an detailed analysis concerning the T*been* construction. Section 6.6 will argue the possibility of the other verbal forms to function as a particle, and Section 6.7 will clarify the syntactic, semantic, and pragmatic characteristics of the three constructions. In Section 6.8, *here*-based constructions will be explored. Section 6.9 will conclude the discussion in this chapter.

6.1　Methodology

There are two caveats regarding the data extraction of three constructions predominantly used in informal speech. First, because the transcription of speech is often inconsistent and arbitrary, we will primarily analyze written data from the *OED* and the COHA in this study, despite the availability of a number of corpora of contemporary natural speech. For instance, the Shogakukan Corpus Network Online provides the following tokens in the spoken subcorpus of the BNC, which superficially look like TV sentences:

(5)　a.　I'm just saying there was mine was Tech …
　　　b.　There's they got there.
　　　　　　　　　　　(Shogakukan Corpus Network Online, BNC)

However, BYU's BNC Online, created by Dr. Mark Davies, adds contextual information, such as pauses and omission of unclear utterances to the same tokens as follows:

(6)　a.　I'm just saying there was (pause) mine was (unclear) Tech …
　　　b.　There's (unclear) (pause) they got there.
　　　　　　　　　　　　　　　　　　　(BYU's BNC Online)

Thus, the transcribed examples of (5) can be parsed as TV sentences, but when contextual information is added, as in (6), it is clear that they are not TV tokens. Therefore, it is possible that the transcription itself—or the transcriber's judgment regarding the insertion of contextual information—can be arbitrary, inaccurate, or inconsistent. For this reason, transcription of natural speech is not analyzed in this study.[3] Although most data in this chapter contain no real utterances in natural contexts but mostly written conversations that reflect usage during their time, results from the analysis of written data are considered more accurate than those of transcribed speech. We investigate the COHA, the COCA, and the SOAP as well, using BYU's online service.

　　One more word of caution should be noted. In the process of parsing,

---

[3] Takaki (2010) seems to have analyzed the BNC through the Shogakukan Corpus Network Online, so he treats tokens of (5) as TV instances. Since his search retrieved only 101 TV tokens, even a few mistaken tokens of this kind may have affected his results. In addition, unlike the analysis of written data of this study in which more than 70% of the TV tokens in present-day English take *there*'s as the existential expression, the use of *there's* accounts for only 30% in his data. Certainly, the credibility of his study should be questioned. Footnote 34 will provide another point to dismiss his data as unreliable.

determining whether a token of speech is a TV or a TP sentence occasionally poses difficulties due to the ambiguity between the two structures. Thus, it is crucial to establish criteria to distinguish these tokens to disambiguate examples such as (7):

(7) a. There's queer things <u>chanced</u> since ye hae been in the land of Nod.   [1818, Scott *Hrt. Midl.* xxx, *OED*]

   b. There's a Coach <u>stopt</u>, I hope 'tis hers.
      [1693 Southerne *Maid's Last Prayer* III. ii, *Lady Susan*, *OED*]

   c. Som of our Preachmen are grown dog mad, <u>ther's</u> a worm <u>got</u> into their toungs, as well as their heads.
      [c1645, Howell *Lett.* II. xxxiv, *OED*]

   d. There's nobody <u>got</u> the right to ask me to stop being active and influential ...   [1915, Day Holman *The Landloper*, COHA]

Tokens (7a), (7b), and (7c) can be parsed both as TV or TP sentences, because some intransitive verbs such as *chance*, *stop*, and *get* have the same past tense and past participle forms. This study, therefore, will assume that sentences with intransitive verbs as in (7a), (7b), and (7c) form TP construction while those with transitive verbs such as in (7d) are TV construction. Following the previously mentioned study by Rydén & Broström (1987), we will assume that tokens with intransitive verbs before 1820, when *be* + pp and *have* + pp were employed 50% of the time, are more likely to be TP sentences, whereas those after 1820 are considered to be TV sentences.[4] Nonetheless, this study assumes that intransitive verbs used in the TP construction in Early Modern English are also used in TP sentences in present-day English. Since all intransitive verbs appearing in the COHA data after 1820 were also used in the *OED*'s TP tokens before 1820, we will categorize all tokens containing intransitive verbs (such as *arrive*, *chance*, *finish*, *get*, *happen*, *rise*, and *stop*) in the COHA as TP sentences. Data collection from the *OED* was conducted through manual examination of over 43,000 quotation texts using the wild card computational system furnished on the *OED*'s CD-ROM to extract *there* + *be* sequences from the dictionary. Consequently, tokens with element(s) between *there* and *be* were excluded, but errors caused by such exclusion are considered to be within an acceptable range because of their rarity. In total, 279 tokens were culled.

---

[4] For example, for the intransitive use of (7), Rydén & Broström (1987) report that when *get* expresses the intransitive meaning of "come" and "go", 93 tokens of *get* were connected with *be* and 53 with *have*, between 1700 and 1826.

Investigation into the COHA's dataset utilized the wild card function provided on the BYU's COHA Online. We applied the following patterns to each of the five verbal forms:

(8) a.   *there + be* * * * * * [verb. Modal]
         e.g. There is a man will come.
    b.   *there + be* * * * * * [verb. Base]
         e.g. There's two men have it.
    c.   *there + be* * * * * * [verb. 3SG]
         e.g. There's a man wants to see you.
    d.   *there + be* * * * * * [verb. ED:]
         e.g. There was a man wanted to see you.
    e.   *there + be* * * * * * [verb. [Have]]
         e.g. There are women have done it.
    f.   *there + be* * * * * * [verb. [Be]]
         e.g. There were three men were eating.

As in the case of the *OED*'s analysis, tokens with elements between *there* and *be* were excluded, and overlapped tokens were also discarded. In addition, because the present analysis retrieves 200 types for each search by the verbal form, there is a possibility that some tokens relevant to the TV construction were sifted out if there were more than 200 types in a pattern. Moreover, when NPs comprised more than five words, TV tokens containing them failed to be retrieved.[5] For the purpose of understanding general tendencies, however, such oversights can be considered to fall within an acceptable range. The present search has yielded a total of 405 tokens.

With the same method used for the extraction of TV tokens, the search for TP and T*been* sentences applied the following patterns for the wild card:

(9) a.   *there + be* * * * * * [verb. EN]
         e.g. There is a man gone overseas.
    b.   *there + be* * * * * * *been*   e.g. There's a book been stolen.

In each search, 1,000 types were gleaned, all of which were manually parsed. Because some patterns rendered more than 1,000 types and tokens with NPs with more than five words were possible, it is also possible that some TP and T*been* tokens could have been overlooked, as was the case of the TV construction. Thus, while the data are not perfectly accurate, it is

---

[5] In fact, almost all the NPs in the *OED*'s TV tokens after 1700 consisted of fewer than six words.

still possible to perceive the trend with a very high precision. Through the search accessed in February, 2013, 88 TP tokens and 36 T*been* tokens were retrieved.   In light of the investigation into ordinary existential sentences in the COHA, number disagreement rates by verbal form were calculated by examining a total of 4,000 sentences with *there* after extracting 200 tokens including *there* every 10 years over the 200-year span via the employment of the wild card.   In addition, retrieval of relevant data from the COCA applied the method outlined above the COHA data extraction.[6]

The next two sections will outline the diachronic shifts of the TV, TP, and T*been* constructions, followed by an analysis of *there's* in Section 6.4.

6.2   The TV construction

According to linguists studying contemporary English, the structure *there + be* + NP + VP is considered ungrammatical (e.g. Lambrecht 1988).   However, the TV construction is quite prevalent, although restricted to use in informal contexts as seen in the examples at the beginning of this chapter.   Previous studies such as McNally (1997) and Montgomery & Chapman (1992) explain that in some dialects, such as Hiberno-English, African-American English, and Appalachian English, this construction is used quite frequently.   Furthermore, Doherty (2000: 71) asserts that it is still widely observed today in North American and British English.[7]   Indeed, in the *OED*'s present-day English data, the construction appears in novels, poems, and magazines in British, American, Canadian, Irish, Scottish, and Australian English.

In fact, the TV construction has a long history in the English language: it has been attested since antiquity with its usage peaking during Early Modern English as in (10):

(10) a.   With hym ther was a Plowman was his brother That hadde ylad
         of dong ful many a fother.[8]   [c1386, Chaucer *Prol.* 529, *OED*]

     b.   There was a Freak took an Ass in the Head, to Scoure abroad upon
         the Ramble.   [1692, R. L'Estrange *Fables* ccxxiv. 196, *OED*]

---

[6]   The search of the COCA in this section was made in November, 2014.

[7]   Lambrecht (1988) claims that it is mistakenly used even by educated speakers, who consider the TV construction not only ungrammatical but also uninterpretable. On the other hand, Erdmann (1980) admits that native speakers exercise their judgment about its grammaticality quite differently, and I have also encountered the same situation.

[8]   There is the same quotation text under the entry of *fother* in the *OED*. This has a comma between *Plowman* and *was his brother*.

    c.   There isn't a mouse in all Epson <u>can</u> be muter, or a guinea-pig dumber.

        [1881, Besant & Rice *The Chaplain of the Fleet* II. xvii, *OED*]

According to Rissanen (1999a: 298–299) and Ukaji (2003), subject zero relative (SZR) sentences including the TV construction were utilized even in formal writing at the end of the eighteenth century despite their close association with colloquialism, and in the course of the nineteenth century a trend to limit the use of SZR sentences to informal speech accelerated.[9] Considering the informality and ungrammaticality that the TV construction entails in present-day English, the course of the diachronic transition is worthwhile to be elucidated.

    The *OED* (s.v. *there* adv., B. 4 e.) states that in present-day English the TV construction is obsolete except in colloquial and ballad styles, adding an account that it is a structure where a relative pronoun is omitted between NP and VP. A number of linguists also adopt this account of the *there* + *be* + NP + Θ + VP structure (e.g. Curme 1912, Jespersen 1927, Prince 1981, van der Auwera 1984, Quirk et al. 1985: 1407, Lambrecht 1988, Denison 1998: 281, Doherty 2000: 71–95, Ukaji 2003, Ando 2005, *inter alia*). Lambrecht (1988: 334) presents the following structure:[10]

---

[9] Ukaji (2003) remarks that among nine types of SZR structures, only five have survived in informal speech at present. Among the five, four types below are known as pseudo-relative clauses, as many linguists have pointed out (e.g. McCawley 1981: 105, 1998: 460, Quirk et al. 1985: 1250, 1387, Huddleston & Pullum 2002: 1035, 1046, 1416):

    (i)   There's a table (that/which) stands in the corner.
    (ii)   Here's the one (that/who) will get it for you.
    (iii) I have an idea (that/which) might work.
    (iv) It's Simon (that/who) did it.

Ukaji's (2003) research on 25 plays and one novel in the period of 1594 to 1614 shows that TV tokens comprise 29.04% of all SZR sentences, whilst Erdmann's (1980) research on British novels published between 1926 and 1975 shows the TV construction accounting for more than half of the 336 attested SZR tokens. These figures indicate that the TV construction has been the most dominant structure in SZR sentences in Early Modern English through present-day English.

    According to Prince (1981), what is common in the four SZR constructions is that the syntactic main clause is propositionally empty, while the syntactic subordinate clause is highly informative.

[10] Lambrecht (1988: 335) advances a different structure of what he calls presentational amalgam construction, in which "one and the same NP functions both as a syntactic object bearing the pragmatic relation of *focus* to the proposition in S₁, and as a syntactic subject, bearing the pragmatic relation of *topic* to the proposition in S₂".

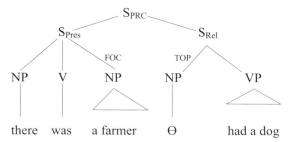

Figure 6-1: Structure of *apo koinou* hypothesis (Lambrecht 1988: 334)

In this study, the structure [*there* + *be* + NP] + [Θ + VP] in Figure 6-1 will be referred to as the *apo koinou* structure.[11] As Lambrecht (1988: 334) uses, the line in a well-known song *There was a farmer had a dog* is a prototypical example. As the term *apo koinou* construction, a structure consisting of two asyndentically connected clauses through an NP with two syntactic functions, indicates, Figure 6-1 shows that *a farmer* functions as the notional subject in the existential part and as the subject of *had a dog*. I will attempt to argue that the TV construction consists of two types of structures, one of which is seen in Figure 6-1 and the other taking the form [*there's*] + [NP + VP] (e.g. *There's something's happened* (COHA, 1949, fiction)), while highlighting the diachronic development and the shift in rate of number disagreement between the verbal form and the NP.

First, the diachronic development of the TV construction, according to the verbal forms (i.e. *there's*, *there is*, *there are*, *there was*, and *there were*) in the *OED* will be demonstrated. See Figure 6-2 and Table 6-1 (also see Appendix 1):

---

[11] Nagucka (1980) hypothesizes a different structure. Without assuming the presence of a relative pronoun, she claims that TV sentences constitute a "semantic unit" of *there* + *be* + NP + VP.

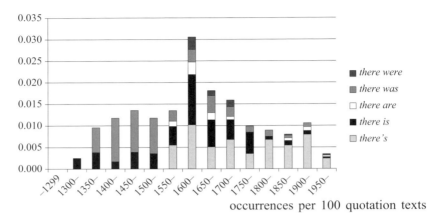

occurrences per 100 quotation texts

Figure 6-2: Occurrences of TV sentences in *OED*

Table 6-1: Raw occurrences of TV sentences in *OED*

	-1299	1300-	1350-	1400-	1450-	1500-	1550-	1600-	1650-	1700-	1750-	1800-	1850-	1900-	1950-
there's							9	21	9	9	5	19	26	18	7
there is		1	2	1	2	3	7	24	11	6	7	2	5	2	1
there are						2	6	3	1	0	0	3	2	1
there was			3	6	5	7	4	6	7	3	2	4	3	2	0
there were							6	2	2			1		1

Figure 6-2 shows the percentage of quotation texts in the *OED* that use the TV construction. Use of the TV construction was clearly frequent between 1600 and 1649, then gradually declined with a sharp drop after 1950. This result is consistent with the widely acknowledged view by Rissanen (1999a: 289–299) and Ukaji (2003) that SZR sentences prevailed in the early years of Early Modern English. Interestingly, in spite of its consistently low occurrences in the *OED* (6.3% of all existential sentences), the contracted form accounted for 44.1% of the total raw occurrences of TV tokens, thus dominating TV sentences since first appearing in the *OED* in 1584. If we represent in graph form the number of TV tokens out of 100 quotation texts of each verbal form, the abundant use of *there's* can be more clearly confirmed as in the following (also see Appendix 1):

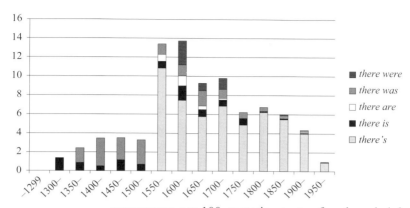

occurrences per 100 quotation texts of each verbal form

Figure 6-3: Occurrences of TV construction according to 100 quotation texts of each verbal form in *OED*   (From Yaguchi 2010a)

Figure 6-3 is an explicit representation of how much more frequently the shortened form *there's* appeared in the TV construction than other verbal forms. Since *there's* was employed mainly in speech or letters in diachronic contexts, we can infer that this construction appeared primarily in speech or letters at least from the beginning of Modern English. Figures 6-2 and 6-3 illustrate that after 1800, the ratio of *there's* to the total occurrences of TV sentences became very high, regardless of the consistently low occurrence of *there's* in the *OED*. This suggests that the construction began to be used primarily in informal contexts after 1800, if one assumes that ample employment of the contracted form characterizes the informality of the construction. This seems consistent with the explanation by Rissanen (1999a: 298–299) and Ukaji (2003) mentioned previously that SZR sentences shifted to uniquely informal use in the nineteenth century.

I would like to address another important point regarding the shortened form, the characteristic lack of number agreement between *be* in existential *there* + *be* and the notional subject, as in the case of (11) ((4a) is repeated as (11a)):

(11) a. There is no womans sides Can bide the beating of so strong a passion.   [1601, Shakespeare *Twel. N.* II. iv. 304, *OED*]
     b. For there's two ravenous Sow-Cats will Eat you.
                    [1689, N. Lee *Princ. Cleves.* III. i. *St. A, OED*]

The present analysis examined this lack of agreement in all the TV tokens in the *OED* according to verbal forms. Table 6-2 shows the ratio of non-agreeing tokens of ordinary *there* + *be* sentences and TV sentences to the total number of ordinary existential sentences and TV sentences in the *OED*:

Table 6-2: Number non-concord in *there* + *be* and TV construction in *OED*[12]   (raw occurrences)

	*there 's**	*there is***	*there are*	*there was****	*there were*
ordinary *there* + *be*	8.1% (211/2,620)	1.2% (230/18,411)	0.01% (1/9,897)	1.9% (157/8,402)	0.3% (11/3,834)
TV construction	16.3% (20/123)	4.1% (3/74)	0% (0/18)	7.5% (4/52)	0% (0/12)

$*\chi^2=8.96$, $**p<.01$ $**\chi^2=4.42$, $*p<.05$ $***\chi^2=9.81$, $**p<.01$

It is true that a statistically significant difference held between *there's*, *there is*, and *there was* in ordinary sentences and TV sentences, but only *there's* will be examined here for the following reason. As previously noted, *there's* appeared mainly in conversation and letters even in writing, while *there is* and *there were* appeared both in formal and informal contexts. Therefore, the significant differences between *there is* and *there was* attested in Table 6-2 can be attributed to their abundance in *OED*'s formal dataset (see Table 4-1 in Chapter 4 and Figure 5-1 in Chapter 5. Total occurrences of *there is* and *there was* account for 65.9% of over 43,000 *there* + *be* tokens), and the extremely low frequency of number non-agreeing tokens in ordinary existential sentences (1.2% for *there is* and 1.9% for *there was*) make the relatively high-frequency, non-agreeing TV sentences (4.1% for *there is* and 7.5% for *there was*) look exceptional. Since the singular forms *there is* and *there was* will be discussed separately in Section 6.6, we will focus on the contracted form here.

The obvious trend one first notices in Table 6-2 is that the rate of number disagreement in the use of *there's* (8.1%) is much higher than in that of other verbal forms in ordinary existential sentences. Indeed, a notable characteristic of *there's* is its behavior as a set phrase, an idea supported by Breivik & Martínez-Insua (2008), who maintain that a lack of number agree-

---

[12] Yaguchi (2010a) uses the percentage of disagreement tokens of *there* + *be* including TV sentences, but, in Table 6-2, I recalculated the data by separating the *there* contact clause tokens from ordinary *there* + *be* tokens for consistency with the other data in this study. As a result, the percentage of ordinary *there* + *be* tokens is a little lower in Table 6-2 than in Yaguchi (2010a). For instance, 8.1% of *there's* data in Table 6-2 is 8.38% in Yaguchi (2010a).

ment of this kind results from the reanalysis of *there's* into a single chunk following a long process of grammaticalization, as discussed in detail in Chapter 5. More important data relevant to this chapter is that the difference in non-concord rate between existential *be* and the notional subject is much larger in TV sentences containing singular verbal forms (in particular, *there's*) than ordinary existential sentences. Following the *apo koinou* hypothesis shown in Figure 6-1, in which we assume a syntactic connection holds between existential *be* and the notional subject, the non-agreement rate between ordinary existential sentences and TV sentences should not differ significantly. The data of *there's* in Table 6-2, however, show a dramatic difference. Based on the number disagreement rates in Table 6-2, I propose that *there's* occasionally functions as a particle, contributing to the formation of the structure of [*there's*] + [NP + VP], consistent with the argument by Yaguchi (2010a). Indeed, Harris & Vincent (1980) and Yasui (1987), though based more or less on their intuition, also present a similar argument without referring to the exclusive employment of *there's*. Erdmann (1980) parses the structure as [*There is*] [*a man wants to see you*] by using *there is* as his example without providing an argument for *there's* being a particle. Following Yaguchi (2010a), this study emphasizes that only *there's* behaves as a particle.

None of these arguments, however, especially those of Yaguchi (2010a), consider the informal use of the construction or identify when *there's* came to function as a particle. First, in order for the particle hypothesis to be tenable, the question of informality should be addressed: is there any possibility that the frequent number disagreement of the shortened form in the TV construction was induced only by the informality that the construction came to connote? In other words, is it possible to argue, contra Yaguchi (2010a), that the common absence of number agreement seen in Table 6-2 can be attributed only to the informal nature of the construction? If so, we cannot fully grant *there's* the status of a particle. This point certainly deserves extensive elaboration. Second, it is necessary to prove when the function of *there's* as a particle started, if my contention is to be valid. It is unfortunate, however, that quotation texts in the *OED* offer insufficient contexts or clues to determine the level of the formality of each token, and that the *OED* contains only 279 TV tokens spanning the whole of the history of English, which makes it rather difficult to accurately analyze all the verbal forms. Hence, it is crucial to conduct a full-scale investigation into the data from Late Modern English and present-day English, when the construction underwent a decline in formality and frequency. It is the COHA's dataset, rather than the *OED*'s quotation texts, that offers the most useful information for identifying a detailed, accurate trend during this period: it contains 405 TV tokens from 1810 to 2009, with uniform distribution of the four genres fiction, magazine, newspaper, and non-fiction across time;[13] the context of each token provides sufficient information to gauge the level of its formality with a certain precision; and it is possible to calculate the ratio of occurrences per one million words, rather than occurrences per 100 quotation texts as in the case of the *OED*. I compiled data for each 40-year span, since in some 10 year spans only a few tokens were retrieved from the COHA. The following graph and Table 6-3 show the diachronic shifts in the TV construction every 40 years in the COHA:

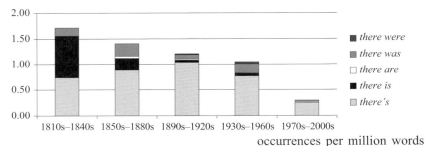

occurrences per million words

Figure 6-4: Occurrences of TV construction in COHA

Table 6-3: Frequency of TV construction in COHA

	1810s–1840s	1850s–1880s	1890s–1920s	1930s–1960s	1970s–2000s
there's	0.92 (35)	0.77 (56)	1.02 (94)	0.71 (69)	0.22 (23)
there is	0.82 (31)	0.23 (17)	0.04 (4)	0.05 (5)	0 (0)
there are	0 (0)	0.04 (3)	0.02 (2)	0.02 (1)	0.02 (2)
there was	0.16 (6)	0.25 (18)	0.10 (9)	0.18 (17)	0.03 (3)
there were	0.03 (1)	0.04 (3)	0.02 (2)	0.04 (4)	0 (0)

per one million words (raw occurrences)

The tendencies noted in Figure 6-4 correspond to those in Figures 6-2 and 6-3 in that *there's* began to play a major role in the TV construction in Late Modern English, especially after the 1850s, and in that after the 1970s, its frequency sharply declined. Certainly, the prominent dominance of *there's*

---

[13] In fact, newspapers were not included in the corpus until the 1860s. In addition, the word counts in the data from the 1810s and 1820s are extremely low compared to those after the 1880s.

appeared later in the COHA than in the *OED* in which, as observed in Figure 6-2, the dominance of *there's* was established around 1800. (The ratio of *there's* to the total TV occurrences is 47.9%, 57.7%, 84.7%, 71.1%, and 82.1% in the 1810s–1840s, 1850s–1880s, 1890s–1920s, 1930s–1960s, and 1970s–2000s periods respectively in the COHA; and 76%, 68.4%, 75%, and 70% in the 1800–1849, 1850–1899, 1900–1949, and 1950–2003 periods respectively in the *OED*.) This difference may be attributed to the low word count in the period from the 1810s through the 1840s (i.e. almost half that from the 1850s through the 1880s) of the COHA, the difference in distributions of genres in the databases, or the distinction between British and American English. Further research is required to clarify this issue.

We now turn to number non-concord by verbal form, which is shown in Table 6-4:

Table 6-4: Number disagreement of ordinary *there* + *be* and TV sentences in COHA

	*there's**	*there is*	*there are*	*there was*	*there were*
ordinary *there* + *be*[14]	10.2% (19/187)	1.0% (9/875)	0.7% (2/299)	3.7% (26/705)	0.8% (2/263)
TV construction	18.4% (51/277)	1.8% (1/57)	0% (0/8)	5.7% (3/53)	0% (0/10)

*χ^2=7.9, **p<.001

As in the case of the *OED*'s dataset in Table 6-2, Table 6-4 conclusively shows that a wider gap between existential *be* and the notional subject in the TV construction than in ordinary *there* + *be* sentences across the singular verbal forms. Only the contracted form was found to be statistically significant in either corpora.[15] Curiously enough, the number non-concord rates

---

[14] For the investigation of ordinary existential sentences in the COHA, number disagreement rates by verbal forms were calculated by an examination of a total of 10,000 sentences with *there* after extracting 500 tokens every 10 years over a 200-year span via the employment of the wild card.

[15] There is an underlying factor to yield the statistical significances of *there is* and *there was* only in the *OED*. For extraction of existential sentences from the COHA, less than 4,000 tokens were analyzed (after discarding locative use of *there* from the retrieved tokens), and, by contrast, the large number of denominators in the *OED*'s data (i.e. more than 43,000 existential tokens) led to realization of the statistical significances of the two items in Table 6-2, since the formality expressed by *there is* and *there was* with high frequency in the *OED* makes the deviating of its TV tokens look significant.

of *there's* in the TV construction underwent a very interesting diachronic change, which is seen in Table 6-5:

Table 6-5: Number disagreement of *there's* in ordinary *there + be* and TV construction in COHA

	1810s–1840s	1850s–1880s	1890s–1920s	1930s–1960s	1970s–2000s
ordinary *there's*[16]	8.2% (16/196)	11.4% (22/193)	12.0% (23/192)	4.1%[17] (8/196)	10.8% (21/194)
TV construction	2.9% (1/35)	5.4% (3/56)	20.2% (19/94)	29.0% (20/69)	34.8% (8/23)

The non-agreement rate of the TV construction including *there's* increased over time to reach more than 30% in contemporary English, in contrast to the consistent 10.2% rate of non-agreement in ordinary existential sentences including *there's*. The construction with the shortened form showed a lower level of non-concord than ordinary existential sentences (10.2% of number disagreement rate on average) until the end of the nineteenth century and then displayed a very high level of number non-concord in the following century.[18] In other words, if one assumes that a high rate of number non-agreement represents the informality of the construction, it is possible to conjecture that its formality level was similar to that of ordinary existential sentences until the turn of the century and came to be considered very informal after 1930.[19] At the same time, however, from a syntactic perspective,

---

[16] For the purpose of this investigation, I collected 100 ordinary existential tokens with *there's* for each 10 years, out of which 200 tokens were randomly selected every 40 years. I excluded irrelevant tokens such as *there's + been* and TV/TP/T*been* tokens from the 200 tokens.

[17] This figure is very low, compared with those of the other periods. I chose another sample, but the figure was almost on the same level. I cannot account for this phenomenon.

[18] The situation concerning TV instances in the COCA is as follows: The ratio of *there's* tokens to the total TV occurrences is 68.1% (32 out of 47 instances) in written texts and 56.7% (76 out o 134 instances) in all texts including speech; the disagreement rate of *there's* in TV tokens is 25.0% (8 out of 32 instances) in written texts and 25.0% (19 out of 76 instances) in all texts including speech. (Unlike the TP and T*been* constructions, because of the possibility that the transcription of speech data may vary according to the transcriber, the rates with and without speech texts are given here.) Thus, in the COCA as well, the TV construction shows tendencies similar to those in the COHA, though the percentages are lower.

[19] Because of the general consensus in the literature that the speakers' educational levels are likely to correlate with the non-concord rate, as discussed in Section 5.1 in Chapter

we can also assume that the independence of the existential predicate from the notional subject progressed in the twentieth century. Again, to fully understand the progression of this change, I would like to propose, along with Yaguchi (2010a), that in some TV sentences *there's* function as a particle in present-day English. As mentioned in connection with Table 6-2, the issue of informality remains: the growing rate of number non-concord can only be attributed to the increased level of informality of the construction. I would like to explore the TV construction's informality in relation to the use of *there's* and its non-agreement rate in Section 6.4, which will provide further quantitative evidence for the syntactic change of the same construction to prove the status of *there's* as a particle in the TV construction in present-day English.

This section has shown the diachronic shift of the TV construction. We have demonstrated that in present-day English, the TV construction has declined in frequency and changed in form: it came to predominantly employ the shortened *there's*, exhibiting more frequent number disagreement than in the nineteenth century.

6.3   The TP and T*been* constructions

This section will examine the diachronic changes and linguistic features of the TP and T*been* constructions. We will first concentrate on the TP construction. As referred to in Section 1.6 of Chapter 1, the TP structure comprises the *there + be + NP + pp* sequence. As (14) of Chapter 1, repeated below as (12a), shows that *is* is employed in the tag question, the use of *be* is mandatory; and the use of *have* is disallowed, as in (12b, c):

(12) a.   There's a change comed over him ... is there not?

[1848, Mrs. Gaskell *Mary Barton* vi, *OED*]

　　b.   There is a letter come to me.

　　c.   *There has a letter come to me.

This construction and its variant with inversion of the notional subject and pp in (13b, c) are attested in earlier English:

5, number non-concord is generally thought to be closely associated with the level of informality.

(13) a.   <u>There was</u> newes <u>come</u> to London, that the Devill ...

[1563, W. Fulke *Meteors* (1640) 10b, *OED*]

b.   <u>Ther was</u> sprongun a greet crye in Egipte.

[1382, Wyclif *Exod.* xii. 30, *OED*]

c.   <u>There is come</u> a Messenger before To signifie their comming.

[1596, Shakespeare *Merch. V.* v. i. 117, *OED*]

Only 34 TP tokens were retrieved in the *OED*, after discarding the inversion tokens as in (13b, c). See Table 6-6, which shows the raw occurrences of the TP construction and those containing *there's* in the *OED*:

Table 6-6: Raw occurrences of TP construction in *OED*

period	1500–1599	1600–1699	1700–1799	1800–1899	1900–
occurrences	2	19	3	6	4
(*there's*)	(1)	(4)	(0)	(4)	(3)

The *OED*, however, contains insufficient data for quantitative analysis, but we can speculate about the transition: after its heyday in the 1600s, the construction declined in use. Moreover, the high ratio of *there's* across time seems to indicate that this construction appeared mainly in speech or letters diachronically. Needless to say, it is necessary to examine the COHA, which contains ampler word counts after 1810, for a more detailed look at the trend in Late Modern English and present-day English. The results of the investigation (a total of 88 tokens) will be shown in the following figure and table, which illustrate the occurrences of TP sentences by the verbal form every 40 years in the COHA since 1810:

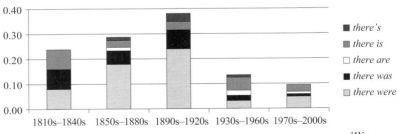

occurrences per one million words

Figure 6-5: Diachronic shift of TP construction in COHA

Table 6-7: Frequency of TP sentences in COHA

	1810s–1840s	1850s–1880s	1890s–1920s	1930s–1960s	1970s–2000s
there's	0.08 (3)	0.18 (13)	0.24 (22)	0.03 (3)	0.05 (5)
there is	0.08 (3)	0.05 (4)	0.08 (7)	0.02 (2)	0.01 (1)
there are	0 (0)	0.01 (1)	0 (0)	0.02 (2)	0.01 (1)
there was	0.08 (3)	0.03 (2)	0.03 (3)	0.05 (5)	0.03 (3)

per one million words (raw occurrences)

The construction increased in frequency up to the 1920s, then underwent a decline. The ratio of *there's* to the total occurrences was quite high, between 25.0% and 68.8%, which is, however, lower than that of TV sentences. Certainly, *there's* was not used as predominantly as in the TV construction. Furthermore, the number disagreement rate of *there's* in TP sentences was not as high as in the TV construction throughout its existence: 4.3% on average in the COHA's dataset. This figure is even lower than the average disagreement rate of *there's* in ordinary existential sentences (10.2%) in the same corpus, as seen in Table 6-4.[20]

Another feature of the TP construction is also worthy of attention: the same types of verbs appear repeatedly. Among the verb types used in this construction, *come* and *gone* accounts for 52.9% and 23.5% of data in the *OED*, and 70.4% and 17.0% in the COHA respectively. In a nutshell, *there + be + NP + come/gone* appears to be a fixed phrase to a considerable degree. Additionally, in the COHA's dataset, only the same types of intransitive verbs appear, such as *arrive, chance, finish, get, happen, rise,* and *stop,* as discussed in Section 6.1. It seems that in the same way that certain types of fixed "pseudo-passive" phrases of perfective such as *be + gone, be + done, be + finished* are still available (c.f. Quirk et al. 1985: 170), only TP sentences using established types of intransitive verbs have survived up to the present.

Let us now examine the T*been* construction, of which only three tokens appear in the *OED*.

---

[20] It is wise to examine written and spoken data in the COCA in order to ascertain the trends mentioned above. The results thus show that the ratio of *there's* to the total occurrences is relatively low, 43.8% (14 out of 32 tokens) and that the number disagreement rate is low, 7.1% (1 out of 14 tokens). Thus, we can confirm parallel inclinations in contemporary English as well.

(14) a.   <u>There's</u> many waur <u>been</u> o' the race, And ...
               [1786, Burns *A Dream* iii, *OED*]

    b.   Then <u>there's</u> the Nailer's <u>been</u> after me ...
               [c1863, T. Taylor in M. R. Booth *Eng. Plays of 19th Cent.*
               (1969) II. 84, *OED*]

    c.   They'd marked my card <u>there was</u> a new dance-hall <u>been</u> opened
               over at Peckham.
               [1962, R. Cook *Crust on its Uppers* ii. 34, *OED*]

It is evident that the T*been* construction rarely occurred in written texts. Indeed, in the COHA's dataset, there are far fewer tokens of T*been* (i.e. 36 tokens) than TP tokens (i.e. 88 tokens). Nonetheless, an investigation of the COHA reveals a general trend in diachronic change, notwithstanding the low frequency of T*been* sentences, as seen in Figure 6-6 and Table 6-8:

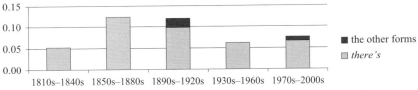

occurrences per one million words

Figure 6-6: Diachronic transition of T*been* construction in COHA

Table 6-8: Frequency of T*been* construction according to verbal forms in
COHA   per one million words (raw occurrences)

	1810s–1840s	1850s–1880s	1890s–1920s	1930s–1960s	1970s–2000s
there's	0.05 (2)	0.12 (9)	0.10 (9)	0.06 (6)	0.07 (7)
the other forms	0 (0)	0 (0)	0.02 (2)	0 (0)	0.01 (1)

It is quite interesting that T*been* sentences show a similar shift to the TP construction in that both peaked in usage between the 1850s and the 1920s, then went into decline. Furthermore, we should note that T*been* sentences are characterized as closely connected to the use of *there's*: Figure 6-6 illustrates the predominant use of the contracted form. In fact, as discussed in Section 1.6 of Chapter 1, Quirk et al. (1985: 1409) and Lakoff (1985: 563) maintain that *there is*, *there are*, *there was*, *there were*, *there has*, and *there have* can hardly replace *there's*, giving the following examples ((15) is repeated below from (16) of Chapter 1:

(15) a.   There are three visitors (?been) waiting to see you.

  b.   There was a new grammar (*been) published recently.

(Quirk et al. 1985: 1409)

  c.   *There is a man been shot.

  d.   *There has a man been shot.

  e.   *There's a man been shot, isn't there?

  f.   There's a man been shot, hasn't there?

  g.   *There've many people been killed this week.

(Lakoff 1987: 563)

Apparently, these examples strongly suggest that the construction is used only with the contracted form and present tense singular.[21] The use of *there's*, accounting for 91.7% in the COHA's dataset, suggests an almost intrinsic link with *there's*. (Out of the 36 tokens in the COHA, two *there was* tokens (1905 and 2000) and one *there is* token (1907) are gleaned.[22]) Once again, it is necessary to examine the rate of number non-agreement between *there's* and the notional subject. Table 6-9 displays the frequent non-agreement in the COHA:

Table 6-9: Number disagreement rates of *there's* of T*been* tokens in COHA

1810s–1840s	1850s–1880s	1890s–1920s	1930s–1960s	1970s–2000s
50.0% (1/2)	11.1% (1/9)	33.3% (3/9)	16.7% (1/6)	28.6% (2/7)

(raw occurrences)

No tendency associated with diachronic change can be found in the data in Table 6-9, in part because of the low frequency of the construction (i.e. 36 tokens), so it is reasonable to estimate an average non-agreement rate of 22.2% as the overall disagreement rate.[23] This high rate is derived from two feasible assumptions. First, existential *there's* seems to be less dependent on NP + *been* than in the TP construction, where the average non-agreement rate is a mere 4.3%. Second, the T*been* construction is more informal than the TP construction, since the shortened form is almost always used.

---

[21] The contrast in grammaticality between (15e) and (15f) will be fully discussed in Section 6.5.

[22] In the *OED*'s token in (14c), *there was* is used. As argued in Chapter 5, *there was* also came to function as a fixed phrase in certain environments in present-day English.

[23] The COCA's dataset also demonstrates a similar tendency: 87.0% (20 out of 23 tokens) of the T*been* tokens are realized in those with *there's* (There is one *there are* token and one *there was* token in speech and one *there was* token in writing); and their disagreement rate is 20.0% (4 out of 20 tokens).

As mentioned at the beginning of this chapter, it is important to consider the structure of the T*been* construction. The structure of example (15f) of *There's a man been shot, hasn't there?*, in particular, needs to be clarified. At this point, we do not have sufficient data to account for the T*been* construction, so I will address this issue in Section 6.5.

This section has focused on the diachronic development of the TP and T*been* constructions in Late Modern English and present-day English. Both structures showed similar diachronic changes: after appearing relatively frequently around the turn of the twentieth century, both declined in frequency in present-day English. We demonstrated, however, that they showed different tendencies in their usage of *there's* and number disagreement.

6.4 Discussion on the use of *there's*

In this section, we address the issues raised in Section 6.2: whether or not the increasingly informal register of *there's* was solely responsible for increased number disagreement rates; and if *there's* became a particle, when did it occur? We will first clarify the syntactic, semantic, and sociolinguistic characteristics of the three constructions in present-day English by exploring the use of *there's* in the TV, TP, and T*been* constructions, and then consider the shift towards informal use of the TV construction.

At this point, I would like to provide background on the data. Present-day English data after 1930 (i.e. the last 80-year-period of the 200-year-spanning COHA) will be mainly analyzed in this section. For the sake of argument, the rationale to highlight the data after 1930, rather than after 1970, needs to be justified. Since the occurrences after 1970 of the three constructions including *there's*, particularly the TP (i.e. five tokens) and the T*been* (i.e. eight tokens), are too low for an accurate quantitative analysis, the target of the analysis should be expanded to the tokens after 1930. The following table shows raw occurrences of the three constructions' tokens after 1930:

Table 6-10: Raw occurrences of TV, TP, and T*been* tokens after 1930 in COHA

	there's	*there is*	*there are*	*there was*	*there were*
TV	92	5	3	20	4
TP	8	3	3	8	1
T*been*	13	0	0	1	0

Indeed, the data after 1930 reflect the tendency towards number disagreement in the TV construction in contemporary English, which declined significantly after this time along with the TP and T*been* constructions. Only eight TP tokens appear with *there's*, so the tendency noted in the following analysis may not reflect the actual situation. Nevertheless, general tendencies can be still derived. (As discussed above, the contemporary data from the COCA showed very similar tendencies for the TV, TP, and T*been* constructions.) Keeping this in mind, we will examine the three constructions from a sociolinguistic perspective.

To begin with, Table 6-11 summarizes the features of the three constructions including *there's* in the COHA:

Table 6-11: Ratio of *there's* to total tokens and its number disagreement rate in COHA (raw occurrences)[24]

		1810s–1840s	1850s–1880s	1890s–1920s	1930s–1960s	1970s–2000s
Ratio of *there's* to total occurrences	TV	47.9% (35/73)	57.7% (56/97)	84.7% (94/111)	71.1% (69/96)	82.1% (23/28)
	TP	33.3% (3/9)	62.0% (13/21)	62.9% (22/35)	23.1% (3/13)	50% (5/10)
	T*been*	100% (2/2)	100% (9/9)	81.8% (9/11)	100% (6/6)	87.5% (7/8)
Number disagreement rate of *there's*	TV	2.9% (1/35)	5.4% (3/56)	20.2% (19/94)	29.0% (20/69)	34.8% (8/23)
	TP	0% (0/3)	0% (0/13)	4.5% (1/22)	0% (0/3)	20% (1/5)
	T*been*	50.0% (1/2)	11.1% (1/9)	33.3% (3/9)	16.7% (1/6)	28.6% (2/7)

Table 6-11 shows three tendencies in present-day English: (1) the rate of number disagreement in TV sentences increased over time with the expanded use of *there's*, and showed high number disagreement most frequently in contemporary English; (2) TP sentences used the shortened form the least and had the lowest number disagreement rate; (3) T*been* sentences are realized by *there's* far more often than their TV and TP counterparts.

First, we return to the issue raised in Section 6.2: whether or not the high number disagreement rate of *there's* is triggered only by the increased informality of the TV construction. I consider it reasonable to compare the

---

[24] As seen in Table 6-11, raw occurrences of TP or T*been* sentences in current English are not high enough to render accurate quantitative results. However, general tendencies are observable.

levels of informality of the three constructions by examining the discoursal context in which each token was used. I examined all instances of the three constructions and counted how many tokens appeared in narration as in (16a) and how many tokens appeared in conversation as in (16b) or first-person narration as in (16c):

(16) a. This may serve to alleviate much of the Uneasiness of old Age, for there is nothing sits so heavy upon the Aged, except Thoughts of an ill-spent Life, …

[1934, Jared Eliot *Upon Field Husbandry*, COHA]

   b. "There's people take it proud to offer up a little money or so to a blind boy can't see his way," he said.

[1963, John Updike *Centaur*, COHA]

   c. I have a dispatch from the Chamber of Commerce of Cincinnati, sent to the Secretary of the Treasury, and by him to me, urging the speedy passage of the bill as it passed the House. It is true there was a doleful sound came up from the caverns of bullion brokers, and from the saloons of the associated banks.

[1869, E. G. Spaulding *A Resource of War*, COHA]

From these data, we assume that third-person narration as in (16a) is the most formal context of these three. The following table displays the data from after 1930 (data prior to 1930 is shown in parentheses) on the use in objective and/or formal contexts:

Table 6-12: Use in narration with third person's perspective after 1930 (before 1930)

	there's	the other forms
TV	0% (0.5%)	9.4% (8.3%)
TP	0% (0%)	13.3% (11.1%)
T*been*	0% (0%)	0% (0%)

The results of the present investigation show that the three constructions were all used primarily in speech, since the tokens with *there's* after 1930 all appeared in a character's conversation or in narration by a character referring to herself/himself as '*I*' or '*we*' in (16b, c). To expand the target to tokens of verbal forms other than *there's*, 9.4% of the TV tokens, 13.3% of the TP tokens, and 0% of the T*been* tokens were used in ordinary third-person nar-

ration as in (16a).[25] These figures suggest that although the three constructions are basically restricted to use in speech or speech-like first-person narration, TV and TP sentences can be objective/formal utterances when verbal
forms other than *there's* are used.

The figures in Table 6-12 seem to indicate the level of objectivity/
formality of each construction after (and before) 1930. It is implausible to
assume that only the presence of *there's* makes a construction casual, so the
TV construction and the TP construction seem to have a similar capacity for
expressing objectivity or formality when verbal forms other than *there's* are
employed.

Returning to the use of *there's* and its number disagreement rate, despite
their similar levels of (in)formality, the two constructions behave very differently, as seen in Table 6-11. On the other hand, the T*been* construction
seems to have been the most subjective/informal of the three, since it fails
to appear in any third-person contexts. Additionally, owing to its limited
use in speech and the abundant use of *there's* (92.9% on average for the
data after 1930), the T*been* construction is considered the most informal
construction of the three. In contrast, however, its disagreement rate (23.1%
on average for the date after 1930) is lower than that of the TV construction
(30.4% on average for the data after 1930). These discrepancies show that
the level of informality itself is not alone correlated with the number non-
concord rate. Rather, it suggests that the wide gap between *there's* observed
in Tables 6-2 and 6-4 cannot be attributed only to the informal nature of the
TV construction.

Hence, I would like to argue that the degree of syntactic connection between *be* in *there's* and VP/pp/*been* determines the number concord rate to a
certain degree. The data for the TP construction offer a clear clue that this
is the case. Certainly, the low number disagreement rate in the TP construction with *there's* indicates compellingly that the relative syntactic significance
of existential *be* affects number concord. In the formation of the TP construction, *be* is an essential syntactic element for the formation of *be* + pp
and is thereby sensitive to the choice of verbal form (i.e. the relatively low
frequency of *there's* of 34.8% on average for the data after 1930 despite the

---

[25] The COCA's dataset exhibits lower rates: 0% (32 tokens, written data only) and
6.7% (1 out of 15 tokens, written data only) for TV tokens with *there's* and the other verbal forms respectively; 0% (8 tokens, written data only) and 10.0% (1 out of 10 tokens,
written data only) for TP tokens; 0% (7 tokens, written data only) and 0% (1 token, written data only) for T*been* tokens.

colloquial use of the construction concerned). This consequently yields a similar number disagreement rate (12.3% on average for the data after 1930) to that of ordinary existential sentences containing *there's* (10.2% on average; see Tables 6-4 and 6-11).

Meanwhile, copula *be* in the existential part of the TV construction is completely independent of the VP, since the presence of *be* makes an ill-formed sentence, according to the grammatical system of present-day English. At the same time, assuming that the grammaticalization of *there's* from an inseparable chunk to a particle progressed in certain linguistic environments in the Modern English period (as will be discussed below), we also assume *there's* in the TV construction to have developed in some instances into an adverbial-like particle, presumably during the course of the nineteenth and twentieth centuries as number disagreement increased in American English. As Tables 6-5 and 6-11 show, the syntactic irrelevance of *there's* thus led to the loss of number concord. Data by Yaguchi (2010a) of quotation texts from the *OED* found that in the 1800–1899 period 13.3% of the TV tokens with *there's* displayed number disagreement, while *there's* was used in 71.4% of all TV tokens; in the 1900–2003 period 41.6% of the TV tokens of *there's* showed number disagreement, while 70.5% of the TV tokens contained *there's*. These figures of the *OED* also support the argument that a new structure had been developed.

Of course, there are also tokens of the *apo koinou* structure in which a relative pronoun is omitted between the NP and the VP as in (17):

(17) a. I've seen her perform before now, and there's not a storm can blow on this coast she won't ride through.
   [1913, Hough Emerson *The Lady and the Pirate Being the Plain Tale of a Diligent Pirate and a Fair Captive*, COHA]

   b. There's not a soul here can or will bake.
   [1971, William Service *Feeling One's Way Across the Chasm*, COHA]

   c. There's old Balaam, was in the Interior—... he's made the riffle on the Injun; great Injun pacificator and land-dealer.
   [1873, 'Mark Twain' & Warner *Gilded Age* xxxi. 279, *OED*]

Negative tokens such as (17a, b) are certainly easier to parse by assuming the presence of a relative pronoun between the NP and the VP. In addition, in (17c), the use of a comma seems to indicate the omission of a relative pronoun. Also, the ratio of *there's* to total occurrences of the TV construction (74.2% on average for the data after 1930) is lower than that of the

T*been* construction (92.9% on average for the data after 1930). Clearly, this sensitivity to the number of the notional subject by other verbal forms strongly supports the *apo koinou* hypothesis. Indeed, using a generative grammar analysis, Doherty (2000) argues for an *apo koinou* structure for the TV construction in present-day English. Hence, it can be assumed that the TV construction was mainly a structure in which a relative pronoun is omitted before the 1890s, due to the fact that number disagreement rates were even lower than those of ordinary existential sentences with *there's* (as Table 6-5 shows) and also that, as Figures 6-2, 6-3, and 6-4 illustrate, verbal forms other than *there's* were more prevalent in earlier English. It is possible to surmise, therefore, that along with the shift of the TV construction with *there's* to purely informal use and the development of *there's* into a particle through the grammaticalization and subjectification of *there* + *is* over time, the structure [*there's*] + [NP + VP] emerged, coexisting with the existing *apo koinou* structure. We can thus postulate that the frequent use of the TV construction with *there's* led to more independent usages of *there's*, which in turn caused its subjectification to function more as an interjectory adverb such as *There goes Tom again!*. In other words, the diluted meaning of *there's* expresses the speaker's intention to draw the listener's attention to prepare for the upcoming talk. The following examples provide evidence ruling out the *apo koinou* structure:

(18) a.   "Who to?" "Why, there's people'll buy anything," said the Patron.   [1954, John Steinbeck *Sweet Thursday*, COHA]

   b.   "There's something's happened," he said gravely.
                    [1949, Roger Phillips Graham, Amazing Stories, COHA]

   c.   Is it staggering to you when you look back on that, given that there's nobody's ever come close to that?   (COCA, spoken)

   d.   There's some'll return and some who'll stay.[26]
                    [1918, Dawson Coningsby *The Glory of the Trenches*, COHA]

The cliticized *'ll* in *people'll* in (18a) and in *some'll* (18d) show there is no omission of a relative pronoun between *people* and *will* and *some* and *will*. The cliticized *'s* in *something's* (18b) and *nobody's* (18c) also exhibits the function of *there's* as a particle. Consequently, we emphasize that the TV construction comprises two structures in present-day English, as the

---

[26] What should be mentioned here is the presence of *who* in example (18d): the writer seems to be aware of the necessity of a relative pronoun for the second notional subject. The subtle nature of *there's* as a particle can be seen here.

examples in (17) and (18) form totally different structures.

Curiously enough, the particle status of *there's* can be confirmed in what is called the list *there*-sentence in present-day English. Observe the next examples in (19) and (20) (which previously appeared as (14) and (15) of Chapter 5 respectively):

(19)   A: Which of the Scandinavian capitals have you visited?
       B: Well, there's Oslo in Norway.

                                                    (Breivik 1990: 153)

(20)   A: Who's attending the meeting?
       B: Well, there's (*are) John, Michael, and Janet.

                                                    (Breivik 1997: 154)

According to Breivik (1990), *there's* in the list existential sentences above functions as a "presentational signal" to bring the referent into the focus of attention, meaning 'I could mention' or 'Don't let's forget'. The important point is that a list existential sentence is predominantly realized by the short-ened form in colloquial English, preventing the plural form from being em-ployed, as in (20). In other words, the intolerance for plural verbal forms in this structure certainly points to *there's* being a fixed phrase, and its inflex-ibility itself is compelling evidence that it functions as a particle. Accord-ing to related semantic and pragmatic arguments, *there's* lists a set of new reference(s) in response to WH-questions, but it is not required syntactically, since it does not express any semantic meaning. It is used as a particle to cue the hearer to prepare for the introduction of a list of reference(s). Thus, *there's* is subjectified to signify the speaker's intentions without expressing existence. In fact, Hartmann (2006) argues that list existentials have a speci-ficational function different from ordinary existentials which have a predi-cational function. Thus, *there's* in list *there*-sentences operates in a distinct way. List *there*-sentence usage is attested in Early Modern English, as in (21) (previously cited as (21) of Chapter 5):

(21)   ... there's your Parragon, Burragon, Phillipine, Cheny, Grogrum,
       Mow-hair.   [1668, Head *Eng. Rogue* II. xii., *OED*]

This data suggests that *there's* behaved as a set phrase from Early Modern English, although it is almost impossible to determine whether it had already attained particle status. In any event, it is reasonable to state that in the same way in which the shortened form functions as a particle in list existen-tial sentences, *there's* in the TV construction works as a particle, signaling the listener to anticipate upcoming talk.

Finally, we discuss the T*been* construction. If it is a variant of TP construction according to its seemingly identical structure to the TP construction (*there's* + NP + pp), we must assume that existential *be* is indispensable, as it is in the TP construction. However, this is clearly not the case in the T*been* construction, as the high rate of number disagreement in the above data shows. Rather, for the same reason, I would like to argue that the *there* + *be* part is independent from NP + *been*. Furthermore, it is significant to note that *been* per se clearly denotes the past participle of the copula *be*, expressing the present tense as default sense when the present tense *there's* is used.[27] Indeed, in some dialects such as Samaná English, *have* is omitted in actual language use while the intended meaning of present perfective is retained, as in (22):

(22) a.   She been married.
b.   We all been raised up speaking English.
c.   They been fixing the road.

(Tagliamonte 1997)

Apparently, the above examples in (22) show that perfective *have* is not necessary in this vernacular dialect. In the T*been* construction, the presence of *have* is not required either. In addition, as stated in connection with (15) in Section 6.3, citing Quirk et al. (1985: 1409) and Lakoff (1985: 563), the use of *there's* is almost always entailed. If one cannot use other verbal forms in this construction, *there's* constitutes part of *there's* + NP + *been* as a fixed sentence unit. At least it is safe to say at this point that the T*been* construction is not a variant of the TP construction. Furthermore, Yaguchi (2015) and Yaguchi (2016a) argue that *there's* in the T*been* construction is a particle, based upon the presupposition that it is the only verbal form available in the same way as *there's* in list existential sentences. This study supports her contention and will elucidate it more clearly in the next section.

Here, it is necessary to account for the 23.1% non-concord rate (after 1930) for the T*been* construction with *there's* and the 30.4% rate (after 1930)

---

[27] It is possible to infer that *there's* in TP sentences with *gone*, a leading marker of the TP construction, may work as fixed phrases in the same way as their T*been* counterpart *been*, since unlike *come*, *gone* can be recognized as past participle without the presence of *be*. However, the average number non-concord rate of TP construction with *gone* is 7.1%, compared with 23.1% of the TP*been* sentences. This difference may be caused by the fact that *been* is a function word, while *gone* is a content word. In addition, unlike *been*, *gone* is not presupposed to always express present tense.

for the TV construction with *there's*. If *there's* in the former construction is a fixed formula, the number disagreement rate should be higher than in the latter construction, because *there's* can be used with any kind of NP in the former. Based on the finding by Biber et al. (1999: 291) demonstrating that the more objective/formal the register is, the lower the ratio of singular nouns to the total use of nouns, it is, by all means, a reasonable inference that the lower number disagreement rate in the T*been* construction can be attributed to the more colloquial nature of the context in which it appears: there are more singular nouns used in T*been* sentences than in their TV counterparts, which induces the lower rate of number disagreement in T*been* tokens despite the presupposed use of *there's* for any kind of NP. Conversely, we can argue that the flexibility in verbal forms other than *there's* and the wide variety of NP types allowed in the TV construction including the *apo koinou* variant represents its richness and potential for expressing objectivity/formality. In a nutshell, partly due to the very informal status of the construction and partly due to the presence of *been* as an explicit marker of the present perfective, the T*been* construction seems to have become a fixed sentence unit before 1810, as shown by the consistently high number disagreement rate in the data in Tables 6-9 and 6-11. More detailed discussion concerning the T*been* construction will be presented in Section 6.5.

Finally, I would like to refer to an interesting phenomenon in the English language, a construction similar to the three constructions discussed above, reported by Montgomery & Chapman (1992). Old speakers (born between 1843 and 1900) of Appalachian English, which still contains a number of linguistic features observed in Chaucer, Spenser, and Shakespeare employed these expressions. In this dialect, not only *there's* but other items such as *they's* and *it's* are used, as seen in (23):

(23)   They's nobody went by hardly ever.

(Montgomery & Chapman 1992)

It is evident that existential *they's*, which contains neither semantic sense nor grammatical significance to the NP, serves as a pragmatic particle to prepare the listener for some new information, syntactically independent of *nobody went by hardly ever*.[28] A similar phenomenon can be seen in the grammaticalized *let's* as a particle as touched upon in the Introduction. Note the following examples of (24) (=(3) of Chapter 1):

---

[28] Montgomery (2006) conducted an extensive discussion on the origin of existential *they* in Appalachian dialect and other regional dialects in the U.S.A.

(24)　a.　<u>Let's</u> <u>you and I</u> take 'em on for a set.

(Hopper & Traugott 2003: 10)
[1929, W. Faulkner, *Sartoris* III. 186, *OED*]

　　　b.　Lets <u>you</u> go first, then if we have any money left I'll go.

(Hopper & Traugott 2003: 11)

　　　c.　<u>Let's</u> <u>us</u> try it out.　　　　　　　(Ando 2005: 882)
　　　d.　<u>Let's</u> wash <u>your</u> hands.　　　　　　(Cole 1975: 268)

As explained in Section 1.3 of Chapter 1, Hopper & Traugott (2003: 10–13) discuss grammaticalization and subjectification of *let* + *us* and show *let's* behaving as an unanalyzable chunk. The use of *us* in (24c) is a total redundancy, but *let's* functions hortatively as a particle. Indeed, *let's* is used at the beginning of a sentence to express the speaker's intentions.

　　Another phenomenon was noted by Shibasaki (2014), who gave examples of *the point is*, *the question is*, *the problem is*, *the fact is*, etc.: the structure X + *be* has a tendency to become a discourse marker when it comes at the beginning of a sentence as in (25):

(25)　But the point is, I know not how to better my selfe.
　　　[1602, *2nd Pt. Return fr. Parnass* v. iii. (Arb.), 68 *OED*, from Shibasaki (2014)]

As this example shows and Shibasaki (2014) states, *the point is* already served as a discourse marker at the beginning of Early Modern English. The grammaticalized and subjectified use of X + *be* can be witnessed amply in present-day English.

　　These three cases make it obvious that the English language allows a phrase to behave as a particle or a set phrase at the beginning of a sentence. Bybee (2001: 2) insisted that main clauses are more likely to undergo syntactic change, while subordinate clauses tend to be conservative because they "contain a considerable amount of detailed information." Certainly, the slot at the beginning of a sentence may be a linguistic environment that gives rise to the grammaticalization of some types of main clause chunks in the English language, a cross-linguistically well-attested pattern of change. The need to collect more linguistic data to support this hypothesis remains a task for future research.

　　In this section, we have shown that while all the three constructions are used primarily in informal speech, *there's* shows different frequencies and number non-concord rates for each construction. Moreover, we have argued that *there's* came to function at times as a particle in the TV construction around the turn to the twentieth century, owing to the syntactic irrelevance of the existential part to the NP + VP complex.

6.5   The T*been* construction and the linguistic status of *there's*[29]

In this section, we explore the nature of the T*been* construction, with the ultimate goal of parsing the sentence *There's a man been shot, hasn't there?* (Lakoff 1876: 563).   In the last two sections, the discussion was based upon the assumption that *there's* in the T*been* construction is composed of *there* + *is*. It is necessary to address the validity of this assumption once more, while we have discussed the situations for the TV and TP constructions in Section 1.6 of Chapter 1.   Furthermore, I will argue that the T*been* construction is a variant of the TV construction with *have* omitted between NP and *been*.

First, we will ensure that *there's* in this construction is the shortened form of *there* + *is*, because *there* + *has* emerged rather late. As we saw in Section 6.3, the *OED* contains only three tokens of the T*been* construction, and the first instance appeared in 1786 as in (26) (previously (14a)):

(26)   There's mony waur <u>been</u> o' the race, And ...

[1786, Burns *A Dream* iii, *OED*]

As discussed in Section 1.6 in Chapter 1, the first token of *there's* as *there* + *has* appeared in 1796 in the CLMETEV, among all the corpora I investigated.   Since only ten-year gap exists between 1786 in (26) and 1796, it may be difficult to support our assumption. However, if we can find an earlier T*been* token, it will confirm our assumption because it is easier to retrieve instances of the shortened form of *there* + *has* than T*been* instances from any corpus due to the ubiquitousness of *there* + *has*. In addition, the data on the quotation texts in the *OED* in Table 1-1 in Chapter 1 show only a few tokens of *there's* as *there* + *has* before 1900, so it is difficult to assume that *there's* already formed *there* + *has* by 1786.

As counter evidence, however, the COHA also offers seven tokens of the *there* + *have* + NP + *been* structure (henceforth, T*havebeen* construction; see Table 1-2 in Chapter 1), two of which are shown below:

---

[29] Earlier Japanese versions of this section appeared as Yaguchi (2016a) and Yaguchi (2017).

(27) a. Wherever poetry has been found, <u>there</u> has music <u>been</u> found also, her inseparable companion.

[1931, *New England Magazine*, COHA]

    b. <u>There</u> have great things <u>been</u> done to mitigate the worst human sights ...

[1953, Ray Bradbury *Golden Apples of the Sun*, COHA]

The presence of the examples as in (27) indicates the possibility that *there's* in the T*been* structure represents *there + has*. However, I would like to argue that this T*havebeen* structure is distinct from the T*been* construction. Here, I will provide evidence for my argument. The T*havebeen* construction is used in rather formal contexts. We can see three tokens using verbal forms other than *there's* of the *there + be + NP + been* structure in the same corpus. Note the following examples:

(28) a. Seems if <u>there was</u> some <u>been</u> done right here in Marsden township.   [1905, Raymond Evelyn *The Brass Bound Box*, COHA]

    b. <u>There is</u> one of them <u>been</u> shook entirely off my house by your well.

[1907, Stockton Frank Richard *The Magic Egg and Other Stories*, COHA]

    c. ... <u>there was</u> a big guy <u>been</u> here exactly three months, drinks water every day at four o'clock in here ...

[2000, Child, Lee *Tripwire*, COHA]

These tokens use non-contracted verbal forms; however, they all appear in conversation. On the other hand, four out of the seven T*havebeen* tokens (57.1%) appear in third-person narration.[30] Considering the ratio of TV and TP sentences with verbal forms other than *there's* in narration (at most 13.3%) (note Table 6-12 in Section 6.4), the rate is rather high. Obviously, the informality associated with the TV, TP, and T*been* constructions is inconsistent with the formality entailed by the T*havebeen* construction. I thus believe that the T*havebeen* construction is an inverted structure with *there* functioning as a full-fledged adverb. It is reasonable to assume that the T*havebeen* and T*been* constructions are different. Thus, the informality of the T*been* construction naturally leads to the conclusion that *there's* should

---

[30] Jespersen (1927: 111–112) shows the following examples:

    there has scarce a day passed but he has visited him. (Keats 4. 184)

    Since the year 1614, there have no States-General met in France. (Carlyle FR 106)

These two also appear in formal contexts.

be the contraction of *there* and *is*.

Here, we show that it is easier to account for the linguistic character-istics of the T*been* construction by presuming it to be a variant of the TV construction with *have* omitted between NP and *been*. I will offer four pieces of evidence to support my hypothesis. First, we note that *have* is sometimes omitted in the TV construction. For instance, Harris & Vincent (1980: 806) give the following examples to explain the tense disagreement in TV sentences:

(29) a.   There's lots of people (have) tried to help him.
     b.   There's two cars (have) left already.

(Harris & Vincent 1980)

The omission of *have* is intuitively filled in by native speakers. Hence, it is reasonable to infer that the T*been* construction comprises *there's* + NP + (*have*) + *been*. Second, there are ten *there* + *be* + NP + *have* + pp tokens as in (30) in the *OED*, while there is no token of *there* + *have* + NP + *have* + pp token in the same dictionary:

(30) a.   There's a strange Magot hath got into their Brain.
                    [c1645, Howell *Lett.* (1688) II. 328, *OED*]
     b.   … that there are Serpents have swallowed children and sheep in-
          tire.   [1662, J. Davies tr. *Mandelslo's Trav.* 147, *OED*]

Thus, the structure *there* + *be* + NP + *have* + pp is attested from early times. This shows that it has been one of the TV patterns. The COHA also contains five examples of the *there's* + NP + *have* + *been* structure as follows:

(31) a.   There's Parkins's Pints has been makin' a great pudder over to
          England, …   [1845, Judd Sylvester *Margaret*, COHA]
     b.   There's your master has been with my master, …
                    [1847, Sargent Epes *Love's Sacrifice*, COHA]

If we parse *there's* as *there* + *has* in (30a) and (31), the redundancy of *has* results in an anomaly. These examples clearly indicate the *there's* (viz. *there* + *is*) + NP + (*have*) + *been* as a feasible structure. Third, as discussed in Section 6.4, T*been* sentences exhibit very different behaviors from TP sen-tences. As discussed in Section 6.4, the verbal form in the TP construction is very important, because *be* gets its number features from its relationship with NP. It is almost impossible to infer that *be* in this case can be fused with *there* to function as a set phrase. Therefore, the T*been* construction has nothing in common with the TP construction despite their surficial resemblance. Fourth, the informal usage of the T*been* construction can be explained by my hypothesis. The omission of *have* as well as the fixed use of *there's* facilitates the informal use of this construction, while the other two constructions presuppose neither any omission nor *there's* as a fixed expression. For these reasons, the T*been* construction is the most casual among the three. All these facts support the argument that the T*been* construction is a variant of the TV construction. If my hypothesis is right, it is reasonable to infer that *there's* in the TV construction behaved as a particle in the form of the T*been* construction earlier than at the beginning of the twentieth century.

Here, it is essential to parse the structure of the T*been* construction. I would like to propose that there are two patterns for the T*been* construction, analogous to those for the TV construction: a particle pattern [*there's*] + [NP + (*have*) + *been*]; and the *apo-koino* pattern [*there's* + NP] + [Θ + (*have*) + *been*]. As discussed above, the use of *there's* is almost entailed in these constructions, but the three examples seen in (28), especially the token from 2000 using *there was* in (28c), and the token using *there was* from 1962 in the *OED* as in (14c) are merely evidence that some T*been* sentences still have the structure [*there* + *be* + NP] + [Θ + (*have*) + *been*]. It is almost impossible to totally rule out the presence of the *apo koino* structure. Of course, I think that the fixed status of *there's* is more likely to induce the particle structure.

At this point, the question how to parse the following sentences remains ((32) appeared as (15d)):[31]

(32)   There's a man been shot, hasn't there?   (Lakoff 1876: 563)

(33) a.   There's a man been shot, there has.   (ibid)
       b.   *There's a man been shot, there is.   (ibid)

These examples raise questions for my hypothesis that the T*been* construction is a variant of the TV construction, since the subjects in the tag questions are realized by *there* and the auxiliaries in the tag questions are realized by *has*. Whether the particle structure or the *apo koino* structure is assumed, the question remains: if *there's* consists of *there* + *is*, why is *there has* used in the tag question? My answer is that *has* is derived from the omitted *has* between NP and *been*, while the presence of *there's* at the be-

---

[31] In the data I retrieved for this Chapter, no tag question tokens were found with the TV, TP, and T*been* structures.

ginning of the sentence implies that it is an existential *there* sentence, which induces the use of *there* as the subject in the tag question. Unfortunately, at present, I have no evidence to prove my hypothesis. We hope that further research on this issue will elucidate this enigmatic construction.

Here, it is worth noting that *there's* has evolved to be reanalyzed as *there*. Remember *let's* behaves like *let* as in (34) (previously as (24c)) and (35) in the COCA and the Corpus of American Soap Opera (=SOAP):[32]

(34)   Let's us try it out.   (Ando 2005: 882)

(35) a.   "Let's us have another one," said the colonel, ...   (COCA, fiction)
     b.   No, let's us handle it from here.   (SOAP)
     c.   Let's us have a talk.   (SOAP)

It is possible to argue that in the examples above, *let's* is reanalyzed as *let*. In the same vein, the reanalyzed *there's* as *there* is featured as in the examples of (36) in the COCA (31 tokens) and SOAP (12 tokens):[33]

(36) a.   There's is nothing magical about the 6000 point mark on the
         Dow.   (COCA, news)
     b.   There's is still hundreds of thousands of dollars not accounted
         for.   (COCA, spoken)
     c.   There's is nothing more we can do here.   (SOAP)
     d.   Wait a second! There's is a big misunderstanding!   (SOAP)

It is clear that *is* is redundant in all the tokens in (36), but if we interpret *there's* as *there*, they become ordinary existential sentences.

6.6   Other verbal forms in the TV construction

It is important to discuss the status of verbal forms other than *there's* and the possibility of their functioning as inseparable phrases in the TV construction. Tables 6-2 and 6-4 are repeated here as Tables 6-13 and 6-14 to show the differences between ordinary existentials and the TV construction:

---

[32] As of July, 2016, there are 25 tokens in the COCA and 12 tokens in the SOAP.
[33] Accessed in July, 2016.

Table 6-13: Number non-concord in *there + be* and TV sentences in the
**   *OED***   (raw occurrences)

	*there's**	*there is***	*there are*	*there was****	*there were*
ordinary *there + be*	8.1% (211/2620)	1.2% (230/18411)	0.01% (1/9897)	1.9% (157/8402)	0.3% (11/3834)
TV construction	16.3% (20/123)	4.1% (3/74)	0% (0/18)	7.5% (4/52)	0% (0/12)

*χ^2=8.96, **p<.01   **χ^2=4.42, *p<.05   ***χ^2=9.81, **p<.01

Table 6-14: Number disagreement of ordinary *there + be* and TV sen-
**   tences in COHA**   (raw occurrences)

	*there's**	*there is*	*there are*	*there was*	*there were*
ordinary *there + be*	10.2% (19/187)	1.0% (9/875)	0.7% (2/299)	3.7% (26/705)	0.8% (2/263)
TV construction	18.4% (51/277)	1.8% (1/57)	0% (0/9)	5.7% (3/53)	0% (0/10)

*χ^2=7.9, **p<.001

As noted in Section 6.2, TV tokens of singular verbal forms, i.e. *there is* and *there was*, show higher disagreement rates than the ordinary *there + be* sequence, both in the *OED* and the COHA. This phenomenon can be attributable to either or both the informal register connoted by these TV tokens and/or the possibility that they take the structure [*there + be*] + [NP + VP]. To find the cause of the higher number non-agreement rates, we first examine *there was* because it displays higher rates of number non-agreement than *there is*, as indicated in Tables 6-13 and 6-14. (An in-depth discussion on the grammaticalization and subjectification of *there was* presented in Section 5.4 of Chapter 5 showed grammaticalized and subjectified behavior in number non-agreement and co-occurrence with definite notional subjects in contemporary British English.) A closer look at the figures in Tables 6-13 and 6-14 reveals that the disagreement rate of TV sentences with *there was* is similar to that of *there's* in ordinary existentials in the *OED* data (7.5% (*there was* TV tokens) vs. 8.1% (*there's* ordinary existential tokens)) and lower than that of *there's* in the COHA data (5.7% (*there was* TV tokens) vs. 10.2% (*there's* ordinary existential tokens)). If *there was* functions as a particle, it should exhibit a higher level of disagreement rate, such as 15% or more. In addition, a comparison of number non-concord ratios in TV tokens with *there was* from before 1930 in the COHA (9.1%) with those from after 1930 (0%) shows no sign of ongoing grammaticalized progress, in contrast to *there's*, which has come to be a particle. For these reasons, we cannot conclude that *there was* functions as a particle in the TV construction, at least in written texts in American English. In other words, it is difficult to determine the feasibility of the structure [*there was*] + [NP + VP] and, instead, we endorse the *apo koinou* hypothesis. The higher number non-concord rate of the TV sentences with *there was* than ordinary *there was* sentences can be attributed to the more informal nature of the former. The same argument applies to *there is*, which shows lower rates of non-agreement than *there was*. Thus, we have confirmed that *there is* and *there was* rarely operate as particles in TV sentences.

6.7   Characteristics of TV sentences in present-day English

This section will present the semantic and pragmatic functions that typical TV, TP, and T*been* sentences serve in present-day English. Five functions will be highlighted: definite notional subjects, negation or negative components, co-occurrences with *come* and *go*, the use of modals, and tense disagreement. During this examination, keep in mind that only a few tokens for each verbal form of the three constructions exist after 1930, especially in the TP and T*been* constructions, as seen in Table 6-10. In this section, therefore, only *there's* and *there was* in the TV and TP constructions and *there's* in the T*been* construction are targeted for analysis, since the other verbal forms show too few occurrences.

First, we examine the tendency towards lexically definite notional subjects as in (37):

(37)   And there was Henry Parkington come down from the Genesee Valley with his bride, ...

[1943, Louis Bromfield *Mrs. Parkinton*, COHA]

The following table shows the result:

Table 6-15: Percentage of definite notional subjects after 1930 in COHA

	there's	*there was*
TV	0%	5.0%
TP	6.3%	12.5%
T*been*	0%	NA

Table 6-15 shows that the TV construction typically contains an indefinite notional subject. Since 7.8% of ordinary existential sentences with *there was* have definite notional subjects in the *OED*'s tokens after 1950, as seen in Table 5-6 of Chapter 5, the 5.0% in Table 6-15 is still low. This suggests that this construction is likely to appear in contexts in which the speaker is presenting new information without much interaction with the listener.[34] The same is true of the T*been* construction, considering that definite notional subjects are no longer in use.

In contrast, the TP tokens with *there was* take definite notional subjects more often (12.5%) than ordinary existential sentences (9.7%) in the UK spoken data seen in Table 5-7 of Chapter 5; thus, TP tokens with *there was* tend to entail interaction between the speaker and the listener more frequently than ordinary existential sentences. Since the occurrences of the TP construction are uniformly low after 1930, as Table 6-10 shows, this analysis should be treated with caution.

Next, tokens of negation or with negative elements will be examined. When negative elements are used, no presentative function can be performed, since no specific referent is available for presentation. However, this does not mean that existential sentences without negative elements always serve presentative functions, but the present analysis presupposes that the frequent use of negative elements is linked to the likelihood of non-presentative function. I considered negation expressions to be those such as (38a) as well as negative words such as *never*, *no*, *nothing*, *none*, *few* and *nobody*. Note the following examples:

(38) a.   There's <u>never</u> anyone sat down at their table …

[1933, Dorothy Thomas *Apple Wood*, COHA]

   b.   I'm afraid there's <u>nothing</u> can be done about it.

[1981, Margaret Truman *Murder in Capital Hill*, COHA]

   c.   "You've beaten them at their own tricks. There's <u>few</u> can say that."

[2000, *Fantasy & Science Fiction* "Conhoon and the Fairy Danc-

---

[34] Takaki (2010) showed that definite subjects and personal pronoun subjects were used very frequently in TV sentences (the average rate is 31.7% in his data) by analyzing the BNC. He then concluded that not only *there's*, but the sequence *there + be* occasionally functions as a particle. This is inconsistent with the findings of this study, which show little use of definite notional subjects in TV sentences with *there's* and *there was*. I think this discrepancy results from flawed data collection methods in Takaki's study, as mentioned in Footnote 3 in this Chapter.

er", COHA]

   d. Ah there's <u>no</u> German battleships come here, sir.

        [1970, *Ryan's Daughter* (movie script), COHA]

   e. "It's begun but there's <u>nobody</u> been killed."

        [1938, Allen Tate *Fathers*, COHA]

Observe the following table, which shows the results of the present investigation:

Table 6-16: Percentage of negation and negative elements after 1930 in COHA

	there's	*there was*
TV	35.8%	4.2%
TP	6.3%	12.5%
T*been*	7.7%	0%

The percentages of tokens with negation and negative elements in existential sentences in the Frown and FLOB corpora are 26.2% and 22.6% respectively. Compared with negative features of ordinary existential sentences, except for TV sentences with *there's*, all three constructions are considered to function presentationally more often, in contrast to ordinary existential sentences, based upon the presupposition that presentative function is realized in affirmative sentences without negative elements (see detailed discussion on this phenomenon in Chapter 7). However, the sequence *there's* + NP + VP, the leading pattern in the TV construction as seen in Table 6-10, showed a very high rate of co-occurrence with *never/no/nobody/nothing* (35.8%), indicating its non-presentative function. We previously noted that TV tokens with *not* or *never* as in (17a, b) and (38a) constitute *apo koinou* structures, but 32 of the 33 negative tokens (data after 1930) in Table 6-16 take *no/nobody/nothing/few/little* such as (38b, c, d, and e), while (38a) is the only example using *never* or *not*. This means that these 32 tokens are less likely to form *apo koinou* structures. It is possible to infer that the weakened capacity of *there's* functioning as a particle could contribute to the weakened presentational function of these constructions, thus failing to highlight a referent.

    Third, the use of *come* and *go* will be examined. (The use of *come* and *go* is irrelevant to the T*been* construction, so T*been* tokens are not taken into consideration here.) As noted in Section 6.3, we have touched upon the characteristics of the TP construction, which center on the use of the past participle of these two verbs. Recall from Section 6.3, that *come* and *gone* account for 52.9% and 23.5% of data in the *OED*'s TP data, and 70.4% and 17.0% in the COHA's TP data respectively. Additional data from the COCA also confirm this trend: 12.5% for *come* and 56.3% for *gone*. We also note an interesting phenomenon in the TV construction: the preterit verbal forms require the co-occurrence of *come* or *go*, as seen in the following examples (39):

(39) a. Well, <u>there was</u> a man <u>came</u> by who wanted me to help him head his cow back to the pasture.

[1956, Kenneth Roberts *Boon Island*, COHA]

b. <u>There were</u> some people <u>came</u> in here at noon from Arkansas.

[1945, William Camp *Skip to my Lou*, COHA]

Table 6-17 shows the percentages of *come* and *go* appearing in the TV tokens.

Table 6-17: Percentage of *come* and *go* in TV construction in COHA

	there's	*there is*	*there are*	*there was*	*there were*
come	4.3%	0%	0%	75.0%	75.0%
go	5.4%	0%	0%	10.0%	0%

Obviously, the preterit verbal forms *there was* and *there were* often co-occur with *come* and *go*, while *there's* and the present verbal forms appear with other verb types. As the more detailed discussion in Section 6.3 showed, *there* + *be* + NP + *come/go* in the TP construction is more or less a fixed unit, and *there* + *was/were* + NP + *came/went* is also a sentence unit to a considerable degree. We hypothesize that the semantic functions of the TV construction with *there was/were* and the TP construction are similar in that they all represent what the referent has *come* or *gone*, but pragmatically different in that the former performs a little less interactively than the latter, as previously discussed. On the other hand, the much lower percentages of TV tokens with the present verbal forms of *come* or *go* clearly contrast with the preterit verbal forms. This may also indicate that the TV construction in the present tense has a different semantic function than that in past tense. In other words, the structure [*there's*] + [NP + VP] is more likely to be used for purposes other than the referent's *come*-and-*go*.

Finally, we address the use of modals and tense non-agreement in the TV construction. The TP and T*been* constructions are excluded from this discussion due to their lack of modals and tense in the pp/*been* phrase. Some TV tokens have modals in the VP as in (40a) or tense non-agreement between the existential expression and VP, as in (40b) ((15) of

Chapter 1):

(40) a.　There's no one <u>can</u> get things going like your dad!
　　　　　　　　　　[1966, Edwin O'Connor *All In the Family*, COCA]
　　　b.　… there's a girl <u>got</u> a room two above me.
　　　　　　　　　　[1949, Kanin Garson *The Rat Race*, COCA]

Table 6-18 shows the percentage of occurrences of modals and tense non-agreement in VP in the tokens from after 1930:

Table 6-18: Percentage of modals and tense disagreement in TV tokens after 1930

	there's	*there was*
modal	32.3%	4.2%
tense disagreement	8.7%	0%

Modal verbs often appear in TV tokens with *there's* (32.3%), as in Table 6-18. The percentage (32.3%) is quite high, which suggests that the TV construction with modals tends to convey the speaker's judgment, since modals frequently used in the TV construction such as *can*, *may*, and *will* entail objective/subjective judgements by the speaker.

　　On the other hand, tense non-agreement raises an interesting point. The rate of tense non-agreement of *there's* in Table 6-18 (8.7%) is often associated with the verb *get*: five out of the eight tense agreement tokens takes *there's* + NP + *got*. Visser (1966: 1298) provides the following example:

(41)　I got a right to know what she said, haven't I?
　　　　　　　　[1904, Booth Parkington *The Flirt* 36, from Visser 1966: 1298]

Apparently, *have* is omitted before *got* in (41). This is usually the case for copies of the auxiliary in the main clause or variants of the supporting form of *do*. The fact that *haven't I* appears in the tag question confirms that the main clause has the auxiliary *have* in its syntactic structure, even if it is not realized. Equally important, *got* itself is closely associated with present perfective even without the presence of the present perfective marker. Indeed, Quirk et al. (1985: 132) explain that in very informal present-day English, '-*'ve got*' is sometimes reduced to '*got*'. The fact that five out of the eight tense disagreement tokens with *there's* in the COHA take *got* suggests the tendency for the NP + VP to covertly carry present tense. As touched upon in Section 6.5 in the discussion of the parsing of the T*been* construction, Harris & Vincent (1980: 806) propose to account for this apparent tense non-agreement by giving the examples below (repeated from (29)):

(42) a.   There's lots of people (have) tried to help him.
   b.   There's two cars (have) left already.

(Harris & Vincent 1980)

Proposing the particle hypothesis without specifying an account of *there's*, Harris & Vincent (1980) argue that present tense auxiliary *have* is omitted in the VP, asserting "[i]n certain idiolects, even the tense marking may be lost" as in (42). Their explanation implies that *there's* and VP agree in tense. Based upon the relatively low tense disagreement rate, as seen in Table 6-18 and the frequent use of *got*, our findings also support their argument that the two parts of the TV construction tend to share the same tense. However, we note that there are genuine cases of tense disagreement, such as (17c). Below is an example of tense non-concord (the third and fourth tokens in (43) are not included in the analysis in Section 6.2 nor in the discussion of Table 6-18, since they could not be retrieved in the data collection using the wild card):

(43)   There's strangers everywheres [sic] else you can think of. There's strangers was born out of the same womb. There's strangers was raised together in the same town and worked side by side all their life through. There's strangers got married and been climbing in and out of the same fourposter together for thirty-five or forty years and they're strangers still.

[1974, Frederick Buechner *Love Feast*, COHA]

This particular example shows the repetition of existential sentences as a rhetorical device to create rhythm to the discourse, which will be discussed in detail in Chapter 8. The first three underlined parts show tense non-agreement, although we take the last one to comprise a T*been* token expressing present perfective. We should thus bear in mind that tense agreement is not an absolute condition in the TV construction.

Finally, I will sum up the findings of this section:

Table 6-19: Functions of TV, TP, and T*been* constructions

	TV with *there's*	TV with *there was*	TP with *there's*	TP with *there was*	T*been*
definite NP	No	Not much	No	Sometimes	No
negation	Yes	Not much	Not much	Not much	Not much
come/go	Not much	Yes	Yes	Yes	NA
modal	Frequent use	Not much	NA	NA	NA
tense agreement	Usually yes	Yes	NA	NA	NA
summary	Non-presentative Non-interactive Judgmental	Presentative Slightly-interactive *come* and *go*	Presentative Non-interactive *come* and *go*	Presentative Interactive *come* and *go*	Presentative Non-interactive

The discussion in this section has outlined the syntactic, semantic, and prag-matic features the TV, TP, and T*been* constructions represent, although the targets of the analysis are limited to cases with *there's* and *there was* due to the low frequency of the other verbal forms. Two kinds of characteristics were found. First, the TV with *there was*, TP, and T*been* constructions per-forms the presentative function of drawing the listener's attention to a new referent more frequently than ordinary existential sentences, to the extent to which the use of negation and negative elements is restricted. The TV construction with *there*'s, the most frequently used sequence, is less likely to serve a presentative function. Second, TV sentences with preterit verbal forms often use *come* and *go*, similar to the TP construction, conveying the referent's movement. In contrast, TV sentences with *there's* occur with a range of verbs. Third, TV sentences with *there's* often appear with modal verbs, but those with *there was* rarely does so. This may indicate that the former is more likely to be used to express the speaker's judgment than the latter. Thus, this section's findings suggest that the functions of the TV construction with *there's* seem distinct from that with *there was*, the TP, and T*been* constructions.

6.8   The *here* + *be* sequence[35]

Before concluding this chapter, it is a matter of importance to tackle one more issue whether or not the *here* + *be* sequence behaves in the same way as its existential counterpart. The constructions of *here* + *be* + NP + VP (=HV) as in (44a), *here* + *be* + NP + pp (=HP) as in (44b), and *here* + *be*

---

[35] An early Japanese version of this section appears as Yaguchi (2017). The data in this section were retrieved from the COHA in March, 2014.

+ NP + *been* (=H*been*) as in (44c) are all observable in present-day English.

(44) a. "Listen, Pere, here's a fellow wants to talk to you."

[1955, Mac Hyman *No Time For Sergeants*, COHA]

b. Here is a man fallen in a fit ...

[1891, Oliver Wendell Holmes *Medical Essays*, COHA]

c. Here's Eugie been walking home with the Burr boy!

[1900, Ellen Anderson Gholson *The Voice of the People*, COHA]

These clearly express deictic contexts distinct from their existential counterparts. In this section, we will compare the syntactic, semantic, and pragmatic features of *here*-based and *there*-based sentences.

The method for extracting *here* tokens in the COHA utilizes the same procedure as that used for the TV, TP, and T*been* sentences (see Section 6.1). Because we used the same corpus, to make a simple comparison of the raw occurrences of tokens can lead to the determination of the characteristics of *here's* and *there's*.

First, the HV, HP, and H*been* constructions occur less frequently in the data than the TV, TP, and T*been* constructions. Table 6-20 shows the total raw occurrences between 1810 and 2009 (and occurrences after 1930):

Table 6-20: Raw occurrences of *here*-based and *there*-based constructions between 1810 and 2009 in COHA (after 1930)

	X + *be* + NP + VP (XV)	X + *be* + NP + pp (XP)	X + *be* + NP + *been* (X*been*)
here-based	80 (22)	62 (13)	0 (1)
there-based	406 (125)	88 (22)	36 (14)

As expected, occurrences of *there*-based constructions outnumbered those of *here*-based constructions across the board. However, the latter do in fact occur very frequently, considering that *here* is generally used much less frequently than *there* in any corpus. As noted in Section 5.5 of Chapter 5, the projected occurrences of ordinary *here* + *be* sentences, i.e. *here's*, *here is*, *here are*, *here was*, and *here were* in the spoken subcorpus of the BNC are only 541, 72, 25, 51, and 3, respectively, whereas the same subcorpus has 16,976 tokens of *there's* alone.[36] It is possible to maintain that, unlike the ordinary *here* + *be* sequences, the occurrences of these three specific con-

---

[36] For another instance, the FLOB contains 647 tokens of *here* and 2,947 tokens of *there*.

structions containing *here* are abundant. Closer scrutiny of the data in Table 6-20 reveals that the XP construction in particular shows only a small difference in frequency between *here*-based and *there*-based tokens.

Another interesting point is that occurrences of the HV, HP, and H*been* constructions decreased in an order parallel to the decreases in the TV, TP, and T*been* constructions. It is notable that the frequencies of these peculiar constructions are strongly associated with the construction. Table 6-21 shows the breakdown of these occurrences by verbal form:

Table 6-21: Breakdown of *here*-based constructions between 1810 and 2009 according to verbal forms in COHA (after 1930)

	here's	*here is*	*here are*	*here was*	*here were*
HV	59 (18)	17 (1)	0	4 (3)	0
HP	36 (13)	11 (0)	3 (1)	11 (3)	1 (0)
H*been*	9 (1)	0	0	0	0

After 1930, occurrences of all three constructions decreased, and H*been* sentences are currently a rare construction in English. *Here's* clearly accounts for the majority of the tokens of the three constructions just as *there's* comprises most tokens of *there*-based constructions. Furthermore, in contrast to the *there*-based constructions, in which *there was* as well as *there's* are both used quite often, *here is*, not *here was*, is the second-most common form of the HV construction after *here's*. The relatively frequent use of *here is* is a clear sign that *here*-based constructions express deictic contexts of here and now. In our examination of definite notional subjects, negative elements, and modals, *here's* and *here is* are analyzed for the HV construction, while *here's*, *here is*, and *here was* are analyzed for the HP construction. The other items were excluded because of their rare uses.

Now we will focalize the contracted form playing the major role in the formation of the *here* + *be* + NP + VP/pp/*been* constructions. Table 6-22 shows the percentage of the use of contracted form in each construction between 1810 and 2009:

Table 6-22: Ratio of *here's* to total use of HV, HP, and H*been* between 1810 and 2009 (*there's*)

HV (TV)	74.1% (68.2%)
HP (TP)	57.4% (43.0%)
H*been* (T*been*)	100% (91.7%)

It is surprising that the percentages of *here's* and *there's* are parallel to each other in the same construction. In other words, the distribution of each verbal form seems to be determined by the construction. X*been* is the most frequent form, followed by XV. Curiously enough, the percentages are even higher in *here's*-based constructions than *there's*-based ones after 1930. Table 6-23 shows the same ratios after 1930:

Table 6-23: Ratio of *here's* to total use of HV, HP, and H*been* after 1930 (*there's*)

HV (TV)	82.6% (73.6%)
HP (TP)	75.0% (34.8%)
H*been* (T*been*)	100% (92.9%)

According to Table 6-23, the frequency of *there's* and *here's* is even higher after 1930, while the relative frequency order X*been*, XV, and XP remains consistent. It seems that besides their less frequent use of *here*-based constructions after 1930, as seen in Table 6-21, the preference for contracted verbal forms in *here*-constructions also suggests that they have become more informal in usage than their *there*-based counterparts.

Next, we examine number non-concord in the contracted verbal phrase. Recall that in Section 5.5 of Chapter 5, we saw that number non-concord rates of *here's* are rather low (1.0% in the BNC's writing, 7.4% in BNC's speech, and 2.2% in COCA's writing). Hence, we concluded that *here's* has not been fully grammaticalized into a single unit. Table 6-24 shows number disagreement for the 1810 to 2009 period:

Table 6-24: Number disagreement in *here's*-based and *there's*-based constructions between 1810 and 2009

	X + *be* + NP + VP (XV)	X + *be* + NP + pp (XP)	X + *be* + NP + *been* (X*been*)
here's-based	0%	1.6%	11.1%
there's-based	18.4%	4.3%	24.2%

Table 6-24 shows the characteristics of the *here's*-based constructions: number non-concord is extremely rare, except in the H*been* construction. This strongly indicates that *here's* has not yet grammaticalized into an inseparable chunk in the HV and HP constructions. However, we have to be careful about the above data in that as in Table 6-21, there are no tokens for the plural verbs *here are* and *here were* in the HV construction. Almost all the notional subjects in the COHA, except for one token of *here was*, feature singular noun phrases. As we noted about the difference in number disagreement between the TV construction and the T*been* construction, the less objective/formal the register of usage, the higher the percentage of singular nouns to the total use of nouns (Biber et al. (1999: 291)). This suggests that the HV construction is very informal. Nonetheless, in contrast to the discussion of *there's* as an inseparable phrase in the TV construction, the possibility of the [*here's*] + [NP + VP] structure is untenable because of the low number disagreement rates of *here's* (e.g. 7.4% even for *here's* in speech data of the BNC) as seen in Table 5-10. Naturally, the HV construction should be parsed as the structure [*here* + *be* + NP] + [Θ + VP], as Ukaji (2003) suggests. In any event, the default structure of X + *be* + NP + VP constitutes the [X + *be* + NP] + [Θ + VP] *apo koinou* configuration, and we can logically conclude that the unique development of *there's* as an unanalyzable phrase made the creation of the [*there's*] + [NP + VP] structure possible.

In the H*been* construction, considering that verbal forms other than *here's* are not employed, *here's* can be assumed to be a fixed phrase analogous to *there's* in the T*been* construction. However, since the H*been* construction became nearly obsolete, after 1930 (i.e. eight occurrences between 1810 and 2009; after 1930, only one occurrence in 1944), it is virtually impossible to argue for the status of *here's* in the H*been* construction in a cogent way.

Next, we turn to the definiteness of notional subjects. As in Table 5-11 of Chapter 5, we found that the abundant use of definite notional subjects is a characteristic of *here* + *be* (in BNC's writing, 27.0% for *here's*, 40.1% for *here is*, and 14.5% for *here are*, 14.3% for *here was*, and 36.2% for *here were*). Here, we will examine the use of definite notional subjects in the three constructions, as seen in (45):

(45)   Here's the guy lives next door, …

[1943, Raymond Chandler *Lady in the Lake*, COHA]

Table 6-25 shows the ratio of definite notional subjects to the total tokens between 1810 and 2009:

Table 6-25: Ratio of definite notional subjects between 1810 and 2009 in COHA

	here's	*here is*	*here was*
HV	46.7%	11.8%	NA
HP	37.1%	45.5%	9.1%
H*been*	77.8%	NA	NA

Table 6-25 shows notably high percentages of definite notional subjects in the present tense forms, in contrast to those of the *there*-based constructions seen in Table 6-15, while the preterit form shows a similar low percentage to its *there*-based counterpart. The preterit form expresses less immediate contexts. In addition, the deictic expression *here* is often compatible with definite notional subjects since any interaction between a speaker and listener takes place in a context of the here and now. This supports my argument in 5.3.3, 5.4, and 5.5 of Chapter 5 that definite notional subjects tend to be used in interactional contexts.

Next, we will consider the presentational feature of *here*-based constructions. Negative elements in *here + be* or the NP, as in (46), are rarely observed:

(46)   Here's none shall affront my grannam!

[1906, Dix, Beulah Marie *Road to Yesterday*, COHA]

Also note the following table:

Table 6-26: Percentage of negated elements in *here*-based constructions of COHA

negation	*here's*	*here is*	*here was*
HV	1.7%	0%	NA
HP	0%	0%	0%
H*been*	0%	NA	NA

The rare use of negative elements suggests the presentative function at work in *here*-based constructions. In a nutshell, the data so far have identified the tendency for deictic *here*-based constructions to co-occur with definite notional subjects in affirmative, presentative sentences.

Next, we turn to the uses of *come* and *go*. It is interesting to compare the *here*-based and *there*-based constructions. Note the following examples and Table 6-27:

(47) a.   ... and here was the Arabian Nights <u>come</u> to life only modern.

[1947, Clyde Brion Davis *Jeremy Bell*, COHA]

b.   ... here's a ringlet <u>gone</u> romping...

[1949, Herman Melville *Pierre or, The Ambiguities*, COHA]

Table 6-27: Percentage of *come* and *go* of *here*-based sentences in COHA

		here's	*here is*	*here are*	*here was*	*here were*
HV	*come*	3.3%	5.9%	NA	NA	NA
HV	*go*	0%	0%	NA	NA	NA
HP	*come*	62.9%	45.5%	NA	81.8%	NA
HP	*go*	17.1%	27.3%	NA	11.1%	NA

The HP construction commonly signals the feature closely associated with the use of *come* and *go* in the same way as in the TP construction. However, for HV tokens with *here was*, although the above table shows NA, the four HV tokens with *here was* contained no *come* and *go*. The deictic construction seems to work very differently from their existential counterpart when *be* is preterit tense. Above mentioned, the combination of *here* and *was* may have a peculiar meaning.

Finally, we examine the use of modal verbs in the HV construction. Observe the following example:

(48)   Here's one <u>will</u> be Dabney's, for you to shine.

[1946, Eudora Welty *Delta Wedding*, COHA]

Table 6-28 shows the results.

Table 6-28: Percentage of modal uses of HV sentences in COHA

Modal	*here's*	*here is*	*here was*
HV	28.3%	23.5%	NA

The percentages of *here's* and *here is* are very similar: 28.3% and 23.5% respectively. As *there's* appears in 32.2% of the TV constructions, as seen in Table 6-18, they also sometimes co-occur with modals. Present-tense XV constructions are likely to often express speaker judgment.

This section investigated the three *here*-based constructions. We saw parallels between them and their *there*-based counterparts in their distribution and uses of shortened forms, *come* and *go*, and modals.

6.9 Summary

This chapter showed the diachronic development and syntactic, semantic, and pragmatic characteristics of the TV, TP, and T*been* constructions, all of which are peculiar structures related to existential sentences employed in informal current English. We found that the TV and TP constructions decreased in frequency from the peak of their usage in Early Modern English, exhibiting a dramatic drop in present-day English, particularly after 1970. The syntactic characteristics of the three differ: (1) TV sentences exhibit a lack of number agreement most frequently in present-day English; (2) TP sentences use the fewest shortened forms, and show the lowest number disagreement rate; and (3) T*been* sentences co-occur with *there's* far more often than their TV and TP counterparts.

This study has argued that the level of syntactic necessity of the existential copula *be* motivates these characteristics. We posited shortened verbal forms to be particles in some tokens, although the *apo koinou* structure is still available in the TV construction. Therefore, the TV construction comprises two structures, i.e. [*there* + *be* + NP] + [Θ + VP] and [*there's*] + [NP + VP]. The longitudinal fusion of *there* + *be* along with the grammaticalization and the subjectification of existential *there* led to *there's* being reanalyzed as a particle in the TV construction.

In the TP construction, the copula *be* is necessary for forming the perfective, consequently so is number agreement despite its colloquial usage. In the T*been* construction, on the other hand, *there's* is a fixed expression, resisting the use of other verbal forms. Additionally, we argue that the T*been* construction, the most informal of the three, is a casual variant of the TV construction: it contains an implicit *have* between NP and *been*, beginning with a fixed particle *there's*. Like the TV construction, the T*been* construction comprises two structures, i.e. [*there's* + NP] + [Θ + (*have*) + *been*] and [*there's*] + [NP + (*have*) + *been*].

The TP and T*been* constructions, as well as the TV construction with *there was*, serve a presentative function more frequently than ordinary existential sentences, but TV sentences with *there's* are less likely to serve a presentative functions, instead co-occurring with negative elements and modals. Moreover, the TP construction and the TV with *there was* are more likely to be used interactively than the TV construction with *there's* and the T*been* construction. The TP construction and the TV with *there was* show more similar patterns with *come* and *go* as well than do the TV construction with *there's* and the T*been* construction.

Our comparison of *there*-based constructions (i.e. TV, TP and T*been* constructions) and *here*-based constructions (i.e. HV, HP, and H*been* constructions) has led us to conclude that the construction determines frequency and function to a certain degree. The more frequent uses of the shortened form *here's* than *there's* in the three *there*-based constructions suggest that the HV and HP constructions are more informal than the TV and TP constructions. Furthermore, we showed that the semantic and pragmatic functions of the three *here*-based constructions tend to be presentative and interactive.

Thus, this chapter showed a more advanced diachronic development of *there's* by focusing on peripheral constructions in English. The fusion of *there* and *is* has made *there's* an inseparable phrase in which *is* is still a syntactically indispensable part of the sentence. This fused structure later evolved into a particle in some environments, causing *there's* to be reanalyzed as *there*. The next chapter will discuss in detail the historical shift of existential sentences with *there* functioning more or less as an adverb.

Chapter 7

There + VP and *there* + *be* + pp Passive

The analyses prior to this chapter have explored the sequence of *there* + *be*, the base structure of a wide variety of syntactic forms, paying special attention to its grammaticalized and subjectified features. It is certain that the construction of *there* + non-*be* verb (henceforth Non-*be* construction) as in (1) is also an important element in present-day English:

(1) In its place <u>there stands</u> a new Ballistic Missile Defence Organisation which employs the same people to do the same things with the same money ...   (BNC, magazine)

The function of the Non-*be* construction is defined as presentative by a number of grammarians (e.g. Aissen 1975, Stowell 1978, Milsark 1979, Hannay 1985, Quirk et al. 1985: 1408, and Huddleston & Pullum 2002, *inter alia*). Quirk et al. (1985: 1408), among others, give the explanation that "*[t]he* existential sentence has been described as 'presentative', in serving to bring something on to the discoursal stage deserving our attention," which "seems especially true of a rather less common, more literary type of existential clause in which *there* is followed by verbs other than *be*." Their explanation evinces the default function of Non-*be* existential sentences in present-day English: they appear much less often than their *there* + *be* counterparts, specializing in the function of focusing on the listener's attention on the existence or occurrence of a new referent primarily in written texts. One is naturally curious about whether or not Non-*be* sentences share the same developmental course as *there* + *be* sentences and whether or not

Non-*be* sentences retained the presentative function from the beginning. The historical development of the Non-*be* construction, however, has not been comprehensively analyzed in previous studies, to my knowledge at least. It certainly deserves being the target of a thorough investigation.

Equally important, the *there* + *be* + past participle (pp) construction, a passivized existential sentence (henceforth Tpp construction), as in (2) is another construction relevant to existential sentences:

(2) At the turn of the century, the very time when Pearson documents the coinage of the term "hooligan" to portray a supposedly new breed of youthful folk-devil, <u>there is found</u> in other sources a mood of contemporary congratulation about the long-term conquest of the problem of order. (BNC, academics)

This construction also often performs a presentative function in contemporary English. Since this passive construction has been given little consideration by linguists with diachronic perspectives (though there are a few previous studies focused upon a limited period of time), I will also make an attempt to elucidate the Tpp construction from synchronic and diachronic points of view.

Though briefly touched upon in the above, I would like to raise several questions. First, have these two constructions retained the same kinds of functions throughout the history of English? Second, were they as rare across time as in present-day English? Or did they once flourish? Third, how were or are their syntactic configurations different from *there* + *be* sentences? Certainly, a detailed examination into the diachronic development of Non-*be* and Tpp sentences may help put the characteristics of *there* + *be* into perspective. In other words, I would like to show how *there* that forms these two sentences with elements of adverbialness is utilized in present-day English against the background that *there* in *there* + *be* has played a syntactic role of nouniness as a subject. This chapter will make an elucidation of the diachronic transition of the Non-*be* and Tpp constructions in frequency and function by examining quotation texts in the *OED* and the COHA.[1]

---

[1] In this chapter, the COHA was accessed in February, 2014, whilst the BNC and the COCA were accessed in August, 2015.

7.1   The Non-*be* construction[2]

7.1.1   Gradient nature of the Non-*be* construction

The Non-*be* construction appeared in Old English in the same way as *there* + *be* sentences. Observe (3):

(3)   Þar com flowende flod æfter ebban.   [a1000, *Byrhtnoth* 65, *OED*]

It can be said that Non-*be* sentences have as long a history as *there* + *be* sentences. In present-day English, only intransitive verbs can appear, although transitive verbs were used in earlier English as will be touched upon in Section 7.3. Quirk et al. (1985: 1408) present three types of intransitive verbs as follows:

(4)   verb of motion (*arrive, remain, pass, come*, etc.)
      verb of inception (*emerge, spring up*, etc.)
      verb of stance (*live, remain, stand, lie*, etc.)

(Quirk et al. 1985: 1408)

Although some previous synchronic studies tend to divide Non-*be* sentences into two, they hardly discuss the issue in details (e.g. Aissen 1975, Milsark 1979: 245–256). For example, Aissen (1975) and Milsark (1979: 245–256) define the two groups as active/stative and outside/inside verbs respectively. The distinction presented by them is basically made based upon whether unaccusative verbs are used or not. In order to show the characteristics of Non-*be* sentences with unaccusative verbs, Chomsky (1999: 15) suggests that a locative phrase should immediately follow unaccusative verbs in present-day English, citing the following examples:

(5)   a.   *There came several angry men into the room.
      b.   There came into the room several angry men.

(Chomsky 1999: 15)

In addition, Aissen (1975) classifies the unaccusative verb as the active verb, stating that it always takes the simple present or past only and that auxiliary elements are excluded:

(6)   *There | did/may/will step | out in front of his car a small child.
              | has stepped | (Aissen 1975)

---

[2] An earlier and shorter version of part of Section 7.1 appeared as Yaguchi (2013).

However, the stative/inside verbs are in principle free from such restrictions as follows:

(7) a.   ... there lay Queequeg in his coffin with little but his composed countenance in view ...   (COCA, fiction)

    b.   ... there has developed an awareness that descriptions of other cultures partly reflect the researcher's own prejudices ...

                                                                    (COCA, academics)

In (7a), the locative phrase comes after the notional subject, and in (7b), present perfective is used.

Contrastively, Quirk et al. (1985: 1408) avoid differentiating even active/outside verbs from stative/inside verbs in respect of syntactic behaviors. They argue that the construction under discussion represents *there* as a grammatical subject and, thereby, takes the question form, such as *Will there come a time...?* and *Did there occur a sudden revolution ...?* (As thoroughly discussed in 4.1 of Chapter 4, when *there* functions fully as subject, it can take a variety of structures: question, subject raising, object raising, the object of the preposition *for*, and tag question.) However, I would like to maintain that the number of syntactic variations of Non-*be* sentences varies according to the meaning that the verb expresses in a context: the more similar meaning to *be* a verb expresses, the wider syntactic variation of *there* as a subject is available; by contrast, when the verb expresses a physical situation or motion of the referent (i.e. conceptualization of unaccusative verbs), it exhibits less flexibility in syntactic variation. For example, although the verb *come* is categorized as a motion verb by Quirk et al. (1985: 1408) as in (4), the same item can be classified as an inception verb depending on the context in which it appears. Observe (8) and (9):

(8)   There came to him his mother and brethren, and they could not come at him for the crowd.   (Bible)

(9) a.   There will come a time when I won't feel the need to make any music, ...   (BNC, magazine)

    a'. There will be a time when I won't feel the need to make any music, ...

    b.   Will there come a time when that might become so acute that the Minister would be prepared to consider an opt-out as opposed to an opt-in donor system?   (BNC, miscellaneous)

Example (8) is a prototypical case of the unaccusative motion verb *come*, whereas in example (9a), *come* metaphorically expresses the emergence or occurrence of the notional subject. In fact, the verb *be* is often used almost interchangeably with *come* as seen in the pair (9a) and (9a′). Although this metaphorical use of *come* is possible in question forms such as (9b), *come* expressing physical motion cannot be employed in question forms such as (10b) in the same way as the unaccusative verb *walk*, which expresses physical motion, is disallowed to appear in question forms such as (10a):

(10) a. *Did there walk into the room a man with a long blond hair?

(Rochemon & Culicover 1990: 132)

   b. *Did there come into the room a man with a long blond hair?

Thus, some verbs can be categorized under more than one type and do not necessarily display consistent syntactic behaviors. It is, therefore, very important to take the contextual meaning of verbs into consideration in the procedure of examining syntactic behaviors. I compiled three kinds of data to obtain acceptability rates according to verb type: researching into previous studies; detecting tokens with syntactic variation of *there* as the subject in the BNC; and by asking four native speakers of English to judge acceptability. All of these were necessary steps in yielding acceptability rates, partly because there are only a few Non-*be* tokens with expanded syntactic patterns in any available corpus and partly because judgment about acceptability by native speakers varies greatly from person to person. As a result of the present research, it was found that the verb types employed in the Non-*be* construction form a gradient in terms of availability of syntactic patterns, which can be diagrammed as follows:

[*be*→*exist*→*be*-stance-type→inception type→physical-stance type→motion type]

Figure 7-1: Subjectness of *there* and verb type

Figure 7-1 shows that *there*, which functions fully as a subject in the sequence of *there* + *be*, expresses less subjectness as the verb type moves towards the right hand end of the scale. The verb *exist* is a peculiar verb. Firstly, its frequency is very high in present-day English (in all the Non-*be* sentences after 1950 in the *OED*'s quotation texts, *exist* accounts for 37.9%);[3] secondly, it constantly performs similar syntactic patterns to *be*, except for tag questions; thirdly, *exist* expresses the essence of existential

---

[3] As will be revealed in 7.1.6, it is not *there* + *exist* that appears the most frequently in the COHA's dataset.

sentences as the term 'existential' is derived from it. Therefore, it has been treated as one independent verb type. (From here on, the term Non-*be* construction will refer to Non-*be* sentences excluding the sequence *there + exist*.)

By contrast, motion type such as *walk* and *pass*, which is located at the right hand end of Figure 7-1, is the least likely to display any syntactic variation. Stance verbs, meanwhile, are divided into two types. When the physical sense of stance verbs is bleached enough to denote more or less the same meaning as *be* or *exist*, they tend to exhibit almost identical patterns to *exist*. They will be called *be*-stance type. The verbs *remain* and *lie*, for instance, often behave semantically in the same way as *exist*. (Nevertheless, they need to be categorized separately from *exist*. I will explain the reason in 7.1.5 and 7.1.6.) On the other hand, when the physical characteristics of stance verbs are profiled, it is more difficult for them to fit into any syntactic patterns other than affirmative. They will be called physical-stance type. Verbs such as *live*, *lie*, *stand*, and *hang* are classified into this group. It should be noted that verbs such as *lie* behave as both *be*-stance and physical types. Observe the following table, which shows how each verb type expands syntactically (Appendix 2 shows the acceptability rates seen in previous studies, the BNC and Altavista and by my informants):

Table 7-1: Syntactic patterns according to contextual meaning of verbs

	be	*exist*	*be*-stance type (*remain, lie*, etc.)	inception type (*occur, emerge, come*, etc.)	physical-stance type (*live, stand hang, lie* etc.)	motion type (*come, pass walk*, etc.)
Affirmative	OK	OK	OK	OK	OK	OK
Question	OK	OK	OK	OK	(?)	*
Subject raising	OK	OK	OK	OK	OK	OK(?)
Object raising	OK	OK	OK	OK(?)	OK(?)	?
for _ to	OK	OK	OK	OK(?)	?	??
Tag Question	OK	??	*	*	*	*

Table 7-1 summarizes what I have argued in the above. The degree of how close to *be* each verb can expand its meaning is fully correlated with the potentiality of its syntactic variety. Motion type verbs are considered to retain adverbial properties in the meaning of *there* the most strongly, rejecting themselves to fit into the structure in which *there* is nominalized.

Thus, this subsection has shown that the syntactic expansion of Non-*be* sentences forms a gradient according to the meaning a verb expresses in the context.

7.1.2   The historical transition of Non-*be* sentences

We now examine the historical development of Non-*be* sentences based on an analysis of the *OED*'s quotation texts. 2,905 tokens were retrieved through manually examining all the quotation texts with *there* after excluding the *there* + *be* tokens used for the analysis in Chapters 4 and 5. Raising tokens of *there* + epistemic verbs + *to* + *be* (e.g. *there* + *seem* (+ *to* + *be*), *there* + *appear* + *to* + *be*) as in (11) were excluded from the data here:[4]

(11) a.   There seem to be certain bounds to the quickness and slowness
       of the succession of those ideas ...

       [1690, Locke *Hum. Und.* II. xiv. 9, *OED*]

   b.   Some fifty years ago ... there seemed a general consensus of
       opinion that inventors were a nuisance.

       [1883, *Law Times* 20 Oct. 409/1, *OED*]

Unquestionably, it would be quite intriguing to analyze data according to the verb type in Table 7-1. However, because the same verb can denote two types, as discussed in 7.1.1, it is virtually impossible to categorically distinguish the data, due to the limited contexts of quotation texts in the *OED*. In addition, it is of importance to see the overall historical trend of *there* + VP, so all tokens were counted across the board, except for *there* + *exist* because of its unique features as previously explained. Observe Figure 7-2, which presents the occurrences of Non-*be* sentences and *there* + *exist* per 100 quotation texts in the *OED* (also see Appendix 1) and Table 7-2 which specifies the raw occurrences in the same dictionary:

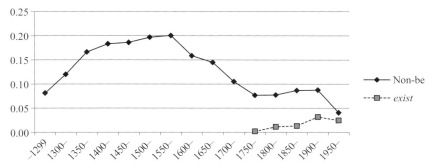

occurrences per 100 quotation texts

Figure 7-2: Frequency of Non-*be* and *there* + *exist* sentences in *OED*

---

[4] In addition to *seem* and *appear*, other raising tokens including *happen*, *chance*, etc.

Table 7-2: Raw occurrences of Non-*be* and *there* + *exist* sentences in *OED*

	-1299	1300-	1350-	1400-	1450-	1500-	1550-	1600-	1650-	1700-	1750-	1800-	1850-	1900-	1950-
Non-*be*	47	48	87	109	98	167	327	327	256	139	109	217	415	199	118
there + *exist*											3	32	63	72	72

In contrast to the diachronic development of *there* + *be* sentences as diagrammed in Figure 4-1 in Chapter 4, the Non-*be* construction saw its heyday at the beginning of the Early Modern English period and experienced a considerable recession in the 1600s and 1700s. From the 1800s to 1949, it remained almost on the same level, and after 1950, however, it marked a dramatic decline. (It should be noted that this drop occurred against the background of the lengthening quotation texts—an increase by 23% from the level of Late Modern English—as mentioned in Chapter 2. Hence, the downward tendency is rather substantial.) On the other hand, from the time that *there* + *exist* appeared in 1785 for the first time in the *OED*, its frequency increased in the 1800s until *there* + *exist* displayed a high frequency in contemporary English, accounting for 37.9% of all Non-*be* tokens after 1950 as mentioned in the above.

7.1.3 Transition of presentative features

At this point, based on three pieces of evidence, I would like to argue that the Non-*be* construction did not always perform a presentative function in Modern English in the way contemporary linguists claim about Non-*be* sentences in contemporary English. The first evidence is that certain types of verbs employed in Non-*be* sentences changed over time. As previously discussed in connection with (4), only intransitive verbs are permissible in the Non-*be* construction in present-day English. We can add one more restriction suggested by Milsark (1979: 254) and Breivik (1981): since "verbs implying or even explicitly expressing appearance—a kind of coming into existence—on the scene," defined by Firbas (1966: 243), are used in the construction under discussion, intransitive verbs which express no 'presentative signal' are unlikely to be employed in contemporary English. In contrast to the presentative verb *appear*, for instance, *disappear* is disallowed to be used, as in (12):

(12) a.   There appeared a man in front of us.
b.   *There disappeared a man in front of us.

---

are excluded. The *OED* contains tokens of *happen to*, *chance to*, *began to*, etc., all of which were also discarded from the present analysis.

(Breivik 1981)

Furthermore, Milsark (1979: 254) and Breivik (1981) explain that the use of *die* and *leave* is not appropriate. Note the following examples:

(13) a. *There died some people in that fire.
     b. *There left several people.

(Breivik 1981)

In the diachronic dataset, however, non-presentative verbs of this kind (e.g. *die, lack, leave, need, want*) were used rather frequently as exemplified in (14):

(14) a. <u>There died</u> also two gallie slaues and foure in the patrone.
        [1585, T. Washington tr. *Nicholay's Voy.* I. xxii. 28, *OED*]
     b. If the strings be out of tune, or frets disordered, <u>there wanteth</u> the harmony.   [1565, J. Calfhill *Answ. Treat. Crosse* 21b, *OED*]

In the case of (14b), the lack of a referent is expressed, which is far from consistent with the existence-or-occurrence-focusing function in contemporary English. Observe Figure 7-3, which illustrates the ratio of these tokens to the total number of Non-*be* sentences in the *OED* (also note Appendix 1):[5]

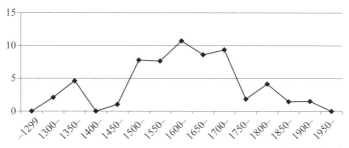

occurrences per 100 Non-*be* tokens

Figure 7-3: Ratio of non-presentative Non-*be* verbs in *OED* (%)

---

[5] Remember that in the case of affirmative tokens of *there* + *lack/want/need* + NP, they hardly express the presentative feature because they do not focus on the existence of a referent, as in the example below:
   There lacked a wrest to the harpe to set all the strynges in a monacorde and tune.
        [a1548, Hall *Chron.*, *Hen. IV* 3, *OED*]
In addition, in negative tokens of *there* + *lack/want/need* + *no/none/nothing* as in the example below, the presence of the referent is not fully focused either:
   There wants no earthly judge-and-jurying: here we stand- Sentence our guilty selves.
        [1879, Brwowning *Ned Bratts* 249, *OED*]
Therefore, instances of this kind are all included in Figure 7-3.

The overall tendency displayed in Figure 7-3 is similar to that in Figure 7-2, except in the Middle English period, despite the fact that the above graph shows a diachronic change in percentage: whereas until 1700, non-presentative verbs were prevalent, they are quite scarce in present-day English. Obviously, earlier English seems to have occasionally failed to entail the presentative function in that a relatively large number of data includes disappearance and non-existence or non-occurrence of the notional subject.

Secondly, Non-*be* sentences did not necessarily occur in main clauses or in the affirmative in early times. When the Non-*be* construction is engaged in focusing on the existence or occurrence of the referent, the speaker's categorical assertion must be expressed to focus on the existence or occurrence of a referent as well as to attract attention from the reader. As a matter of fact, it is essential to discuss the syntactic forms by which the presentative function is realized in actual language use. I would like to present four syntactic characteristics. First, it should appear in declarative sentences; for focusing on the existence of some referent must be conducted affirmatively. Thus, native speakers of present-day English reject the question form of the Non-*be* construction as grammatical as in (15) as well as in (10):

(15) a. ?Did there live in that Hall anyone important?

(Pérez Guerra 1999: 74)

    b. ??Into which room did there come a man? (Coopmans 1989: 745)

Second, by the same token, Lakoff (1987: 574) argues that negation of the Non-*be* construction is inconsistent with the presentative nature as in (16):

(16) *There didn't emerge from the cocoon a beautiful black and red butterfly.   (Lakoff 1987: 574)

For the same reason, the presence of negative elements such as *no*, *none*, *nothing*, *few*, *little*, etc. is likely to restrict the presentative function as in (17).

(17) ?There came into the room no man.

Third, to be presentative, propositions appear in main clauses. Aissen (1975) claims that Non-*be* sentences cannot appear in embedded clauses of unassertive predicates or in subject clauses as shown in the following:

(18) a.?* It's likely that while they were eating there ran out of the woods a grizzly bear.

    b.??That there arose many trivial objections during the meeting is surprising.

(Aissen 1975)

Owing to the fact that the presentative function of the Non-*be* construction is concerned with introducing a new referent into the discourse and focusing on it, it is least prone to express a proposition in an embedded clause.[6] Similarly, it can be reasonably inferred that the Non-*be* construction with a presentative purpose avoids appearing in the subordinate clause as in (19):

(19) ?If there walks into the room a lady with beautiful blond hair, I will be surprised.

Fourth, the presentative function should express the categorical attitude of the speaker/writer and thereby does not fit with raising, which is likely to be used to avoid assertion. Aissen (1975), Hannay (1985: 10), and Nakajima (1997: 486) point out that Non-*be* sentences rarely occur with raising verbs:

(20) a. ?There is believed to stand in the corner of the room a handball trophy.
                                                                    (Aissen 1975)
       b. There happened to be a stranger sitting next to me.
       b'. *There happened to sit a stranger sitting next to me.
                                                                (Hannay 1985: 10)
       c. *I think there to run into the kitchen the big rats.[7]
                                                            (Nakajima 1997: 486)

As a matter of fact, several tokens with non-presentative forms of negation and within *if*-subordinate clauses were observable from around 1300. In fact, the earliest subject raising token of an existential sentence in the *OED*

---

[6] Aissen (1975) regards the form of Subject + *say/believe* (assertive predication) + (*that*) + *there* + VP as grammatical. Since the discussion here is all about non-presentativeness, I consider that any Non-*be* token in an embedded clause hardly performs a presentative function in the discourse, even if it is recognized as grammatical. The acceptability rates in previous studies reflect the degree of how grammatical native speakers judge a target item to be. They do not consider how it is used in actual communication or whether they really use it or not.

[7] For instance, Kathol & Levine (1992: 208) cite the following example of object raising for a motion verb as an acceptable instance:
   We wouldn't have expected there to leap from behind so many hiding places so few Jansissaries.
I would like to point out that this is a negative sentence with repetition of the intensifier *so* in *so many* and *so few*, which is more likely to be accepted as grammatical for any linguistic phenomenon than affirmative short sentences. According to Nishihara (personal communication), the longer the targeted sentence, the more acceptable rating a native speaker tends to give it.

was not a *there* + *be* sentence, but a Non-*be* sentence, as discussed in Chapter 4. Here, I will repeat the same token (13) of Chapter 4 as (21):

(21)   And by discente Þer is not like to ffalle gretter heritage to any man than to Þe kyng.
    [c1460, Fortescue *Absol.& Lim. Mon.* x. 134, *OED*, by Yaguchi (2016b)]

It is worth pointing out that (21) is also a token of negation.

A glance at the *OED*'s dataset, however, detects a number of tokens used in these kinds of environments where the construction under discussion rarely serves to highlight existence or occurrence, as exemplified in the following:

(22) a.   <u>Why should there want</u> a Marmady? a mite?
                                    [1605, *Play of Stucley* l2b, *OED*]
    b.   <u>Should there come</u> a slant of wind, I'm off.
                                    [1892, Clark Russell *List, Ye Landsmen* i, *OED*]
    c.   <u>For if ther fell him eny schame,</u> It was thurgh his misgovernance.   [1390, Gower *Conf.* II. 150, *OED*]
    d.   The little boye espying the bush to wag, … <u>imagined that there lay</u> some wilde beast.   [1568, Grafton *Chron.* I. 7, *OED*]
    e.   <u>There doth not occurre</u> to me, at this present, any use thereof, for profit.   [1626, Bacon *Sylva* §401, *OED*]
    f.   <u>There came no fruit at all,</u> because the shopkeepers had mutined and agreed not to buy any fruit.
                                    [1650, Howell *Giraffi's Rev. Naples* ₁. 12, *OED*]

The Non-*be* construction in the examples above is used in question (22a), *if*-clause (22b, c), embedded clause (22d), negation (22e), and quasi-negation (22f).[8] In these examples, *there* is by no means effective in exercising presentative, existence-or-occurrence-focusing functions in that the Non-*be* sentences in (22) can be interpreted more or less as objective statements.[9] As

---

[8] It is possible to argue that there is some difference in meaning between "*there* + *do/did* + *not* (*never*) + VP" as in (22e) and "*there* + VP + *no* + noun" as (22f). However, since neither engage in the presentative function, they are non-presentative. I consider nouns denoting negatives such as *nothing*, *none*, *few*, and *little* to have the same meaning as *no* and, thereby, counted them as non-presentative.

As discussed in Footnote 97, tokens with negative elements of *there* + *lack/want/need* + *no/none/nothing* can be non-presentative, but they are not included in Figure 7-4.

[9] Negative tokens such as (22e) and (22f) comprise 64.8% of all the non-presentative cases.

a matter of fact, the Non-*be* construction appearing in non-presentative syntactic environments demonstrates an interesting transition. Observe Figure 7-4 showing the percentages of Non-*be* sentences in embedded and subordinate clauses, raising form, question form, or negation form (also note Appendix 1):[10]

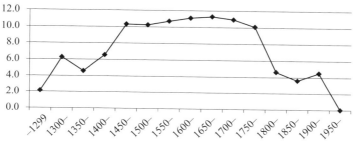

Figure 7-4: Ratio of Non-*be* tokens in embedded and subordinate clauses, raising form, question form, and negation form to total use of Non-*be* construction in *OED* (%)

Apparently, non-presentative use of Non-*be* sentences was quite common until the 1700s. Then it decreased in Late Modern English and became out of fashion in contemporary English. It is, in fact, worthy of attention that both Figures 7-3 and 7-4 show an almost identical trend: non-presentative use is virtually nonexistent in contemporary English, while it was quite common in the 1500s, 1600s and 1700s. The results of these detailed quantitative investigations eventuate in the conclusion that Non-*be* sentences did not exclusively serve a presentative function in Modern English. Instead, it is a reasonable inference that they behaved in more or less a similar manner to *there* + *be*.

Here, it is wise to observe the transition of frequency of ordinary existential sentences of present-day English employed non-presentatively. The following table gives the ratios of existential sentences in negation form, question form, raising form, and embedded and subordinate clauses to the total occurrences of all the *there* + *be* sentences in the COHA:[11]

---

[10] As a matter of fact, the *there* + VP + (*to*) + *be*, such as *there* + *seem* + (*to*) + *be*, *there* + *appear* + *to* + *be* raising tokens are excluded from the analysis as mentioned above. However, the tokens using Non-*be* sentences, i.e. *there* + [Raising] + *to* + verb such as (20a, b′, c) and (21) are included in the analysis.

[11] As in the case of Chapter 6, by an examination of a total of 4,000 sentences with *there* after extracting 200 tokens including *there* every 10 years over the 200-year period

Table 7-3: Ratio of ordinary existential sentences in negation form, question form, raising form, and embedded and subordinate clauses in COHA   (raw occurrences)

period	1810s–1840s	1850s–1880s	1890s–1920s	1930s–1960s	1970s–2000s
%	45.9 (96/209)	45.9 (111/242)	31.0 (68/218)	39.1 (99/253)	42.0 (103/245)

It is obvious that there are great differences in ratio between Non-*be* sentences in the *OED* and ordinary existential sentences in the COHA: the former exhibits below 12% at its peak as Figure 7-4 shows, while the latter shows a level of around 40%. This indicates that Non-*be* sentences tended to serve presentatively more often than *there + be* throughout English history, if one assumes that the ratio of non-presentative use is in inverse correlation to that of presentative use. However, the use of non-presentative verbs seen in Figure 7-3 (around 10% between 1500 and 1700) also shows that some Non-*be* sentences did not function presentatively. In other words, the accounts presented by contemporary linguists concerning the default, presentative, existence-occurrence-focusing function of the Non-*be* construction are applicable only to contemporary English in the strictest sense, or to nineteenth and twentieth century English in a less rigid sense, judging from the tendencies observed in Figures 7-3 and 7-4. Also, it is possible to surmise that the literary nuance of the Non-*be* construction has considerably strengthened since 1800 because its rarity, as seen in Figure 7-2, may help provide a rhetorical impact on the discourse. It seems that the construction concerned is primarily involved in adding literary and formal nuance to the discourse and simultaneously serving a presentative function in contemporary English. Thus, the investigations so far have revealed how *there* functioning to focus on the presence/occurrence of a referent came to what it is now.

7.1.4   Positions of locatives

Here, it is significant to demonstrate how Non-*be* sentences are different from ordinary existential sentences in the frequency and the position of locatives. A particular issue is frequently addressed in previous studies: the position of locative phrases in Non-*be* sentences. We have discussed the restriction presented by Chomsky (1999: 15) in respect to the locative phrase co-occurring with unaccusative verbs in present-day English. (5) will be repeated as (23):

---

via applying the wild card, the ratios were calculated.

(23) a.   *There came several angry men into the room.

     b.   There came into the room several angry men.

(Chomsky 1999: 15)

Before analyzing the feature above, the distinction between tokens with a locative phrase and those without should be checked. Example (24a) is the type which contains a locative phrase, while (24b) exemplifies tokens without:

(24) a.   There came immediately <u>on us</u> a great storm of hail.

[1976, J. James *Bridge of Sand* iii. 62, *OED*]

     b.   But at the same time there appears a general disposition of these masses, producing one comprehensive form.

[a1786, A. Cozens *New Method in Drawing Landscape* 7, *OED*]

The following graph shows the diachronic change: the 'total' line is the same as the Non-*be* line in Figure 7-2, and the 'locative' line shows tokens with the explicit presence of locative phrases in Non-*be* sentences of the *OED* (*there* + *exist* excluded), while Table 7-4 specifies the percentage of the tokens with locative phrases to the total occurrences of Non-*be* sentences in the same dictionary:

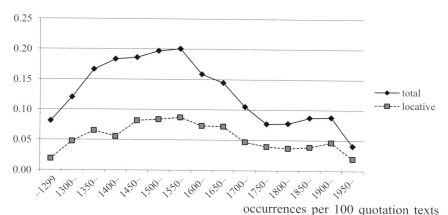

occurrences per 100 quotation texts

Figure 7-5: Diachronic transition of presence of locative phrase

Table 7-4: Ratio of locative presence to total Non-*be* tokens in *OED*

period	−1299	1300−	1350−	1400−	1450−	1500−	1550−	1600−	1650−	1700−	1750−	1800−	1850−	1900−	1950−
%	23.4	39.6	39.1	30.3	43.9	42.5	43.4	46.2	50.0	44.6	51.4	47.5	44.3	52.8	48.3

The use of locatives has consistently remained at around half the level of occurrences of Non-*be* sentences since the beginning of Modern English. On the other hand, ordinary existential sentences contain locatives less than one third of the time in present-day English, as in Table 7-5:[12]

Table 7-5: Ratio of locative use to total ordinary existential sentences in COHA
(raw occurrences)

period	1810s–1840s	1850s–1880s	1890s–1920s	1930s–1960s	1970s–2000s
%	46.9 (98/209)	50.0 (121/242)	31.7 (69/218)	34.0 (86/253)	26.9 (66/245)

Apparently, Tables 7-4 and 7-5 indicate that while Non-*be* and ordinary existential sentences shared similar ratios of around 40 percent in the 1800s, the presence of locative phrases is becoming less common in ordinary existential sentences in contemporary English. Hence, suffice it to say that in current English Non-*be* sentences are more likely to need the explicit presence of locative phrases than ordinary *there* + *be*, although in the 1800s ordinary *there* + *be* occurred with locatives as often as Non-*be* sentences.

Syntactically, there are three slots available for Non-*be* sentences in present-day English.

(25)   Type A: LOC + *there* + VP + NP
Within the towne of Rome there stood An image cut of cornel wood.   [1870, Morris *Earthly Par.* I. ₁ 440, *OED*]
Type B: *there* + VP + LOC + NP
There went through me so great a heave of surprise that I was all shook with it.   [1893, Stevenson *Catriona* 296, *OED*]
Type C: *there* + VP + NP + LOC
There rose a greate derth thorow out all that same londe.
[1526, Tindale *Luke* xv. 14, *OED*]

It should be heeded that the meaning of the verb in the context is a crucial factor in the process of considering the grammaticality of Type C. In the case of Type C, not only the inception type verbs, but also *be*-stance and physical-stance types fit into this slot perfectly well; meanwhile, motion type verbs are least likely to appear there as shown above. Therefore, the frequency of Type C is considered to be in inverse relation to the frequency of the use of motion type verbs, which is applicable at least to present-day English. Type B, by contrast, is used for motion type verbs or for express-

---

[12] The COHA data in this chapter include only *there* + *be* tokens, excluding those with modals and adverbial elements between *there* and *be*, since those things can have an impact on the position of locatives. The method of data collection is shown in Footnote 11.

ing relatively literal nuance as in (26) because the reader feels as if it is an inversion:

(26)   There stood on our shelves volumes of the Zohar ..., and other cabalistic works.   [1978, I.B. Singer *Shosha* i. 8, *OED*]

The transition of the position of locatives of Non-*be* sentences in the *OED* is shown in Figure 7-6 and that of ordinary existential sentences in the COHA is shown in Figure 7-7 (also see Appendix 1):

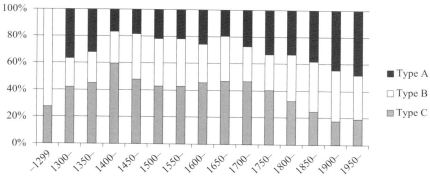

Figure 7-6: Ratio of three positions of locatives in Non-*be* sentences in *OED*

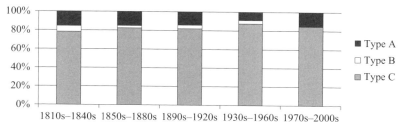

Figure 7-7: Ratio of three positions of locatives in *there* + *be* sentences in COHA

The above two graphs exhibit the contrastive distributions of the three positions. First, present-day English shows the most distinctive differences. Non-*be* sentences depend on Type A and Type B, while ordinary existential sentences make the best of the Type C structure. Second, Type B is often utilized by Non-*be* sentences, but not by ordinary existential sentences. Third, Type C of Non-*be* sentences was quite prevalent until the 1800–1849 period (30% or more), but decreased gradually to the extent that in present-day English it remains below 20%. In other words, Non-*be* sentences specialize in the presentative function, culminating in the ample use of Type A and Type B positions of locatives.

As examined above, the presence of locative phrases in ordinary existential sentences itself is not as frequent as in their Non-*be* counterparts, but once a prepositional phrase is used, it tends to come at the end of the sentence. Biber et al. (1999: 950) also show a similar result. This profiles a prototypical sequence of ordinary existential sentences as *there* + *be* + NP + LOC, in contrast to LOC + *there* + VP + NP or *there* + VP + LOC + NP of Non-*be* sentences, in writing. Thus, the Non-*be* construction is inclined to distinguish itself from ordinary existential sentences in the word order explicitly in present-day English. Returning to Figure 7-6, the relatively frequent employment of Type C in the Early Modern English period may also show that Non-*be* sentences were more similar in function to ordinary existential sentences at that time than at present.

7.1.5 *there* + *exist* and *there* + *remain*

Here, it is important to pay attention to *there* + *exist*, the sequence following similar patterns to ordinary existential sentences: it often exhibited syntactic features expressing a non-presentative function. Note the following examples:

(27) a. … but this sign should not be employed <u>unless there exists</u> exact analogy between mathematical addition and logical alternation.

   [1874, W.S. Jevons *Princ. Science: Treat. Logic* I. v. 81, *OED*]

  b. It would not be fair to say that they are hated, <u>that there exists</u> well-defined Negrophobia among us.

   [1898, T.J. Morgan *Negro in Amer.* vi. 125, *OED*]

(27a) is a case used in an *if*-clause, and (27b) is a case in an embedded clause. The ratio of non-presentative tokens to all the *there* + *exist* tokens is shown in the following table:

Table 7-6: Ratio of non-presentative tokens of *there* + *exist* in *OED*

period	−1799	1800–1849	1850–1899	1900–1949	1950–
there + *exist*	0% (0/3)	25.0% (8/32)	14.3% (9/63)	19.4% (14/72)	27.8% (20/72)

(raw occurrences)

It is apparent that *there* + *exist* showed a very high frequency in constituting non-presentative features since the 1800s, as Table 7-6 exhibits (note that Non-*be* sentences form non-presentative syntactic features at less than 5% after 1800 in the *OED*). This is conclusive evidence to show that *there* + *exist* is often utilized non-presentatively like *there* + *be*; of course, it should be mentioned that *there* + *exist* is more likely to function presentatively than ordinary existential sentences (around 40% of *there* + *be*'s non-presentative ratio in present-day English, as Table 7-3 shows). Furthermore, the examination into the position of locatives discloses another interesting point. See the following three patterns:

(28)   Type A
       In America ... there exists a body of men who are known as 'Business Doctors', men who are called in to give advice upon the proper conduct of business.   [1909, *Modern Business* Jan. 606/1, *OED*]
       Type B
       A totem is a class of material objects which a savage regards with superstitious respect, believing that there exists between him and every member of the class an intimate and altogether special relation.
                                    [1888, in *Encycl, Brit.* XXIII. 467/1, *OED*]
       Type C
       There exists no dual society in the world today and all attempts to find one are attempts to justify and/or cover up imperialism and revisionism.   [1969, A.G. Frank *Latin Amer.* (1970) xiv. 221, *OED*]

Table 7-7 shows the ratios of the presence of locatives to the total tokens in *there* + *exist*:

Table 7-7: Ratio of locatives to total tokens of *there* + *exist* in *OED*

period	1800–	1850–	1900–	1950–
%	62.5	47.6	56.9	38.9

As discussed above, *there* + *exist* manifests similar syntactic characteristics to ordinary existential sentences except for tag question as in Table 7-1. The frequency of the presence of locatives (38.9% after 1950 in the *OED*) is higher than that of ordinary *there* + *be* sentences (27.8% for the 1970s–2000s period) in current English, but it is still lower than that of Non-*be* sentences (48.3% after 1950 in the *OED*). In other words, *there* + *exist* shows a median frequency between *there* + *be* and Non-*be* sentences. Additionally, the distribution of the three positions by the *there* + *exist* sequence shows an interesting trend (see Appendix 1):

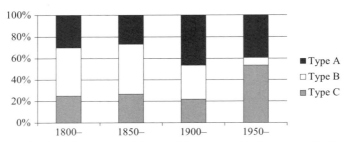

Figure 7-8: Ratio of three positions of locatives in *there* + *exist* in *OED*

Up to 1949 the distributions of the three slots for *there* + *exist* and Non-*be* sentences were relatively alike, but after 1950 the slot immediately after *be* of Type B yielded its share (7.1%) to Type C (52.6%), whereas Type B in Non-*be* sentences account for more than 30% in the same period. Apparently, *there* + *exist* has come to behave similarly to *there* + *be* only after 1950 in light of the rare appearance of locative phrases between *be* and NP (Type B). Thus, it is reasonable to conclude that *there* + *exist* lost the characteristics as a Non-*be* construction in the ratio of non-presentative function, the ratio of the use of locatives, and the ratio of Type B structure and gradually came to behave similarly to *there* + *be* after 1950.

Interestingly enough, *there* + *remain*, semantically similar to *there* + *exist* and frequently employed in current English and the second most frequently used sequence among Non-*be* sentences after *there* + *exist* in the data after 1950 of the *OED*, showed a different distribution from *there* + *exist*.[13] Note the following table:

Table 7-8: Ratio of non-presentative tokens of *there* + *remain* in *OED*

period	−1799	1800–1849	1850–1899	1900–1949	1950–
there + *remain*	7.1% (1/14)	22.2% (4/18)	9.7% (3/31)	12.5% (4/32)	0% (0/24)

(raw occurrences)

None of the 24 *there* + *remain* tokens displayed non-presentative features in the *OED*'s current English data after 1950, while 27.8% of *there* + *exist* tokens did so as Table 7-6 shows. In the 1850 to 1949 period, by contrast, *there* + *remain* appeared non-presentatively often enough, although its non-

---

[13] It decreased a great deal in frequency in present-day English from its zenith in Early Modern English.

presentative ratio was slightly lower than that of *there* + *exist*: in the 1850 to 1899 period, 9.7% of *there* + *remain* appeared in non-presentative forms while 14.3% of *there* + *exist* did so; in the period of 1900 to 1949, 12.5% of *there* + *remain*, while 19.4% of *there* + *exist*. Based upon the fact that even *there* + *remain* expressing a similar meaning to *there* + *exist* came to perform a predominantly presentative function in current English, we can justifiably conclude that the presentative function of the Non-*be* construction, except for *there* + *exist*, has been strengthened in current English.[14]

The subsections so far have found that the Non-*be* construction decreased in frequency and, instead, began to specialize in the function of presentatively focusing on the referent, especially after 1950 and that *there* + *exist* increased in frequency in present-day English, acquiring similar syntactic and semantic functions to *there* + *be*. I have argued that contemporary linguists' explanations are inapplicable to Non-*be* sentences in earlier English.

7.1.6 The data of the COHA

It is important to confirm the validity of what has been discussed in the previous subsections by analysing the COHA. Due to the high word count of the COHA, I chose verb types whose occurrences exceed 100 after applying "*there* [v*]". The following table shows the occurrences:[15]

---

[14] Of course, it would be interesting to investigate what kind of positions locative phrases *there* + *remain* takes. However, the occurrences of locatives for *there* + *remain* are far lower than those of Non-*be* and *there* + *exist*, so I have refrained from discussing locatives due to the inaccuracy caused by scarce data.

[15] Tokens which fail to constitute the Non-*be* structure such as *For thou shalt there remain immured*, ... were not excluded in the data of Table 7-9. However, due to the paucity in irrelevant data of this kind, the general trend is successfully identified.

In addition, *there* in some instances may be used as a locative adverb. However, as mentioned in Section 1.7 of Chapter 1, the distinction between locative and existential is hard to demarcate.

Table 7-9 Raw occurrences of *there* + verb in COHA

THERE CAME	5,439
THERE COMES	934
THERE STOOD	824
THERE GOES	763
THERE EXISTS	712
THERE REMAINED	666
THERE REMAINS	646
THERE LAY	586
THERE FOLLOWED	490
THERE AROSE	416
THERE EXISTED	404
THERE LIES	350
THERE SAT	268
THERE LIVED	266
THERE STANDS	241
THERE ROSE	234
THERE COME	224
THERE BEGAN	205
THERE REMAIN	201
THERE WENT	194
THERE FELL	184
THERE EXIST	173
THERE GREW	162
THERE GO	126
THERE HUNG	122
THERE OCCURRED	117

I picked up a tenth of the above instances from the 23 sequences (and excluded tokens which do not form the target construction) and all *there* + *exist* sequences (i.e. *there* + *exist*, *there* + *exists*, and *there* + *existed*) to calculate the total frequency of Non-*be* and *there* + *exist* in the COHA. As a result, I retrieved 1,345 tokens and 1,289 tokens from Non-*be* sentences and *there* + *exist* sentences respectively. As Table 7-9 shows, the occurrences of the *there* + *come* sequence are extremely high (49.1% of all tokens) in the COHA whilst it is only 7.0% in the *OED*'s dataset of Table 7-2. Hence, the following analysis may display *come*-oriented tendencies. Consider the following graph (also see Appendix 1):

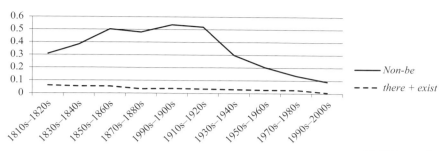

occurrences per 10,000 words

Figure 7-9: Frequency of Non-*be* and *there* + *exist* sentences in COHA

I would like to refer to five respects relevant to the differences between the *OED*'s and the COHA's datasets. First, the above graph shows that occurrences of the Non-*be* construction declined after 1910 after it had increased between the 1810s and the 1890s. This boost of occurrences in the 1800s can be witnessed in the *OED*'s dataset of Figure 7-2 in that it also show a slight increase between 1800 and 1900.[16] Thus, this confirms the declining trend of Non-*be* sentences. Second, *there* + *exist* is not the most frequent item and gradually decreased, which is inconsistent with the data in the *OED*. The *OED* contains many quotation texts cited from science papers, where *there* + *exist* is frequently employed, which seems to cause the differences. Nevertheless, in terms of syntactic configuration, it still shows its own unique characteristics. We will examine this later in this subsection.

Third, the ratios of non-presentative instances (i.e. the use of negation form, question form, and raising form, and in embedded and subordinate clauses) remain around 3% till the year 2009 in the COHA as in Table 7-10, while that of the *OED* is also around 4% from the 1800s to 1949 and lowers to zero in the 1950–2003 period as in Figure 7-4:

Table 7-10: Ratio of non-presentative Non-*be* tokens in COHA

period	1810s–1840s	1850s–1880s	1890s–1920s	1930s–1960s	1970s–2000s
%	5.8 (8/139)	5.6 (20/358)	3.5 (17/486)	2.9 (7/243)	3.4 (4/119)

(raw occurrences)

Thus, the presentative characteristics of Non-*be* sentences are observable in the COHA as well, because the figures in the above table are very low, com-

---

[16] The lower occurrences between the 1810s and 1840s in the COHA may have been caused by the lack of newspaper genre, as mentioned in Section 2.1 and Section 6.2.

pared with the level of 40% for ordinary existential sentences in the COHA's contemporary data in Table 7-3.

Fourth, the use of locatives shows slightly lower percentages than the Non-*be* data in the *OED* (around 50%) as in Table 7-4, but slightly higher percentages than the *there + be* data after the 1930s in the COHA (a declining tendency from around 50% in the 1800s to around 30% in the 1900s) as in Table 7-5. Observe the following table:

Table 7-11: Ratio of locatives to total tokens of Non-*be* construction in COHA (raw occurrences)

period	1810s–1840s	1850s–1880s	1890s–1920s	1930s–1960s	1970s–2000s
%	38.1 (53/139)	48.0 (172/358)	49.2 (239/486)	40.7 (99/243)	33.6 (44/119)

The tendency observed in the above table bears a resemblance to that of Non-*be* sentences in the *OED* as in Table 7-4, while the latter shows slightly higher percentages.

Fifth, the positions of locative phrases demonstrate dissimilar tendencies. Observe Figure 7-10 (also note Appendix 1):

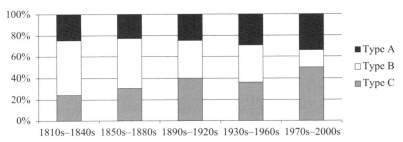

Figure 7-10: Ratio of three positions of locatives of Non-*be* sentences in COHA

The results of Figure 7-10 show contradictory tendencies to the data of the *OED* in Figure 7-6. Although Type A increased in frequency in the same way as in the *OED*, Type C also increased unlike the decrease observed in the *OED*'s dataset (Figure 7-6). On the other hand, the frequency of Type B is lower in the above figure than that in the *OED*'s data especially between the 1970s and the 2000s, but compared with null use by *there + be* in the COHA's data in the same period as in Figure 7-7, 16.0% in the above data can be said to contain the characteristic of Non-*be* sentences. The discrepancies noted here seem to be ascribable to the ample use of *there +*

come. As discussed about the polysemic nature of *come* in connection with (8) and (9), *come* in *there* + *come* often functions as a verb similar to *be*, and therein, the impact of *there* + *come* (49.1% of all the investigated tokens) seems to affect the results. Although the analyses so far have revealed a diminished use in frequency, frequent presentative use, frequent use of locatives, and their frequent appearance immediately after the Non-*be* verb in contemporary English, factors behind the increased use of Type C are required to be investigated in further research.

Finally, the comparison of *there* + *exist* tokens with *there* + *remain* tokens shows that *there* + *exist* shows very similar features to *there* + *be* sentences. For the sake of accuracy, I randomly chose 331 tokens of *there* + *remain* and 286 tokens of *there* + *exist* in accordance with the occurrences of the respective sequences' verbal forms seen in Table 7-9. Note the following table (see Appendix 1):

Table 7-12: Type A, B, C positions of locatives and non-presentative ratio of *there* + *exist* and *there* + *remain* in COHA

	1810s–1840s	1850s–1880s	1890s–1920s	1930s–1960s	1970s–2000s
exist Type A/B/C	32.1%/46.4%/21.4%	33.3%/44.4%/22.2%	31.6%/39.5%/30.0%	25%/15%/60%	35.7%/14.3%/50%
remain Type A/B/C	33.3%/25%/41.7%	20.8%/37.5%/41.7%	27.8%/36.1%/36.1%	29.4%/35.3%/35.3%	38.5%/15.4%/46.2%
exist non-presentative	47.1% (16/34)	55.3% (47/85)	35.3% (24/68)	34.4% (22/64)	54.3% (19/35)
remain non-presentative	17.9% (7/39)	12.3% (9/73)	8.3% (9/108)	2.7% (2/75)	8.3% (3/36)

(raw occurrences)

According to the above table, the declining tendency of locatives of *there* + *exist* to take Type B position is clearly observable in the same way as the *OED*'s data of Figure 7-8 shows. *There* + *remain* also exhibits a similar trend. (As seen in Figure 7-10, Non-*be* sentences in the COHA also show similar tendencies.) On the other hand, frequent non-presentative tokens of *there* + *exist* are witnessed throughout the time, which differentiates its function from that of *there* + *remain*. What is notable is that compared with the ordinary *there* + *be* sentences as seen in Table 7-3, these non-presentative ratios of *there* + *exist* are similar or even higher, whereas those of *there* + *remain* are significantly low. Thus, the *there* + *exist* construction proves to be different from its semantically kin sequence *there* + *remain* in light of semantic and pragmatic function.

In this subsection, we have confirmed the characteristics of Non-*be* sentences in the *OED* by analysing the COHA. Despite some dissimilar tendencies in the positions of locatives, the general tendencies of Non-*be* sentences and the uniqueness of *there* + *exist* have been verified in the COHA as well.

7.2   The passive existential construction

The present section will explore the historical development of the *there* + *be* + pp + NP sequence as passive existential sentences. As briefly explained in 5.3.2 of Chapter 5, there are two main types of constructions to passivize existential sentences in present-day English (e.g. Milsark 1974, Quirk et al. 1985: 1409, Chomsky 1999: 20, Radford 2000). Quirk et al. (1985: 1409) provide the following examples:

(29) a.   There was a gold medal presented (to the winner) by the mayor.
b.   There was presented (to the winner) by the mayor a gold medal.

(Quirk et al. 1985: 1409)

According to Quirk et al. (1985: 1409), *there* + *be* + NP + pp of (29a) is more common than *there* + *be* + pp + NP of (29b) in contemporary English. Radford (2000) explains that (29a) is construed to express a dynamic situation of the notional subject's change of state as well as a static situation, while (29b) denotes only the dynamic situation of the notional subject.

Curiously enough, Chomsky (1999: 15) claims restrictions in passivizing existential sentences in respect to the position of the locative prepositional phrase as follows:

(30) a.   There was a large book placed on the table.
b.   There was placed on the table a large book.
c.   *There was placed a large book on the table.

(Chomsky 1999: 15)

According to Chomsky (1999: 15), the restriction seen in (30) and that in (5) regarding unaccusative verbs share common features.

It is widely agreed that passive existential sentences have been present since Old English and that the sequence *there* + *be* + pp + NP as in (29b) and (30b) was prevalent in Middle English, but conceded to the *there* + *be* + NP + pp in Early Modern English (e.g. Ukaji 2000: 321–328). For example, Yanagi (2011) provides Middle English data via the analyses of the Parsed Corpus of Early English Correspondence (PCEEC) and the Penn-Helsinki Parsed Corpus of Middle English, Second Edition (PPCME2). He explains that there are four slots for a notional subject to appear in passive existential sentences (also see Subsection 5.3.2 of Chapter 5).

(31)   There will [A] be [B] baked [C] for the party [D].

Table 7-13: Syntactic positions of notional subjects in Middle English

	Position A	Position B	Position C	Position D
PCEEC	23.4%	23.4%	46.8%	4.3%
PPCME2	5.6%	36.4%	32.2%	20.3%

(From Yanagi 2011)

Position B represents *there* + *be* + NP + pp such as (29a) and Positions C and D are for *there* + *be* + pp + NP such as (29b). (Position A is not subject to discussion here partly due to its unavailability in present-day English and partly due to the condition of this study's exclusion of modal elements.) It would be interesting to examine both constructions. However, as Breivik (1990: 122) and Pfenninger (2009: 235) point out, the former poses some ambiguity yielding the three feasible structures. Note the following examples:

(32)   There were some letters written by her grandfather.
  a.   There were [some letters] written by her grandfather at his death bed.
  b.   There were [some letters written by her grandfather at his death bed].
  c.   There were [some letters written by her grandfather] in the small box.

The sequence *there* + *be* + NP + LOC can feature three structures: example (32a) expresses the passive existential structure, but in (32b) and (32c), the scopes of the NPs as notional subjects span from *some letters* to *written by her grandfather at his death bed* and from *some letters* to *written by her grandfather* respectively. As a result, the structures of (32b) and (32c) by no means form passive existential sentences. Since the *OED* fails to provide sufficient contexts as mentioned in Chapter 2, it is difficult to retrieve only genuine passive existential sentences. Therefore, the present study will treat only the *there* + *be* + pp + NP construction, which is called Tpp construction in this study.

7.2.1   The *OED*'s dataset

In the *OED*, the construction concerned started to appear in Middle English as in (33):

(33) a.   <u>Þar was conuerted</u> thusand fiue.

[a1300, *Cursor M.* 19134 (Cott.), *OED*]

   b.   <u>Thare was crakked</u> many a crowne Of wild Scottes, and alls of tame.   [1352, Minot *Poems* 4, *OED*]

I will put this construction to the subjectness test following the same procedures used for the Non-*be* construction in Section 7.1. The acceptability judgments presented in previous studies are as follows:

(34) a.   ? Was there found among the ruins a skeleton?   (Bresnan 1994)

   b.   *How many packages were there placed on the table?

(Chomsky 1999:15)

   c.   There are likely to be awarded several prizes.

(Chomsky 1999: 20)

   d.   We expect there to be awarded several prizes.

(Chomsky 1999: 20)

   e.   I expect there to be hung on this wall a portrait of our founder.

(Bresnan 1994)

As for the object raising demonstrated in (34d, e), Chomsky (1999: 20) and Bresnan (1994) judge it as acceptable, but two of my four informants regard it as unacceptable. I give 'OK(?)' as in the table below (also see Appendix 2):

Table 7-14: Syntactic patterns of Tpp construction

	ordinary *there + be*	Tpp *there + be +* pp
Affirmative	OK	OK
Question	OK	?
Subject raising	OK	OK
Object raising	OK	OK(?)
for _ to	OK	?
Tag Question	OK	?

As seen in Table 7-14, *there* in the Tpp construction does not show an identical subjectness to *there* in ordinary existential sentences, in that it is unlikely to be employed in question and *for-to* forms. This result suggests that *there* in the Tpp construction connotes the vestige of adverbial properties to a certain degree as in the case of Non-*be* sentences.

The present study extracted all 771 Tpp tokens from the *OED*, after excluding the data of subject raising such as (35):

(35)   There is required to be therein [in their hearts] moche cautele and sobrenesse.   [1511, Elyot *Gov.* ₁. iv, *OED*]

The following graph is the result of the research (also see Appendix 1):

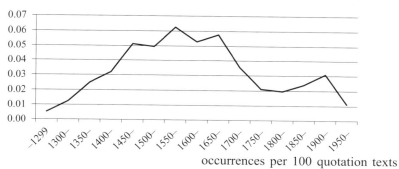

occurrences per 100 quotation texts

Figure 7-11: Frequency of Tpp sentences in *OED*

Table 7-15: Raw occurrences of Tpp sentences in *OED*

−1299	1300−	1350−	1400−	1450−	1500−	1550−	1600−	1650−	1700−	1750−	1800−	1850−	1900−	1950−
3	5	13	19	27	42	102	109	102	47	30	55	114	70	33

Obviously, the frequency of the Tpp sentence was relatively low throughout English history, compared with the Non-*be* sentence. A careful scrutiny of the data, however, demonstrates that in the Early Modern English period, it was more abundantly used than at any other time, and then declined in the 1700s. Whereas through 1750 to 1949 its frequency remained almost unchanged, it decreased after 1950, in the same way as the Non-*be* construction. Another thing I want to note is that in the 1850–1949 period, there was a slight increment in just the same way as the Non-*be* construction. It can be conjectured that the Tpp and Non-*be* constructions regained some popularity in writing in the same period. Hence, the overall inclination is evidenced to show a strong resemblance to that of the Non-*be* construction, although the decline of the Tpp construction occurred slightly later than the Non-*be* construction. If tokens of the other passive form *there* + *be* + NP + pp were added, the whole picture would, of course, be totally different, because *there* + *be* + NP + pp tokens were dominantly employed since Modern

English.

Next, it is important to observe the degree to which the Tpp construction has served presentively. As in the case of Non-*be* sentences, passive existentials appear with *never/nor/not* and *no/none/nothing/few/little* or in raising form or embedded and subordinate clauses in Modern English. Consider the following quotation texts:

(36) a.   There is not left in him one inch of man.

     [1594, Kyd *Sp. Trag.* ɪᴠ. in Hazl. *Dodsley* V. 114, *OED*]

  b.   There was made no more doubt to leuie the Campe.

      [1579, Fenton *Guicciard.* (1618) 256, *OED*]

  c.   … and this has been from time to time improved until there is now produced from the Canadian mattes by a fire process metallic nickel which is from 99% to 99.3% pure.

      [1895, *Mineral Industry* III. 458, *OED*]

Examples (36a) and (36b) are instances of the Tpp construction with negative elements, while (36c) exemplifies a token in a subordinate clause. The following graph shows the ratio of non-presentative sentences which include negative elements of *never/nor/not* and *no/none/nothing/few/little* or those appearing in raising and embedded and subordinate clauses to the total Tpp tokens in the *OED* (also note Appendix 1):

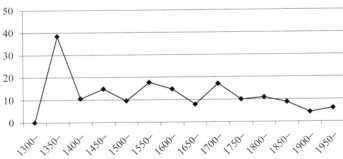

Figure 7-12: Ratio of Tpp tokens in embedded and subordinate clauses, raising form, question form, and negation form to total Tpp tokens in *OED* (%)

The graph above illustrates that non-presentative tokens account for between 10% and 20% in Early Modern English, except for the 1650–1699 period, but show less than 10% in present-day English. (The early data in the 1300s may be too scarce to identify an accurate tendency.)

Considering that the ratio under discussion for ordinary *there* + *be* sentences is about 40% in the COHA as shown in Table 7-3, the Tpp construction is more likely to have assumed a presentative function throughout English history than present-day ordinary existential sentences.[17]   Indeed, it is possible to surmise that the Tpp construction plays a rhetorical role as presentative formula because of its rarity in contemporary English. However, compared with Non-*be* sentences, which yield a non-presentative level of less than 5% after 1800 and posit no non-presentative tokens after 1950 in the *OED*, Tpp sentences still retain some of the characteristics of ordinary *there* + *be* sentences to occasionally function non-presentatively.

Finally, it is significant to investigate the positions of locative phrases. Before conducting an analysis, it is necessary to show how often locative phrases appear in the passive construction concerned. Observe the graph below, which shows the frequencies of all Tpp sentences and those with prepositional phrases and the table below, which shows the ratios:

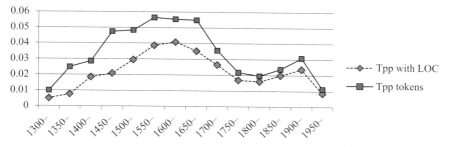

occurrences per 100 quotation texts

Figure 7-13: Frequency of all Tpp tokens and those without locative in *OED*

---

[17] Toyota (2008: 110–113) shows that negation-based *there*-passive sentences including the *there* + *be* + NP + pp such as (36a) faded away in the Helsinki, ARCHER, London-Lund, and LOB corpora as time passed by supplying the following data:

Occurrences of the passive structure within the scope of negation

	Without negation	With negation	Total
EME	12 (44.4%)	15 (55.6%)	27 (100%)
LME	9 (64.3%)	5 (35.7%)	14 (100%)
PDE	12 (100%)	0 (0%)	12 (100%)

(Toyota 2008: 112)

His data suggest that the present-day English environment is more suitable for the presentative function than earlier English, although accuracy is not guaranteed due to the low raw occurrences.

Table 7-16: Ratio of Tpp with locative to all Tpp tokens in *OED* (%)

period	1300–	1350–	1400–	1450–	1500–	1550–	1600–	1650–	1700–	1750–	1800–	1850–	1900–	1950–
%	50.0	30.8	64.7	44.0	61.0	68.5	73.7	63.9	74.5	77.4	81.8	83.3	77.1	75.8

The ratio of Tpp tokens with locative phrases to the total Tpp tokens increased gradually until Early Modern English and rose to 80% or more in the 1800s. Compared with Figure 7-5 and Table 7-4, the Tpp construction occurs with the prepositional phrase more strenuously than the Non-*be* construction and the *there + be* construction in present-day English, which proves that the Tpp construction is closely linked with the locative phrase.

We are now in a position to make sure whether Chomsky's (1999: 15) account concerning the location of the locative phrase as in (30) is valid or not. Note the following examples:

(37) a. There is thus gradually built up a picture of increasing epidermal hyperplasia which at length becomes heaped up into a papilloma composed of the keratinising remnants of former follicles.
[1964, G. H. Haggis et al. *Introd, Molecular Lancet* 31 Dec. 1457/2, *OED*]

   b. Type A: LOC before *there*
You must know that all along the north-west frontier of India there is spread a force of some thirty thousand foot and horse, ...   [1893, Kipling *Many Invent., Lost Legion, OED*]

   c. Type B: LOC immediately after pp
Last year there was imported into London from Newcastle and Sunderland 692093¼ chalders of coals.
[1778, *Chron.* in *Ann. Reg.* 161/1, *OED*]

   d. Type C: LOC after NP
There was set A penalty of blood on all who shared So much of water with him as might wet His lips.
[1818, Shelley *Marenghi* xii, *OED*]

While (37a) contains no locative phrase, (37b) is a prototypical Tpp sentence with a prepositional phrase appearing before *there* (Type A): (37c) is a case of a prepositional phrase immediately following pp (Type B), and (37d) is a case of a prepositional phrase placed after the notional subject (Type C). The following graph indicates the chronological change of how Type C such as (37d) came to disappear from the English language (also see Appendix 1):

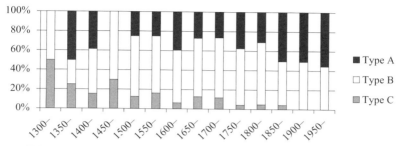

Figure 7-14: Ratio of three positions of locatives in Tpp sentences in *OED*

Type C was rarely seen in Late Modern English and is completely unavailable in present-day English. We can verify Chomsky's (1999: 20) contention that the position of a prepositional phrase after the NP became unacceptable in present-day English. The fact that a locative phrase always appears before the notional subject certainly suggests that Tpp sentences are a construction which highlights the notional subject based on the well shared view that new information comes at the end of a sentence. In any event, the Tpp is a marked construction in terms of constituent order in present-day English.

7.2.2   The COHA's dataset

In this subsection, the tendencies observed in the *OED* will be confirmed by analyzing the COHA. Because there are only 771 tokens in the *OED*, the COHA, which contains 2,392 Tpp tokens, helps furnish more detailed data after 1810.[18] See the following graph to show the trend in Late Modern English and present-day English (Also note Appendix 1):

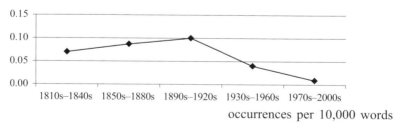

occurrences per 10,000 words

Figure 7-15: Frequency of Tpp construction in COHA

---

[18] The methodology used here is as follows: 1,000 types of the sequence *there* + *be* + pp {there [vb*] [v?n*]} are retrieved, and tokens including the root form *be* are discarded. Unlike the analysis of the *OED*, tokens with some element(s) between *be* and pp are screened out.

The Tpp construction shows an increase from the 1810s to the 1920s and then a decrease after 1930. In the latest period, the frequency is extremely low. We can confirm a parallelism in trend between Figure 7-11 and the above figure. (It deserves mentioning that the *OED*'s 771 items of data are very reliable.) I would like to point out that the Tpp construction shows a declining tendency in current English, which is very similar to that of the Non-*be* construction. It seems safe to say that the Tpp construction has also become a rare construction now playing a literal role.

Second, a non-presentative inclination will be considered.[19] The following graph shows the trend after 1810 in the COHA:

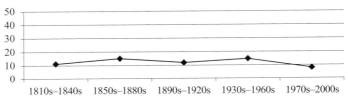

Figure 7-16: Ratio of Tpp tokens in embedded and subordinate clauses, raising form, question form, and negation form to total Tpp tokens in COHA (%)

The ratio fluctuates between 11.2% and 15.2% until the 1960s, and reduced slightly to 8.0% after the 1970s. The gaps in percentage between Figure 7-12 and the above graph may be attributed to different distributions of genres in each corpus or the factor that in the process of extracting the COHA's data, tokens with some element(s) between *there* and *be* and between *be* and pp are excluded, causing a decrease in the number of total occurrences of the TPP construction. However, it is possible to state that non-presentative tokens comprise around 10% after Late Modern English. Needless to say, this level is much lower than that of *there* + *be* (around 40% in the COHA).

Third, the use of locatives will be shown. Compared with the *OED*'s Tpp data, the frequency is a little lower, while compared with Non-*be* data, the frequency is higher until the 1960s. In contemporary English, the percentages are on a similar level (*OED*'s data is 48.3%). As for ordinary exis-

---

[19] The methodology used here is as follows:1,000 types of the sequence *there* + *be* + pp + *not*/*no*/*none*/*nothing*/*little*/*few* {*there* [vb*] [v?n*] *not*/*no*/*none*/*nothing*/*little*/*few*} and conjunctive + *there* + *be* + pp {[c*] *there* [vb*] [v?n*]} are retrieved, and tokens including the root form *be* and tokens which do not constitute the Tpp construction are discarded. Unlike the analysis of the *OED*, tokens with some element(s) between *be* and pp are sifted out.

tential sentences, they show a declining tendency from 46.9% in the 1810s–1840s period to 26.9% in the 1970s–2000s period. See the following table:

Table 7-17: Percentage of locatives of Tpp sentences in COHA

1810s–1840s	1850s–1880s	1890s–1920s	1930s–1960s	1970s–2000s
61.6%	68.4%	61.2%	62.4%	46.2%
(90/146)	(199/291)	(276/451)	(113/181)	(18/39)

(raw occurrences)

Next, the positions of locatives will be shown. See the next figure:

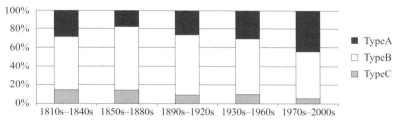

Figure 7-17: Ratio of three positions of locatives in Tpp sentences in COHA

The positions of locatives also show infrequent use of Type C, similar to the *OED*'s trend.

Thus, in spite of the lower frequencies of the presence of locatives in contemporary English, we were able to verify the findings from the *OED*'s dataset: decreasing tendency, moderate non-presentative use, and rare use of Type C position of locatives.

This section has shown that the Tpp use of *there* peaked around 1550 and declined after that, functioning presentatively as a marked usage because of its rarity in present-day English. The present restriction which demands that the locative phrase appear before the notional subject was placed at the turn of the twentieth century.

7.3   Transitive verbs

As Jespersen (1927: 112) maintains, it is well acknowledged that transitive verbs were also used in Modern English. In the *OED*, a Middle English token is also observable as in (38a):

(38) a.   Ouer-thwart this for-seide longe lyne, <u>ther crosseth</u> hym a-nother
     lyne.   [c1391, Chaucer *Astrol.* I. §5, *OED*]

    b.   There met him a ship of the Carthaginians, garnished with in-
        fules, ribbands, and white flags of peace.

                                [1600, Holland *Livy* xxx. xxxvi. 765, *OED*]

Ukaji et al. (2000: 325–326) state that transitive verbs, such as *accompany*,
follow, and *meet*, started to appear in Late Middle English as in (38a), adding that the verbs employed should express the semantic elements of 'come'
and 'go'. I have found *approach, accompany, accost, befall, cross, enter,
follow,* and *meet*, all of which denote 'come' and 'go' and appear only a few
times in the *OED*.[20] It is unfortunate that a quantitative analysis cannot be
conducted due to an insufficient number of tokens. It is in 1841 that the latest transitive token (*there + approach*) appeared in the *OED*:

(39)   There approached them a third sheykh, with a dapple mule.

                                [1841, Lane *Arab. Nts.* I. 46, *OED*]

7.4 Summary

This chapter showed the diachronic change of the Non-*be* and Tpp constructions through the investigation of quotation texts in the *OED* as well as in
the COHA. As far as the *OED*'s dataset is concerned, whilst ordinary existential sentences expanded in frequency and syntactic variation throughout
the history of English as noted in Chapters 4 and 5, the Non-*be* construction
declined in frequency in Late Modern English, specializing in the presentative function in current English. I discussed that contemporary linguists'
explanations and intuitions about the presentative feature of the Non-*be* construction have validity only for nineteenth and twentieth century English. In
other words, it is inferable that *there + be* sentences and the Non-*be* construction overlapped in non-presentative syntactic and semantic functions until around 1800, and thereafter the former showed further grammaticalization
strengthening the nature of *there* as subject, which was reflected in syntactic
variation such as object of the preposition *for*, and the latter started to lose
its syntactic potentials, constituting presentative forms of affirmative, non-
raising structure in the main clause. On the other hand, *there + exist*, one
of the major players of the *there + VP* construction in current English, also
behaved in a similar way to *there + be* syntactically as well as semantically

---

[20] The phrase *take place* is excluded in spite of the fact that *take* is a transitive verb,
because *take place* means to 'occur', which expresses the emergence of something.

after 1950, after emerging in 1785 in the *OED*. Thus, it was found that the *there* + VP sequence came to function in the present state after the end of Late Modern English.

The Tpp construction to represent dynamic/verbal situations appeared with a consistently low frequency in the history of the English language, while it showed a relatively increased appearance in Early Modern English. *There* in the construction concerned retains adverbial-like properties as well as nominal ones in present-day English, and the ratio of its presentative use is increasing in present-day English. The restriction for word order seems to have been established only at the end of Late Modern English, which places importance on the referent, rather than its location, in terms of the value as new information, unlike *there* + *be*, whose locative phrase is more likely to come at the end of the sentence.

Thus, it was demonstrated that the Non-*be* and Tpp constructions are marked usages in contemporary English, in contrast with ordinary existential sentences. The general characteristics derived from the *OED*'s dataset were confirmed by analyzing the COHA's data. The following table summarizes the common features observed in contemporary English in the *OED*'s and COHA's datasets:

Table 7-18: Summary of investigations in Chapter 7

	Non-*be*	Tpp	ordinary existentials	*there exist*
Presentative vs. Non-presentative (Non-presentative %)	More likely to be presentative (0 to 3.4%)	More likely to be presentative (6.1% to 8.0%)	More likely to be non-presentative (42.0%)	More likely to be non-presentative (27.8% to 54.3%)
Use of locatives (%)	Frequent (33.6% to 48.3%)	Very frequent (46.2% to 75.8%)	Infrequent (26.9%)	Frequent (38.9% to 40.0%)
Position of locatives Type B (%)	Moderately frequent (15.9% to 32.3%)	Frequent (44.4% to 50.0%)	None (0%)	Infrequent (7.1% to 14.3%)
Position of locatives Type C (%)	Depending on corpus (19% to 50%)	Infrequent (0% to 5.6%)	Frequent (84.8%)	Moderately frequent (50% to 53.6%)

The above table reveals characteristics of Non-*be* sentences, Tpp sentences, ordinary existential sentences, and *there + exist* sentences.

Thus, this chapter demonstrated what kind of syntactic, semantic, and pragmatic characteristics ordinary existential sentences, Non-*be* sentences, and Tpp sentences have exhibited in both diachronic and synchronic contexts. Although ordinary existential sentences expanded in frequency and syntactic variation, Non-*be* sentences, in which the adverbial nature of *there* has been strengthened, decreased in the same categories. Tpp sentences, meanwhile, have retained both elements *there* as subject and as adverb. As additional research, we overviewed transitive verb use involving Non-*be*, which disappeared from present-day English.

Chapter 8

Dialectal Differences and Changes
in Contemporary English[1]

The English language undergoes a different developmental course in each speech community. As a result, existential sentences also change in different ways on both sides of the Atlantic. This chapter investigates the current status of *there + be* existential sentences in contemporary English by observing differences between contemporary British and American English. We will show that there are more differences than generally thought. We will also show that the frequency of existential sentences began to decrease at the end of the 1900s, presumably after peaking in written from between 1960 and 1990, in both dialects. In addition, we will elaborate on how these changes are taking place.

8.1 Differences between British English and American English

This section explores distinctions between British English and American English. In 8.1.1, it will be shown that British English utilizes existential sentences more often than American English. In 8.1.2, frequencies according to the verbal forms will be demonstrated. In 8.1.3, number non-concord will be discussed. In 8.1.4, definite use of notional subject will be discussed. 8.1.5 will conclude the present section.

---

[1] An earlier, shorter version of this chapter appeared as Yaguchi (2014).

8.1.1 Frequency and rhetorical use

First, it is important to grasp how frequently existential sentences are used in current English. Written data of the 15 genres from the FLOB and the Frown and spoken data from the BNC and the COCA are examined and compared.[2] All tokens of *there's*, *there're*, *there is*, *there are*, *there was*, *there were*, *there* + auxiliary + *be*, *there* + *be* + *going* + *to* + *be*, *there* + *have* (*had*) + *been*, raising, and others (e.g. *there being*, *there* + *be* + pp, *there is likely to be*, *there is supposed to be*) are counted in each genre in all selected corpora.

The following graph shows the results of the investigation (also note Appendix 1):

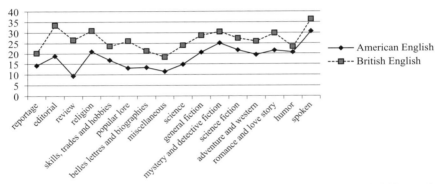

occurrences per 10,000 words

Figure 8-1: Frequency of existential sentences in Frown, FLOB, BNC, and COCA

In any genre of writing or speech, *there* + *be* sentences obviously appear more often in British English than in American English. Judging from parallels between the American English data line and the British English data line, as seen in Figure 8-1, genre may be considered a more important factor than dialectal difference in determining frequency. Nevertheless, we can clearly assert that British speakers/writers seek to employ *there* + *be* more copiously than their American counterparts in any genre.

The frequent employment of existential sentences naturally covers not only informal use but also boosted rhetorical use. We will see their very typical rhetorical use. The following examples represent two types of rhe-

---

[2] The BNC and the COCA were accessed in March, 2012.

torical use of existential sentences; see (1) and (2), which appeared as (36) and (37) of Chapter 4 respectively:

(1)   <u>There are two reasons</u> for interpolating an insulating layer between a hot working lining and the 'outside.' These are: (a) to cool the back face, e.g., to preserve the mechanical integrity of an enclosing metal shell or for reasons of safety outside a wall or roof; and (b) to reduce the heat flux through the lining and hence improve process fuel economy. Both motives may apply at the same time, though the second usually predominates.   (Frown, science)

(2)   Later <u>there would be time for</u> the pain and pleasure lust lends to love. Time for body lines and angles that provoke the astounded primitive to leap delighted from the civilised skin, and tear the woman to him, <u>There would be time for</u> words obscene and dangerous. <u>There would be time for</u> cruel laughter to excite, and for ribbons colourfully to bind limbs to a sickening, thrilling subjugation. <u>There would be time for</u> flowers to put out the eyes, and for silken softness to close the ears. And time also in that dark and silent world for the howl of the lonely man, who had feared eternal exile.   (FLOB, general fiction)

(1) and (2) exemplify the use of an existential sentence as an organizer of the discourse. Example (1) shows that by presenting how many points the writer intends to raise in the subsequent discourse, she/he can convey her/his message clearly and effectively. *There* + *be* fulfills this purpose by revealing the number of points she/he intends to make in advance. By contrast, *there* + *be* in (2) is used rhetorically to organize the text through repetition of the same phrase. A close examination of the FLOB and the Frown discloses that British writers make use of such linguistic devices more often than their American counterparts. The following table demonstrates the raw occurrences of numbering seen in (1) and of repetition seen in (2) in reportage, editorial, science, and general fiction in the FLOB and the Frown. (As these four genres almost share the same word count within the same genre in these two corpora, a simple comparison of the raw occurrences will exhibit the representative situation of the differences.)

Table 8-1: Raw occurrences of rhetorical use of existential sentences in FLOB and Frown

	Reportage Numbering	Reportage Repetition	Editorial Numbering	Editorial Repetition	Science Numbering	Science Repetition	General Fiction Numbering	General Fiction Repetition
FLOB	1	1	2	1	6	12	0	5
Frown	0	0	0	1	3	6	0	1

These four genres were selected based on the assumption that the writer will attempt to use numbering and repetition strategy in order to make an editorial and academic point more effectively and to describe scenes more rhetorically in reportage and general fiction than in the other genres. Indeed, numbering and repetition occur more abundantly for these four genres in the FLOB than in the Frown, except for repetitious editorial use.

In addition, inversion is another rhetorical use. Inversion, as seen in (3), is more often encountered in British English than in American English. Inversion of this kind certainly adds rhetorical impact to the discourse, as shown in Table 8-2:

(3) Had there been a hundred stacked corpses in there it would have been a less gruesome sight. (Frown, mystery and general fiction)

Table 8-2: Raw occurrences of inversion

	FLOB	Frown
Inversion	10	6

Evidently, British writers are more inclined to take advantage of the rhetorical use of existential sentences than American writers.

This subsection has shown that existential sentences are utilized more abundantly in British English than in American English. There are, of course, a number of linguistic strategies and devices available for organizing texts, but British writers are more likely to operate the *there + be* construction to achieve that aim.

8.1.2 Verbal form

It is intriguing to consider what kind of linguistic elements contributes to creating the distinction of frequency between the two standard varieties. An in-depth investigation into how each verbal form, i.e. *there's*, *there is*, *there are*, *there was*, and *there were*, comprises textual formation may enable us to identify what causes the differences in characteristics between British English and American English.

One point of caution should be taken into consideration. As shown in Figure 8-1, occurrences greatly fluctuate according to genre in the FLOB and the Frown: the frequency of existential sentences varies between 18 and 36 occurrences per 10,000 words in British English, and between 9 and 30 occurrences per 10,000 words in American English. Moreover, the sizes of the sub-corpora that represent each genre differ drastically: they vary between 12,000 words (i.e. science fiction) and 160,000 words (i.e. science). Therefore, an analysis of the data from the FLOB and the Frown combined would not render accurate results, because some large-sized sub-corpora, such as science (160,000 words), have a more decisive impact on the calculation of frequency than others and thus may distort the real outcome. For this reason, I determined the average frequencies for the 15 genres according to verbal form as part of the process of calculating frequencies in the FLOB and Frown, as shown in the following table (highlighted ratios are higher than the total ratio of 1.60; see Appendix 1):[3]

Table 8-3: Occurrences of existential sentences according to verbal forms in writing

	FLOB	Frown	Br/Am Ratio
there's	1.8	1.8	1.03
there is	6.2	3.4	1.81
there are	3.9	2.5	1.56
there was	6.6	3.4	1.96
there were	2.3	2.1	1.12
there + modal + *be*	2.2	1.6	1.39
there + *have* + *been*	1.2	0.6	1.96
others	0.7	0.3	0.78
total**	25.0	15.7	1.60

t=1.824, df=28 **p<.05   occurrences per 10,000 words

The ratio of the total number of occurrences of *there* + *be* in British English (25.0 occurrences per 10,000 words) to the number of occurrences in American English (15.7 occurrences per 10,000 words) is 1.60 on average. The

---

[3] The tokens of *there're* and *there* + *be* + *going* + *to* + *be* are included in the category of 'others' because of their low occurrences.

difference in total occurrences proved to be statistically significant.[4] It is clear that *there + is* and *there + was*, in particular, are used more abundantly in British English (6.2 and 6.6 occurrences per 10,000 words respectively) than in American English (3.4 and 3.4 occurrences per 10,000 words respectively), as the ratios of British English to American English (1.81 and 1.96 respectively) substantially exceed that of the total number of occurrences (1.60). Present perfective *there + have + been* likewise shows a higher frequency in British English than in American English. This finding leads to the conclusion that the frequent use of *there + is*, *there + was*, and *there + have + been* is characteristic of British English in written texts. From now on, to focus on the five verbal forms, the tokens with auxiliary elements will be excluded from the analysis.

Next, the written data will be investigated according to genre. It is effective to examine fiction and academic writing by using the BNC and the COCA, both of which boast ample word counts, since these enable research into frequency according to verbal form as well as genre. I selected these two genres from among the written texts because the style of fiction appears to be the most similar to speech among all writing categories in the two corpora, owing to its narrative nature and inclusion of people's conversation, whereas academic writing differs the most from speech in terms of its distinct difference in information-density and the writer's detachedness, as shown in the following table (the marked ratios of American English to British English exceed the overall ratio of 1.44 in fiction and 1.89 in academic respectively; also see Appendix 1):

---

[4] The *t*-test score was calculated based on the total occurrences of each group among the 15 genres.

Table 8-4: Frequency according to verbal forms

	BNC Fiction	COCA Fiction	Br/Am Ratio	BNC Academic	COCA Academic	Br/Am Ratio
there's	4.4	3.6	1.22	0.2	0.3	0.67
there is	2.1	2	1.05	9.6	4.7	2.04
there are	1.6	1.5	1.07	5.4	2.9	1.86
there was	10.9	6.2	1.76	3.7	1.8	2.06
there were	3.2	2.3	1.39	2.1	2	1.05
there + modal + *be*	0.5	0.3	1.67	1.7	0.5	3.40
there + *have* + *been*	0.8	0.4	2.00	1.2	0.5	2.40
there + *be* + *going* + *to* + *be*	0.03	0.04	0.75	0.01	0.01	1.00
others	0.3	0.2	1.50	0.5	0.2	2.50
total	23.83	16.54	1.44	24.41	12.91	1.89

occurrences per 10,000 words (accessed in March, 2012)[5]

The results in Table 8-4 clearly show that the BNC makes more frequent use of existential sentences than the COCA for both genres. In fiction, British English evidently employs *there was* much more frequently than does American English, whereas in academic, the former uses *there is* and *there was* more often than the latter does. Therefore, we can confirm that the abundant use of singular verb forms characterizes British English.

Next, the speech data in the BNC, the COCA, the UKspoken, and the SBCSAE will be analyzed. Before details can be discussed, we need to address the following four points. First, spoken data in the COCA is basically comprised of transcripts of TV talk shows, thus lacking variety of genre, and may be very formal owing to the public setting. Second, the BNC consists of two parts that contain various contexts and topics, namely, dialogue and monologue spoken mainly in standard English (6.85 million words) and dialogue in many regional varieties (4.9 million words). Third, the data in the UKspoken sub-corpus (7.9 million words) from WordBanks is informal according to its description: it contains speech by an equal number of male and female participants recorded from telephone calls, service encounters, discussions, consultations, lectures, radio phone-ins, research interviews, television discussion, etc. In fact, Yaguchi (2010b) found that the UKspoken is more informal than the BNC. Fourth, the SBCSAE (249,000 words) com-

---

[5] I retrieved 1,000 tokens of *there's*, *there is*, *there are*, *there was*, *there were*, *there* + modal + *be*, *there* + *have* + *been* and then discarded the tokens which do not form existential sentences. Afterwards, I calculated the frequencies.

piles both formal and informal texts, such as telephone conversations, card games, food preparation, on-the-job talk, classroom lectures, sermons, story-telling, town hall meetings, and tour-guide speech. Hence, it is noteworthy that these four speech corpora correspond neither in terms of genre nor in terms of formality.

First, we will examine frequency according to verbal form. The following table shows the results (also see Appendix 1):

Table 8-5: Frequency of existential sentences according to verbal forms in speech[6]

	BNC Spoken	COCA Spoken	UKspoken	SBCSAE
there's	16.2	9.7	17.8	15.7
there is	4.5	5.1	4.6	3.1
there are	4.3	6.1	4.5	2.8
there was	6.2	4.5	6.8	5.9
there were	1.8	2.1	2.3	1.5
there + auxiliary + *be*	1.3	1.2	0.7	1.3
there + *have* + *been*	0.8	1.4	0.8	0.4
there + *be* + *going to* + *be*	0.2	0.4	0.2	0.7
others	1	0.2	0.7	0.4
total	36.3	30.7	38.4	31.7

occurrences per 10,000 words (accessed in March, 2012)

Table 8-5 confirms that overall frequency in speech is higher than in writing (all corpora show more than 30 occurrences per 10,000 words in Table 8-5; all corpora show less than 30 occurrences per 10,000 words in Tables 8-3 and 8-4) and that British English uses existential sentences more often in speech than American English, although the difference between the two dialects is smaller in speech. In fact, the ratio of total occurrences of the UKspoken, which contains the highest occurrences, to those of the COCA, which contains the lowest occurrences, is 1.25, whereas that of the FLOB and Frown is 1.60. The disparateness between British English and American

---

[6] I retrieved 3,000 tokens of each verbal from for the UKspoken using the Shogakukan Corpus Network and 1,000 tokens of each verbal for the BNC's and COCA's spoken sub-corpora and discarded irrelevant tokens. Then I calculated the frequencies. Therefore, the figures in Table 8-5, other than those of the SBCSAE, are all projected frequencies. The detailed data of the UKspoken appear in Section 5.4 of Chapter 5.

English that the analysis of written data disclosed, namely, the more frequent use of singular verbal forms of *there's* and *there was* by British English as opposed to American English, can be attested by the above-mentioned speech data. On the other hand, as far as *there is* is concerned, the COCA uses it the most.

Here, it is interesting to see the above data from a different perspective, although the analysis followed is irrelevant to the distinction between British English and American English. I calculated the percentages of each verbal form in the four corpora as shown in the following table:

Table 8-6: Percentage of existential sentences according to verbal forms in speech   (accessed in March, 2012)

	BNC Spoken	COCA Spoken	WordBanks UKspoken	SBCSAE
there's	44.6%	31.6%	46.4%	49.5%
there is	12.4%	16.6%	12.0%	9.8%
there are	11.8%	19.9%	11.7%	8.8%
there was	17.1%	14.7%	17.7%	18.6%
there were	5.0%	6.8%	6.0%	4.7%
there + auxiliary + *be*	3.6%	3.9%	1.8%	4.1%
there + *have* + *been*	2.2%	4.6%	2.1%	1.3%
there + *be* + *going to* + *be*	0.6%	1.3%	0.5%	2.2%
others	2.8%	0.7%	1.8%	1.3%

Speech clearly demonstrates a unique characteristic: the use of *there's* is very frequent in any (sub-)corpus. By contrast, the distribution within the same dialect shows a broad distinction between the COCA and the SBCSAE: the highest use of *there is* and *there are* in the COCA contrasts with the lowest use of them in the SBCSAE. The abundant use of *there is* and *there are* in the COCA is rather similar to their occurrence in academic texts, as seen in Table 8-4. In addition, the breakdowns shown in Table 8-6 suggest that objectivity/formality increases in the order of the SBCSAE, the UKspoken, the BNC, and the COCA, when one assumes that the frequent use of *there is* and *there are* and the infrequent use of *there's* and *there was* is an indicator of objectivity/formality, as it is in writing. In this sense, *there's* and *there was* make a great contribution to the formation of interactive, dynamic texts in speech.

8.1.3 Number disagreement

It is significant to investigate number disagreement. As discussed in Chapters 5 and 6, *there's* and the notional subject often disagree in number in speech, as seen in (4) (e.g. Quirk et al. 1985: 1405, DeWolf 1992, Meechan & Foley 1994, Carter 1999, Cheshire 1999, Crawford 2005, *inter alia*):

(4) There's a few people now and then going past, but no one stops ...

(BNC, spoken)

As mentioned in Chapters 5 and 6, Breivik & Martínez-Insua (2008) provide an explanation for this phenomenon, stating that the phrase *there's* is recognized as a single phrase after a long process of the grammaticalization of the sequence *there + be* or the existential *there* itself, thereby disagreeing with the notional subject in number. Hence, it is important to compare the disagreement rates and investigate the dialectal differences in the two standard varieties of English. Because of the nature of the writing they represent, disagreement rarely occurs in the FLOB and the Frown; therefore, the present analysis examines speech data from the BNC and the COCA, the UK-spoken in WordBanks, and the SBCSAE, as shown in the following table:

Table 8-7: Disagreement rate according to verbal forms in speech (%)

	BNC Spoken	COCA Spoken	UKspoken	SBCSAE
there's	14.1	12.7	21.3	24.5
there is	4.0	2.7	3.4	5.6
there are	0.9	0.2	1.0	0
there was	15.8	5.4	12.5	15.9
there were	0.8	0.4	3.0	0

(accessed in March, 2012)

Apparently, the non-concord rate of *there's* is outstandingly high across the board, which is in accordance with its thoroughly discussed tendency. Curiously, regarding the assumption that the level of informality of a text correlates with the rate of number disagreement of *there's*, the informality of the data from the UKspoken and the SBCSAE may be reflected in these very high rates (21.3% and 24.5% respectively). Meanwhile, the COCA's speech presents the lowest rate (12.7%), which suggests the (sub-)corpus' formality. It may not be coincidental that the order of formality based on the number disagreement rate is exactly the same as suggested in 8.1.2. Therefore, this order is reasonably justified.

Apart from the high number disagreement rates of *there's*, it is striking that the disagreement rate of *there was* (15.8%) is higher than that of *there's* (14.1%) in the BNC's spoken data, despite the formality of that corpus compared with the UKspoken and the SBCSAE. The BNC's compilation of regional varieties may account for this phenomenon, as discussed by Anderwald's (2001) study, which reveals that the use of *was* in place of *were*, or the use of *were* in place of *was*, are widely observed in regional varieties in Britain. In fact, a number of previous studies have found that the existential sentence constitutes a syntactic structure that is the most prone to invite variation between *was* and *were* in past tense among any variety of English in the world. For instance, Tagliamonte (1998) and Tagliamonte & Baayen (2012) report that the forms of *there* + *was* + plural notional subject and *there* + *were* + *not* + singular notional subject are ubiquitously prevalent, regardless of regional distance. However, Anderwald (2001) states that speakers aged between 35 to 59 in the London area, whose variety may be closest to standard English, have a clear preference for *were* generalization, not *was* generalization. This variation factor may have intruded the data presented in Table 8-7, rendering the frequency of disagreement of *there was* remarkably high, as the data of regional varieties comprises 41.7% of the BNC's spoken sub-corpus. Yet, while the BNC's formal spoken settings, such as education and business, account for 58.3% of the total word count of the spoken data, 15.8% of non-concord regarding *there was* tokens is still high. Evidently, the 15.9% of the SBCSAE is also high, whereas the 12.5% of the UKspoken is relatively high. It would be practical and reasonable to assert that standard English is inclined to allow the fusion of *there* and *was*, except in formal speech. At the same time, it is notable that the outcome of our discussion regarding the grammaticalization of *there was* in British English in Section 5.4 of Chapter 5 is confirmed in informal American English as well.

8.1.4   Interpersonal function

This subsection explores how often lexically definite notional subjects appear in British and American English. First, the underlying factor is repeated to cause the use of definite notional subjects, as discussed in Chapter 5. Because the main function of existential sentences is to introduce a new referent into the discourse, the notional subject usually takes on an indefinite form. However, recent studies argue that, if the referent has previously been evoked in the discourse but judged by the speaker to be beyond the consciousness of the hearer at the time of utterance, a lexically definite form of

NP can be employed (e.g. Breivik 1990, Abbott 1993, Ward & Birner 1995, Biber et al. 1999: 953, *inter alia*). For example, Biber et al. (1999: 953) maintain that one of the discoursal effects of the existential *there* followed by a definite notional subject is "to bring something already known back to mind, rather than asserting that it exists," as seen in (5) (previously (12) of Chapter 5):

(5)   "Do you know the town of Makara? Is there a medical station there?" But he said that Makara patients had always been brought to him at Kodowa. There wasn't even a trained nurse, only a couple of midwives. Then he brightened. "There is the cotton factory," he said. (fiction)   (Biber et al. 1999: 953)

The interaction between the speaker/writer and the listener/reader is indeed entailed in the employment of a definite notional subject, in that the speaker/writer signals a message of which the listener/reader should also know the referent, in contrast to the discoursal function that provides an objective introduction to a new referent, as seen in (4). Furthermore, list *there*-sentences that were discussed in Chapters 5 and 6 often also involve definite notional subjects, the usage of which sends a similar signal to the listener. Interestingly, the present study has found that the definite form of notional subject appears more frequently in writing in British English than in American English, as shown in the following table:

Table 8-8: Frequency of definite notional subjects[7]

FLOB	Frown	Ratio Br/Am
1.20	0.67	1.79

occurrences per 10,000 words

Compared to the ratio (1.60) of the total occurrences of existential sentences in the FLOB to the total occurrences of existential sentences in the Frown, as seen in the discussion relevant to Table 8-3, the ratio 1.79 above in Table 8-8 may be considered high. It is clear that more existential sentences are used in interactive modes in writing in British English than in American English.

The following table demonstrates the difference in genre and verbal forms in the BNC, the COCA, the UKspoken data in WordBanks, and the

---

[7] The figures are the average occurrences in 15 genres. The raw occurrences are 108 in FLOB and 62 in Frown. If it is calculated based upon the raw occurrences, the ratio of British English to American English is 1.74.

SBCSAE (the occurrences of highlighted frequencies exceed 0.5 per 10,000 words):

Table 8-9: Frequency of definite notional subjects

	BNC Spoken	COCA Spoken	WordBanks UKspoken	SBCSAE	BNC Fiction	COCA Fiction	BNC Academic	COCA Academic
there's	1.37	0.6	1.54	1.29	0.39	0.3	0	0
there is	0.26	0.25	0.35	0.16	0.1	0.12	0.51	0.18
there are	0.11	0.13	0.09	0	0.06	0.03	0.07	0.04
there was	0.56	0.39	0.65	0.32	0.75	0.47	0.12	0.05
there were	0.07	0.07	0.1	0.04	0.19	0.09	0.04	0.01
total	2.37	1.44	2.73	1.81	1.49	1.01	0.74	0.28

occurrences per 10,000 words (accessed in March, 2012)

The examination of the occurrences of definite notional subject use has evidently disclosed the following four points: (i) within the same dialect, speech employs more definite notional subjects than writing; (ii) British English' speech sub-corpora contain higher occurrences than American English' speech sub-corpora; (iii) in fiction, British English uses them more than American English; and (iv) academic writing, which represents the most detached style, utilizes the lowest occurrences in both dialects. Again, it is notable that the difference in frequency of *there's* and *there was* contributes to the distinction between British English and American English in speech. In writing, too, *there was* and *there is* differ in frequency, appearing more often in fiction and in academic respectively. Therefore, it can be concluded that the interactive use of *there + be*, especially in the singular forms of verb, is employed more frequently in British English than in American English.

8.1.5   Summary

A clear difference was found in the use of existential sentences between British English and American English in writing from the 1980s to the 1990s. The former makes more frequent use of existential sentences than the latter, particularly in singular verbal forms, thus exhibiting more rhetorical employment to organize texts or add archaic nuance to them, and more interpersonal utilization. In speech, although number disagreement does not differ significantly between the two standard varieties, British English makes more use of existential sentences and definite notional subjects than American English. The singular verbal forms make the differences.

8.2 Change in present-day English

This section clarifies how existential sentences are changing in the late twentieth century. First, a comparison of the written data in the LOB and the Brown, which both represent English from the 1960s, will be made with the written data in the FLOB and the Frown, which both represent English from the 1990s, in order to investigate how existential sentences changed as part of the diachronic transition of the two dialects in the 30-year span of the latter half of the twentieth century. The frequencies according to the genre of the LOB and the Brown are shown in the following graph (also note Appendix 1):

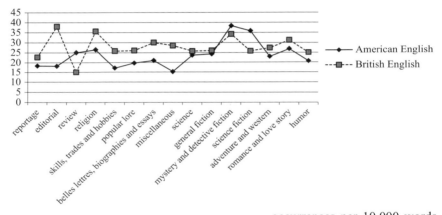

occurrences per 10,000 words

Figure 8-2: Frequency of existential sentences in LOB and Brown

The overall frequencies of both dialects are higher in the LOB and the Brown than in the FLOB and the Frown: the frequency of the LOB is between 15 and 38 occurrences per 10,000 words, and that of the Brown is between 15 and 39 occurrences per 10,000 words (it should be noted that existential sentences have 18 to 34 occurrences per 10,000 words in the FLOB and 9 to 26 occurrences in the Frown.) Unlike what Figure 8-1 suggests, the frequency of British English is not always higher than that of American English across all 15 genres. The following table which analyzed the same features as Table 8-3 shows the components of the LOB and the Brown (the marked ratios exceed the total ratio of 1.16; see Appendix 1):

Table 8-10: Occurrences of existential sentences according to verbal forms in writing in the 1960s occurrences per 10,000 words

	LOB	Brown	Ratio Br/Am
there's	1.5	1.6	0.93
there is	7.3	5.2	1.41
there are	3.7	3.1	1.21
there was	8.0	7.4	1.08
there were	2.7	2.4	1.15
there + auxiliary + *be*	3.0	2.1	1.39
there + *have* + *been*	1.4	1.2	1.17
others	0.6	0.5	1.37
total	27.3	23.6	1.16

Three points stand out regarding the total occurrences reported in Table 8-10. Firstly, the total frequencies of British English and American English are higher for the 1960s (27.3 and 23.6 occurrences per 10,000 words respectively) than for the 1990s (25.7 and 15.7 occurrences per 10,000 words respectively). Although the difference between the FLOB and the LOB was not statistically significant ($t = 0.750$, df = 28, $p > .05$), the Frown and the Brown show statistical significance regarding their differences in total occurrences ($t = 3.544$, df = 28, $**p < .01$). American English evidently reduced the use of existential sentences significantly. Secondly, the difference in total frequency between British English and American English from the 1960s is not as large as the ratio of 1.16 suggests (the statistical significance was not obtained: $t = 0.640$, df = 28, $p > .05$). Compared to the ratio of the 1990s, which is 1.60 (British English to American English), the close scrutiny of the relationship between frequency and verbal form shows that, although *there is* and *there are* are used relatively often in British English, hardly any distinctive difference in frequency between the two dialects can be observed, unlike the case of data from the 1990s, as discussed in Section 8.1. However, the comparison between the data from the 1990s and that from the 1960s demonstrates that occurrences of *there is* and *there was* were greatly reduced in American English (5.2→3.4 occurrences per 10,000 words (35% down); and 7.4→3.4 occurrences per 10,000 words (54% down) respectively). Thirdly, it is notable that in spite of the declining tendencies of *there is* and *there was*, *there's* did not decrease but did increase instead in both dialects (1.5→1.8 occurrences per 10,000 words between LOB and FLOB; and 1.6→1.8. occurrences per 10,000 words between FLOB and Frown). This indicates the increased role of *there's* in current English in writing.

Next, the frequency of definite notional subjects will be compared, as shown in the following table:

Table 8-11: Frequency of definite notional subjects in the 1960s[8]

LOB	Brown	Ratio Br/Am
1.86	1.83	1.01

occurrences per 10,000 words

British English and American English from the 1960s mark similar occurrences in the use of the definite notional subject, while at the same time positing much higher occurrences (both being 1.8-occrrences-per-10,000-words level) than in the 1990s (1.20 and 0.67 occurrences per 10,000 words respectively), as seen in Table 8-8. It may be argued that interactional use is declining in both dialects, and particularly in American English.

Next, spoken data will be examined. Fortunately, spoken British English data from the 1960s and 1970s are available in the form of the LLC.[9] It is certainly possible to acquire a general trend concerning the change of existential sentences in contemporary British English speech despite of the fact that the LLC compiles one particular vernacular in the London area. The following table presents the data gleaned from this corpus:

---

[8] The figures are the average occurrences in 15 genres. Because of frequent use of definite notional subjects in science fiction, romance, and humor in the Brown where the total word count is low, the figure is rather high. The raw occurrences are 180 and 145 in the LOB and the Brown respectively. Based upon the data of the raw occurrences, the raito of British English to American English is 1.24. Compared with the FLOB and Frown (the ratio: 1.74 as in Footnote 7), the difference is not great.

[9] To be more accurate, data from 1958 to 1988 is included in the corpus under discussion. However, most of the data were collected in the 1960s and the 1970s.

Table 8-12: Occurrences of existential sentences, disagreement rate, and occurrences of definite notional subjects according to verbal forms in London speech in the 1960s and 1970s

	Occurrences per 10,000 words	Number disagreement rate (%)	Definite notional subject (%)
there's	12.9 (562/435,000)	7.65 (43/562)	1.38 (60/562)
there is	5.1 (220/435,000)	0.91 (2/220)	0.55 (24/220)
there are	5.1 (220/43,5000)	0.00 (2/220)	0.16 (7/220)
there was	5.4 (234/43,5000)	2.99 (7/234)	0.69 (30/234)
there were	2.0 (86/43,5000)	3.49 (3/86)	0.14 (6/86)
there + auxiliary + *be*	2.4 (104/43,5000)		NA
there + *have* + *been*	0.7 (29/43,5000)		NA
others	1.1 (48/43,5000)		NA
total	34.6		2.92

(raw occurrences)

In comparison to the contemporary British data in Table 8-5, the frequency of existential sentences in the 1960s and the 1970s (34.6 occurrences per 10,000 words) is almost on the same level as that in the BNC, which contains data recorded between the 1980s and 1993 (36.3 occurrences per 10,000 words). The LLC seems to contain more formal conversations than the BNC when the disagreement rate and the frequency of *there's* are assumed to be in correlation with the degree of informality: the frequency of *there's* is 12.9 occurrences per 10,000 words in the LLC and 16.2 occurrences per 10,000 words in the BNC; the number non-concord rate of *there's* is 7.65% in the LLC and 14.1% in the BNC.[10] The phrasal status of *there was*

---

[10] It is of course also possible to postulate that these gaps may reflect the change in the concept of linguistic stigma: number disagreement may have been considered to be a

cannot be confirmed by the above data, and the disagreement rate (2.99%) is even lower than that of *there were* (3.49%). On the grounds that London is an area where *were* generalization prevails in standard English in the place of *was* (cf. Anderwald 2001), the relatively high disagreement rate of *there were* (3.49%) may reflect the trend in London-area vernacular. In any event, the number non-concord rates are very low, perhaps because the speakers were well-educated and/or perhaps because they spoke formal English in the experimental data collection environment.

By contrast, the total use of definite notional subjects was more frequent in the 1960s and the 1970s (2.92 occurrences per 10,000 words) than in the BNC (2.37 occurrences per 10,000 words), as is shown by the comparison between Tables 8-9 and 8-12. It is possible to conjecture that existential sentences called more strongly for lexically definite notional subjects in the 1960s and 1970s than in the 1980s and early 1990s, both in terms of speech and writing, which implies that existential sentences reduced their interactive use. Further research is strongly required.

The present section has elicited the contemporary data that show how existential sentences decreased in frequency in writing regardless of dialect. Especially American English has drastically decreased the use of existential sentences. The data in Tables 8-3 and 8-10 reveal that the decrease in the use of singular forms of *there is* and *there was* caused a declining tendency in both dialects, but particularly in American English: the reduction of the use of two singular verbal forms seems to have expanded the distinction between the two dialects in the 1990s. Hence, the detailed examination in this section addressed the necessity of modification for the increasing tendency of *there + be* existential sentences after 1950 in the *OED*, as discussed in Chapters 4 and 5: around the 1990s, existential sentences showed a declining tendency in written texts and this decline was caused by the less frequent use of the singular forms *there is* and *there was*. However, it should be emphasized that the use of *there's* increased in both dialects, which seems to indicate the tendency that the default form to lead the pragmatic, interactive use is in the process of switching to the contracted form even in writing. In addition, existential sentences have come to function in

---

stigma in the 1960s and the 1970s among educated speakers in the LCC, which thus may have triggered its low occurrences in the 1960s and the 1970s, but it is more acceptable in contemporary English at present, as Svartvik & Leech (2006: 196) insist. In fact, further research is required to find out how the level of informality is realized with the use of *there's* and number disagreement.

objective/detached ways as a result of their lower frequency in the 1990s. It seems that the sequence "*there* + *be* + indefinite NP + (LOC)" became the norm again, after the previous inclination was observed to use lexically definite notional subjects to express intersubjectivity from around 1850, as discussed in connection with Figure 5-4 in Chapter 5.

8.3   Summary

This chapter clarified the distinctions in the use of existential sentences between British and American English and the tendency of frequency reduction in the 1990s in written texts, after they peaked sometime between 1950 and the 1990s. *There + be* appears more frequently in the former than in the latter, in both speech and writing. The abundant appearance of singular verbal forms in British English contributes to this phenomenon. In addition, it is notable that existential sentences except for ones with *there's* decreased between the 1960s and the 1990s in writing from both dialects, but American English in particular. This decline was caused by the reduced occurrences of singular verbal forms of *there is* and *there was*, while the contracted form increased in the same period. At the same time, the interactive use of existential sentences also greatly declined, especially in American English. Existential sentences became more objective in nature in the 1990s. As discussed in Chapters 6 and 7, colloquial TV, TP, T*been* sentences, literal Non-*be*, and Tpp constructions decreased in contemporary English. Contemporary English writers who have time to hone their work may eschew the use of the existential *there* itself. As a result, it was found that the directionality of existential sentences changed during the latter half of the twentieth century.

Conclusion

Because of the longitudinal history of *there* existential sentences, which were already attested in Old English, a number of syntactic variations are observed in current English: some constructions are often used orally as well as in written texts, some only remain in use in informal vernaculars, whereas others appear only in literal contexts. Obsolescent but not yet obsolete constructions as well as grammaticalized items are almost always a hindrance, countering attempts to formulate a theory. This study has demonstrated the diachronic transition of existential sentences by paying special attention to the verbal form, according to the assumption that the fusion of *there + be* as well as *there* itself has propelled syntactic and semantic changes over time.

Firstly, this study revealed the historical development of *there* as a subject through the analysis of the *OED*. An extensive period, spanning 1,000 years, was required to obtain the full syntactic patterns featured in contemporary English. It was found that while question and subject raising were already seen in Middle English, the form of *for + there + to + be* could only be observed in Late Modern English. Along with the syntactic expansion of *there* as a subject, existential sentences increased in frequency. The grammaticalized and subjectified characteristics of *there + is* as the shortened form *there's* were witnessed in terms of number disagreement, use of definite notional subjects, and resistance to passivization, when it appeared for the first time in the *OED* in 1584. The list *there*-existential using *there's* was even detected in Early Modern English. These phenomena are attributable to the reanalysis of *there's* as an inseparable phrase. All the data evidently lead to the reasonable surmise that it operated as an inseparable unit in Middle English speech, even before the emergence of the contracted form in writing.

Secondly, this study set out to prove that *there's* does not only work as a phrase in which *be* functions as verb, but also occasionally as a particle, in which the presence of *is* is hardly recognized. To prove this, the study analyzed three constructions considered obsolete in formal English and that are, in fact, used in informal vernacular quite frequently: namely, the *there + be + NP + VP*, *there + be + NP + pp*, and *there's + be + NP + been* constructions. Examination of the number non-concord between the verbal form and the NP, formality, and the choice of verbal forms led to the conclusion that *there's* occasionally works as a particle in *there's + NP + been* sentences. This fact indicates the following three points. First, despite the fact that the *there + be + NP + VP* construction's default structure is [*there + be + NP*] + [Θ + VP], the special nature of *there's* as a particle makes it possible to generate the structure [*there's*] + [NP + VP]. Second, the *there + be + NP + pp* construction is unique, in that the presence of *be* is profiled consistently, which disallows *there + be* to fuse syntactically. Third, the *there's + NP + been* construction is a variant of the *there + be + NP + VP* construction, in which along with the fixed use of *there's*, *have* is omitted after NP. This study also compared these *there*-based constructions with their *here*-based counterparts. This revealed three points. First, although the frequency of the former is higher than that of the latter, the frequency order within the construction exhibits the same trend: occurrences decrease in the order of the *X + be + NP + VP*, *X + be + NP + pp*, and *X + be + NP + been* constructions. Second, except for deixis representation, the *there*-based constructions and the *here*-based constructions share a number of syntactic and semantic features within the same construction. Third, the *here*-based constructions are likely to function presentatively, while the *there*-based constructions do not necessarily so.

Thirdly, the *there + VP + NP* and *there + be + pp + NP* passive constructions, both literal constructions in present-day English, were examined in depth. Apparently, *there* in these two constructions exhibits syntactic patterns that differ from the ordinary existential *there*. Their diachronic developments were clarified, which showed that both peaked in frequency in Modern English and declined in the *OED* after 1950. While their occurrences were reduced, *there + VP + NP* strengthened its function as a presentative formula in current English. The passive construction also functioned more presentatively throughout Modern English and present-day English compared with ordinary *there + be* sentences. It was illustrated that the positions of locative phrases in *there* + VP + NP and *there* + *be* + pp + NP passive constructions show distributions that are totally different from those of ordinary sentences.

Fourthly, it was demonstrated that existential sentences except for ones with *there's* were on the wane in frequency in writing from the 1990s, after they had kept expanding until the latter half of the twentieth century. American English exhibited a more explicit tendency of reduction than British English: it uses singular verbal forms of *there is* and *there was* less frequently than its British counterpart, which caused the decrease of frequency. At the same time, the interactive use of existential sentences also declined in frequency. Again, this reduction of use is more noticeable in American English. Hence, this study discussed that although each dialect takes its own course in the development of existential sentences in contemporary English, the two standard dialects show similar tendencies to reduce frequency and interactive use of them.

In addition, the following points were found in the process of the above-described analyses. First, the *there* + *have* + NP + pp sequence did not take root as perfective in present-day English, although these tokens can be attested in American English up to 1953. Second, the raising that involved existential sentences consistently increased in frequency throughout the history of English. Third, unlike *there's*, *here's* shows no full-fledge sign of forming a single unit, although it exhibits grammaticalizing features to a certain extent. Fourth, the sequence *there* + *exist* came to closely resemble ordinary existential sentences in syntactic and semantic aspects after 1950.

Appendix 1

Raw occurrences of quotation texts in *OED*

-1299	1300-	1350-	1400-	1450-	1500-	1550-	1600-	1650-	1700-	1750-	1800-	1850-	1900-	1950-
57,904	39,973	52,291	59,475	52,664	84,876	163,118	205,983	176,842	132,244	141,989	280,240	477,473	226,874	291,668

Word Count of COHA (Accessed in January, 2012)

1810s	1820s	1830s	1840s	1850s	1860s	1870s	1880s	1890s	1900s	1910s	1920s	1930s	1940s	1950s	1960s	1970s	1980s	1990s	2000s
1,181,022	6,927,005	13,773,987	16,046,854	16,493,826	17,125,102	18,610,160	20,872,855	21,183,383	22,541,232	22,655,252	25,632,411	24,413,247	24,144,478	24,398,180	23,927,982	23,769,305	25,178,952	27,877,340	29,479,451

Figure 4-1: Frequency of *there* + *be* sentences in *OED*

-1299	1300-	1350-	1400-	1450-	1500-	1550-	1600-	1650-	1700-	1750-	1800-	1850-	1900-	1950-
0.32	0.45	0.91	0.79	0.84	0.95	1.13	1.54	1.77	1.62	1.52	1.58	1.95	2.70	2.91

occurrences per 100 quotation texts

Figure 4-4: Ratio of raising tokens to total number quotation texts in *OED**

	1500-	1550-	1600-	1650-	1700-	1750-	1800-	1850-	1900-	1950-
adj	0.000	0.000	0.000	0.001	0.002	0.000	0.001	0.001	0.000	0.004
pp	0.001	0.000	0.002	0.002	0.000	0.001	0.003	0.004	0.005	0.010
to be	0.000	0.003	0.006	0.003	0.002	0.003	0.005	0.007	0.009	0.005
verb	0.000	0.003	0.004	0.008	0.008	0.011	0.010	0.015	0.026	0.028
existential	1.145	1.340	1.712	1.928	1.730	1.612	1.672	2.057	2.814	2.981

occurrences per 100 quotation texts

*The figures are calculated by using the denominators seen in Figure 4-5.

Figure 4-5: Ratio of subject raising of *there* + *be* + *to* + *be* (+ pp), *there* + *be* + adj + *to*, *there* + *be* + pp + *to*, and *there* + verb + *to* to total use of existential sentences *in OED* (%)   (raw occurrences)

	1500–	1550–	1600–	1650–	1700–	1750–	1800–	1850–	1900–	1950–
verb	0	0.23 (5/2,186)	0.26 (9/3,527)	0.44 (15/3,410)	0.44 (10/2,288)	0.7 (16/2,289)	0.62 (29/4,687)	0.73 (72/9,823)	0.94 (60/6,385)	0.93 (81/8,696)
to be	0	0.23 (5/2,186)	0.34 (12/3,527)	0.15 (5/3,410)	0.09 (2/2,288)	0.17 (4/2,289)	0.3 (14/4,687)	0.36 (35/9,823)	0.33 (21/6,385)	0.17 (15/8,696)
pp	0.1 (1/972)	0	0.14 (5/3,527)	0.09 (3/3,410)	0	0.04 (1/2,289)	0.17 (8/4,687)	0.17 (17/9,823)	0.17 (11/6,385)	0.34 (30/8,696)
adj	0	0	0	0.03 (1/3,410)	0.09 (2/2,288)	0	0.04 (2/4,687)	0.03 (3/9,823)	0.02 (1/6,385)	0.14 (12/8,696)

The denominators are different from the occurrences seen in Table 4-1. The occurrences of verb types are added to the data in Figure 4-5. Due to the large numbers of the denominators of existential sentences as a whole, the ratios remain almost the same.

Figure 5-1: Frequency of *there* + *be* sentences according to verbal forms in *OED*

	–1299	1300–	1350–	1400–	1450–	1500–	1550–	1600–	1650–	1700–	1750–	1800–	1850–	1900–	1950–
there's							0.05	0.14	0.09	0.10	0.07	0.11	0.10	0.20	0.26
there is	0.10	0.18	0.44	0.33	0.33	0.50	0.60	0.77	0.84	0.69	0.71	0.67	0.80	1.10	1.09
there are		0.01	0.00	0.01	0.01	0.04	0.17	0.28	0.45	0.45	0.43	0.35	0.47	0.68	0.76
there was	0.16	0.19	0.37	0.34	0.40	0.32	0.22	0.25	0.25	0.24	0.22	0.33	0.40	0.47	0.54
there were	0.07	0.07	0.10	0.11	0.10	0.09	0.10	0.12	0.14	0.13	0.09	0.13	0.19	0.25	0.26

occurrences per 100 quotation texts

Figure 5-2: Number non-concord in each verbal form in *OED* (%)

	–1299	1300–	1350–	1400–	1450–	1500–	1550–	1600–	1650–	1700–	1750–	1800–	1850–	1900–	1950–
there's							3.6	7.5	7.1	5.3	5.9	11.1	9.7	11.1	6.9
there is	0	2.7	2.2	2.1	2.9	4.7	3.7	2.1	2.5	1.3	1.4	0.8	0.6	0.4	0.5
there are		0	0	0	0	0	0	0	0	0	0	0	0	0.1	0
there was	0	2.6	1	2.5	6.1	3.7	4.2	2.3	2.9	3.8	3.2	0.4	1.5	1.3	1.3
there were	0	0	0	1.5	0	0	1.2	1.3	1.2	0	0	0.3	0.3	0	0

Figure 5-3: Passives of *there* + *be* according to verbal forms in *OED* (%)

	–1299	1300–	1350–	1400–	1450–	1500–	1550–	1600–	1650–	1700–	1750–	1800–	1850–	1900–	1950–
there's							0.0	0.7	0.6	0.0	0.0	0.0	0.2	0.0	0.3
there is	3.5	0.0	3.0	3.6	1.2	3.3	4.6	2.8	2.7	2.3	1.7	1.8	1.8	1.4	1.0
there are		0.0	0.0	0.0	0.0	2.8	4.4	1.4	3.0	1.5	1.3	0.7	1.0	1.5	0.6
there was	1.1	3.9	4.1	3.9	8.5	7.4	9.7	8.0	5.0	4.7	3.2	1.8	1.1	1.8	0.4
there were	0.0	3.8	2.0	3.1	9.6	11.8	7.2	8.9	7.5	2.3	2.3	2.4	1.4	0.7	1.1

Figure 5-4: *There + be* **sentences with definite notional subjects in** *OED*
(%)

	-1299	1300-	1350-	1400-	1450-	1500-	1550-	1600-	1650-	1700-	1750-	1800-	1850-	1900-	1950-
there's							0	0.7	0.6	0	0	0	0.2	0	0.3
there is	3.5	0	3	3.6	1.2	3.3	4.6	2.8	2.7	2.3	1.7	1.8	1.8	1.4	1
there are		0	0	0	0	2.8	4.4	1.4	3	1.5	1.3	0.7	1	1.5	0.6
there was	1.1	3.9	4.1	3.9	8.5	7.4	9.7	8	5	4.7	3.2	1.8	1.1	1.8	0.4
there were	2.6	3.8	2	3.1	9.6	11.8	7.2	8.9	7.5	2.3	2.3	2.4	1.4	0.7	1.1

Figure 6-2: Occurrences of TV sentences in *OED*

	-1299	1300-	1350-	1400-	1450-	1500-	1550-	1600-	1650-	1700-	1750-	1800-	1850-	1900-	1950-
there's	0.0000	0.0000	0.0000	0.0000	0.0000	0.0000	0.0055	0.0102	0.0051	0.0068	0.0035	0.0068	0.0054	0.0079	0.0024
there is	0.0000	0.0025	0.0038	0.0017	0.0039	0.0035	0.0043	0.0117	0.0062	0.0045	0.0049	0.0007	0.0010	0.0009	0.0003
there are	0.0000	0.0000	0.0000	0.0000	0.0000	0.0000	0.0012	0.0029	0.0017	0.0008	0.0000	0.0000	0.0006	0.0009	0.0003
there was	0.0000	0.0000	0.0057	0.0101	0.0097	0.0082	0.0025	0.0029	0.0040	0.0023	0.0014	0.0014	0.0006	0.0009	0.0000
there were	0.0000	0.0000	0.0000	0.0000	0.0000	0.0000	0.0000	0.0029	0.0011	0.0015	0.0000	0.0000	0.0002	0.0000	0.0003

occurrences per 100 quotation texts

Figure 6-3: Occurrences of TV construction according to 100 quotation texts of each verbal form in *OED*

	-1299	1300-	1350-	1400-	1450-	1500-	1550-	1600-	1650-	1700-	1750-	1800-	1850-	1900-	1950-
there's							10.84	7.47	5.77	6.87	4.90	6.23	5.49	3.98	0.92
there is		1.37	0.87	0.51	1.16	0.71	0.72	1.52	0.74	0.65	0.69	0.11	0.13	0.08	0.03
there are							0.73	1.04	0.38	0.17			0.13	0.13	0.05
there was			1.55	2.96	2.35	2.58	1.11	1.17	1.59	0.94	0.64	0.44	0.16	0.19	
there were							2.53	0.79	1.17				0.11		

occurrences per 100 quotation texts of each verbal form

Figure 7-2: Frequency of Non-*be* **and** *there + exist* **sentences in** *OED*

	-1299	1300-	1350-	1400-	1450-	1500-	1550-	1600-	1650-	1700-	1750-	1800-	1850-	1900-	1950-
Non-be	0.08	0.12	0.17	0.18	0.19	0.20	0.20	0.16	0.14	0.11	0.08	0.08	0.09	0.09	0.04
exist											0.00	0.01	0.01	0.03	0.02

occurrences per 100 quotation texts

Figure 7-3: Raw occurrences and ratio of non-presentative Non-*be* **verbs in** *OED*

	-1299	1300-	1350-	1400-	1450-	1500-	1550-	1600-	1650-	1700-	1750-	1800-	1850-	1900-	1950-
non-presentative	0	1	4	0	1	13	25	35	22	13	2	9	6	3	0
Non-be	47	48	87	109	98	167	327	327	256	139	109	217	415	199	118
%	0.00	2.08	4.60	0.00	1.02	7.78	7.65	10.70	8.59	9.35	1.83	4.15	1.45	1.51	0.00

Figure 7-4: Raw occurrences and ratio of Non-*be* tokens in embedded and subordinate clauses, raising form, question form, and negation form to total use of Non-*be* construction in *OED*

	-1299	1300-	1350-	1400-	1450-	1500-	1550-	1600-	1650-	1700-	1750-	1800-	1850-	1900-	1950-
Non-*be*	47	48	87	109	98	167	327	327	256	139	109	217	415	199	118
non-presentative	1	3	4	7	10	17	35	36	28	15	11	10	15	9	0
%	2.13	6.25	4.60	6.42	10.20	10.18	10.70	11.01	10.94	10.79	10.09	4.61	3.61	4.52	0.00

Figure 7-5: Diachronic transition of presence of locative phrase

	-1299	1300-	1350-	1400-	1450-	1500-	1550-	1600-	1650-	1700-	1750-	1800-	1850-	1900-	1950-
total	0.081	0.120	0.166	0.183	0.186	0.197	0.200	0.159	0.145	0.105	0.077	0.077	0.087	0.088	0.040
locative	0.019	0.048	0.065	0.055	0.082	0.084	0.087	0.073	0.072	0.047	0.039	0.037	0.039	0.046	0.020

occurrences per 100 quotation texts

Figure 7-6: Raw occurrences of three positions of locatives in Non-*be* sentences in *OED*

	-1299	1300-	1350-	1400-	1450-	1500-	1550-	1600-	1650-	1700-	1750-	1800-	1850-	1900-	1950-
Type C	3	8	14	25	34	61	61	69	60	29	23	33	44	18	11
Type B	8	4	7	10	24	50	50	43	43	16	15	35	67	39	19
Type A	0	7	10	7	13	31	31	39	25	17	19	34	69	46	28

Figure 7-7: Raw occurrences of three positions of locatives in *there* + *be* sentences in COHA

	1810s-1840s	1850s-1880s	1890s-1920s	1930s-1960s	1970s-2000s
Type C	76	99	64	70	56
Type B	6	3	3	3	0
Type A	15	18	11	7	10

Figure 7-8: Raw occurrences of three positions of locatives in *there* + *exist* in *OED*

exist	1800-	1850-	1900-	1950-
Type C	5	8	9	15
Type B	9	14	13	2
Type A	6	8	19	11

Figure 7-9: Frequency of Non-*be* and *there* + *exist* sentences in COHA

	1810s–1820s	1830s–1840s	1850s–1860s	1870s–1880s	1890s–1900s	1910s–1920s	1930s–1940s	1950s–1960s	1970s–1980s	1990s–2000s
Non-*be*	0.31	0.38	0.50	0.48	0.54	0.52	0.30	0.20	0.14	0.09
there + *exist*	0.06	0.05	0.05	0.03	0.04	0.03	0.03	0.03	0.03	0.01

occurrences per 10,000 words

Figure 7-9: Raw occurrences of Non-*be* and *there* + *exist* sentences in COHA

	1810s	1820s	1830s	1840s	1850s	1860s	1870s	1880s	1890s	1900s	1910s	1920s	1930s	1940s	1950s	1960s	1970s	1980s	1990s	2000s
Non-*be*	9	16	47	67	83	86	81	108	119	116	119	132	78	67	52	46	35	32	25	27
there + *exist*	7	42	94	68	94	86	67	66	74	89	65	98	59	87	56	70	65	65	25	12

* The real occurrences aof Non-*be* can be projected to be ten times the figures here.

Figure 7-10: Raw Occurrences of three positions of locatives of Non-*be* sentences in COHA

	1810s–1840s	1850s–1880s	1890s–1920s	1930s–1960s	1970s–2000s
Type A	13	39	59	29	15
Type B	27	80	84	34	7
Type C	13	53	96	36	22

Table 7-12: Raw Occurrences of Type A, B, C positions of locatives of *there* + *exist* and *there* + *remain*

	1810s–1840s	1850s–1880s	1890s–1920s	1930s–1960s	1970s–2000s
exist					
Type C	6	8	11	12	7
Type B	13	16	15	3	2
Type A	9	12	12	5	5
remain					
Type C	5	10	13	6	6
Type B	3	9	13	6	2
Type A	4	5	10	5	5

Figure 7-11: Frequency of Tpp sentences in *OED*

–1299	1300–	1350–	1400–	1450–	1500–	1550–	1600–	1650–	1700–	1750–	1800–	1850–	1900–	1950–
0.005	0.01	0.02	0.03	0.05	0.05	0.06	0.05	0.06	0.04	0.02	0.02	0.02	0.03	0.01

occurrences per 100 quotation texts

Figure 7-12: Ratio of Tpp tokens in embedded and subordinate clauses, raising form, question form, and negation form to total Tpp tokens in *OED* (%)

1300–	1350–	1400–	1450–	1500–	1550–	1600–	1650–	1700–	1750–	1800–	1850–	1900–	1950–
0.0	38.5	10.5	14.8	9.5	17.6	14.7	7.8	17.0	10.0	10.9	8.8	4.3	6.1

Figure 7-13: Frequency of all Tpp tokens without locative in *OED*

1300–	1350–	1400–	1450–	1500–	1550–	1600–	1650–	1700–	1750–	1800–	1850–	1900–	1950–
0.0	38.5	10.5	15.4	9.5	19.1	14.7	7.8	17.0	10.0	10.9	9.2	4.2	6.1

occurrences per 100 quotation texts

Figure 7-14: Raw occurrences of three positions of locatives in Tpp sentences in *OED*

	1300–	1350–	1400–	1450–	1500–	1550–	1600–	1650–	1700–	1750–	1800–	1850–	1900–	1950–
Type C	1	1	2	3	3	9	5	8	4	1	2	4	0	0
Type B	1	1	6	7	15	33	44	38	21	14	27	42	26	8
Type A	0	2	5	0	6	14	32	17	9	9	13	47	27	10

Figure 7-15: Frequency of Tpp construction in COHA

1810s–1840s	1850s–1880s	1890s–1920s	1930s–1960s	1970s–2000s
0.0700	0.0870	0.0999	0.0403	0.0093

occurrences per 10,000 words

Figure 7-15: Raw occurrences of Tpp construction in COHA

1810s–1840s	1850s–1880s	1890s–1920s	1930s–1960s	1970s–2000s
313	657	926	402	94

Figure 7-16: Ratio of Tpp tokens in embedded and subordinate clauses, raising form, question form, and negation form to total Tpp tokens in COHA

1810s–1840s	1850s–1880s	1890s–1920s	1930s–1960s	1970s–2000s
11.2%	15.2%	12.0%	14.8%	8.0%

Figure 7-16: Raw occurrences of Tpp tokens in embedded and subordinate clauses, raising form, question form, and negation form to total Tpp tokens in COHA

	1810	1820	1830	1840	1850	1860	1870	1880	1890	1900	1910	1920	1930	1940	1950	1960	1970	1980	1990	2000
negative/ subordinate clauses	0	8	20	16	32	16	29	22	35	21	30	22	30	15	13	6	6	3	1	0
total	4	53	105	152	157	130	172	198	222	272	196	236	157	98	90	57	46	27	13	8

Figure 7-17: Raw occurrences of three position of locatives in Tpp sentences in COHA

	1810s–1840s	1850s–1880s	1890s–1920s	1930s–1960s	1970s–2000s
Type C	13	28	25	11	1
Type B	51	135	177	67	9
Type A	26	36	74	35	8

Figure 8-1: Frequency of existential sentences in Frown, FLOB, BNC, and COCA

	report-age	editorial	review	religion	skills, trades	popular lore	belles lettres	misce aneous	science	general fiction	mystery	science fiction	adven-ture	romance	humor	spoken
American English	14.2	18.8	9.3	21.0	16.7	13.0	13.3	11.4	14.8	20.6	25.1	21.6	19.4	21.4	20.5	30.7
British English	20.2	33.5	26.6	30.9	23.6	26.1	21.2	18.2	24.0	28.8	30.5	27.4	25.9	29.9	23.2	36.3

occurrences per 10,000 words

Figure 8-1: Raw Occurrences of existential sentences in Frown and FLOB

Frown	report-age	editorial	review	religion	skills, trades	popular lore	belles lettres	miscel-laneous	science	general fiction	mystery	science fiction	adven-ture	romance	humor
there exis-tential	126	102	32	72	121	126	201	69	238	120	121	26	113	125	37
total word count	88,625	54,300	34,235	34,358	72,395	96,620	150,921	60,386	160,924	58,377	48,184	12,032	58,385	58,300	18,046
FLOB															
there exis-tential	179	184	93	109	182	231	334	111	388	170	147	34	151	174	44
total word count	88,595	54,362	34,185	34,265	76,336	88,569	154,924	60,370	160,972	58,329	48,232	12,026	58,192	58,271	18,101

Table 8-3: Raw occurrences according to verbal forms in writing in Frown and FLOB

Frown	report-age	editorial	review	religion	skills, trades	popular lore	belles lettres	miscel-laneous	science	general fiction	mystery	science fiction	adven-ture	romance	humor
there's	23	11	9	1	15	16	6	6	4	10	18	0	24	21	9
there is	23	29	10	30	26	41	68	22	96	16	10	3	9	5	7
there are	24	26	7	14	42	24	29	12	54	9	11	1	2	17	4
there was	18	12	2	2	18	16	46	5	30	35	40	6	46	43	11
there were	11	4	2	7	18	12	28	7	9	22	23	5	14	21	4
there auxiliary	9	14	0	7	6	9	12	6	28	9	8	8	8	9	2
there have	6	4	0	0	4	7	0	6	11	2	9	1	6	6	1
there verb	3	0	0	1	2	3	3	1	23	1	0	0	0	0	0
raising	2	1	2	3	0	1	3	3	2	1	0	0	0	0	0
others	0	1	0	1	1	0	0	1	5	2	1	0	2	1	0
FLOB	report-age	editorial	review	religion	skills, trades	popular lore	belles lettres	miscel-laneous	science	general fiction	mystery	science fiction	adven-ture	romance	humor
there's	10	8	10	0	16	9	2	1	1	26	27	0	18	18	4
there is	46	70	38	38	66	60	90	36	169	8	7	4	13	16	8
there are	35	38	14	11	45	54	53	28	80	14	8	4	15	6	7
there was	31	20	10	21	17	36	77	16	54	80	67	15	56	56	11
there were	18	5	2	14	13	22	46	10	21	17	15	4	23	9	4
there auxiliary	24	19	4	6	13	30	34	10	39	17	11	3	12	10	2
there have	4	6	4	13	4	7	18	7	10	8	7	1	8	4	4
there verb	0	2	2	3	2	0	5	1	2	2	0	1	0	0	2
raising	1	4	3	0	4	2	7	1	4	0	2	0	3	2	2
others	0	2	2	1	2	4	2	1	3	0	3	1	2	2	0

Table 8-4: Raw occurrences of existential sentences according to verbal forms in fiction in BNC and COCA

Fiction	*there's*	*there is*	*there are*	*there was*	*there were*
BNC	963	993	982	991	990
COCA	959	990	991	996	992

Table 8-4: Raw occurrences of existential sentences according to verbal forms in academic in BNC and COCA

Academic	*there's*	*there is*	*there are*	*there was*	*there were*
BNC	987	987	988	996	1,000
COCA	995	995	990	998	998

Table 8-5: Raw occurrences of existential sentences according to verbal forms in speech in BNC and COCA

Spoken	*there's*	*there is*	*there are*	*there was*	*there were*
BNC	950	941	946	994	948
COCA	919	969	980	986	991

Table 8-5: Raw occurrences of existential sentences according to verbal forms in speech (SBCSAE)

SBCSAE	*there's*	*there is*	*there are*	*there was*	*there were*	*there +* auxiliary + *be*	*there +* have + *been*	*there + be + going to + be*	others
total word count 249,000	391	76	70	146	36	32	10	18	7

Figure 8-2: Frequency of existential sentences in Brown and LOB

	report-age	editorial	review	religion	skills, trades	popular lore	belles lettres	miscelaneous	science	general fiction	mystery	science fiction	adven-ture	romance	humor
British English	22.7	38.0	15.0	35.6	25.8	26.0	30.0	28.5	25.8	26.0	34.2	25.8	27.4	31.2	25.0
American English	18.3	18.1	25.0	26.5	17.1	19.7	21.0	15.2	23.7	24.3	38.3	35.8	22.9	26.9	20.6

occurrences per 10,000 words

Figure 8-2: Raw occurrences of existential sentences in Brown and LOB

Brown	report-age	editorial	review	religion	skills, trades	popular lore	belles lettres	miscel-laneous	science	general fiction	mystery	science fiction	adven-ture	romance	humor
existential *there*	159	103	87	91	126	194	315	96	393	145	183	43	136	154	35
total word count	88,000	54,000	34,000	34,000	72,000	96,000	150,000	60,000	160,000	58,000	48,000	12,000	58,000	58,000	18,000
LOB															
existential *there*	203	201	51	118	195	229	461	172	411	152	163	31	158	182	44
total word count	88,000	54,000	34,000	34,000	76,000	88,000	154,000	60,000	160,000	58,000	48,000	12,000	58,000	58,000	18,000

Table 8-10: Raw occurrences according to verbal forms in Brown and LOB

Brown	report-age	editorial	review	religion	skills, trades	popular lore	belles lettres	miscel-laneous	science	general fiction	mystery	science fiction	adven-ture	romance	humor
there's	2	4	1	0	12	7	7	0	1	8	16	7	26	12	4
there is	45	38	31	45	47	60	99	27	142	10	12	0	11	13	4
there are	21	21	16	16	40	42	48	28	80	5	8	1	3	8	4
there was	29	9	12	8	4	30	72	6	48	82	103	21	67	77	17
there were	23	8	8	5	5	17	37	5	42	18	21	7	11	23	0
there auxiliary	23	14	8	9	11	10	31	17	37	13	11	4	6	8	3
there have	9	4	6	2	4	14	12	5	13	4	11	2	8	11	3
there verb	1	4	2	2	3	6	3	5	14	4	0	0	3	1	0
raising	5	1	3	2	0	7	3	0	7	0	1	1	1	1	0
others	1	0	0	2	0	1	3	3	9	1	0	0	0	0	0
LOB	report-age	editorial	review	religion	skills, trades	popular lore	belles lettres	miscel-laneous	science	general fiction	mystery	science fiction	adven-ture	romance	humor
there's	4	0	2	0	5	13	3	0	0	10	18	2	29	27	3
there is	47	88	25	49	87	66	132	65	156	14	12	4	11	10	12
there are	28	35	11	24	41	52	51	30	81	10	6	0	3	9	6
there was	38	15	7	15	21	38	144	20	57	68	79	13	73	102	11
there were	32	9	4	7	10	19	48	9	26	18	27	5	19	11	4
there auxiliary	34	37	1	16	19	15	28	23	39	11	9	5	8	10	7
there have	17	12	0	5	7	12	20	18	21	6	9	1	9	9	0
there verb	0	2	1	0	0	9	17	3	12	8	1	0	4	1	1
raising	2	2	0	1	2	3	14	3	13	5	2	0	1	3	0
others	1	1	0	1	3	2	4	1	6	2	0	1	1	0	0

Appendix 2

Question
a. Do you remember? Did there hang on the wall a Mexican serape? (Bresnan 1994)
b. Did there occur a sudden revolution …? (Quirk et al. 1985: 1408)
c. *Did there walk into the room a man with a long blond hair?
(Rochemon & Culicover 1990: 132)
d. ?Was there found among the ruins a skeleton? (Bresnan 1994)
e. On the wall hang a Mexican serape.
Do you remember? *Did on the wall hang a Mexican serape?
(Bresnan 1994)

Subject raising
a. Somewhere in me there seems to live an unrequited penchant for
fixedness. (Altavista)
b. There seemed to emerge a common thread of humanity and soul-
searching in all of these stories that follow. (Altavista)
c.(?)There seemed to walk into the cafeteria a very famous actress.
(Informants)
d. There seems to be found among the ruins a skeleton.
(Informants)
e. On this wall is likely to be hung a portrait of our founder.
(Bresnan 1994)

Object raising

    a. If this provision was consolidated in the new city centre college, the council would <u>expect there to remain</u> a role for Stow College, ...   (Altavista)

    b. Therefore we might <u>expect there to occur</u> injustices, and persecutions, and corporate indictments and tribulations when these systems turn to evil.   (Altavista)

    c. We <u>believe there to have walked</u> into the room a man with a funny hat.   (Nishihara 1999)

    d. *I <u>think there to run</u> into the kitchen the big rats.
                                      (Nakajima 1997:486)

    e.??I expect there to be found among the ruins a skeleton.
                                          (Informants)

    e′. I <u>expect there to be</u> hung on this wall a portrait of our founder.
                                        (Bresnan 1994)

    f. *I expect on this wall to be hung a portrait of our founder.
                                        (Bresnan 1994)

for there to

    a. Is it not possible <u>for there to live</u> within the same church family persons with honest disagreements about matters of interpretation?   (Altavista)

    b.(?)It is natural <u>for there to have emerged</u> at some point a self-critical voice.   (Informants)

    c.??It is surprising <u>for there to have walked</u> into the cafeteria a very famous actress.   (Informants)

    d.??It is surprising <u>for there to be found</u> among the ruins a skeleton.
                                          (Informants)

    e. *It is surprising for on this wall to be hung a portrait of our founder.   (Informants)

Tag question

    a. *There lived elephants in Japan, didn't there?   (Informants)

    b. *There occurred a sudden revolution, didn't there?   (Informants)

    c. *There came a man from the village, didn't there?   (Informants)

    d. ?There was found among the ruins a skeleton, wasn't there?
                                          (Informants)

    e. On this wall was hung a portrait of our founder, wasn't it?
                                          (Informants)

there + exist

a. First, <u>does there exist</u> an infinite number of systems capable of producing living organisms like human beings?

(Collins WordBanks)

b. <u>Does there exist</u> a reparatory reconstructive force to take its place?   [1852, *Fraser's Mag.* XLV. 325, *OED*]

c. For example, <u>there seems to exist</u> an impression that Russia has all of the works from the Bremen collection.   (BNC)

d. One would normally <u>expect there to exist</u> an inverse relationship, derived, inter alia, from the short-run production function, between unemployment and the logarithm of output.   (BNC)

e. In many the majority may have no religion at all, and may be totally skeptical about the necessity <u>for there to exist</u> any such thing.   (BNC)

f. ??There exists a unicorn, doesn't there?   (Informants)

References

Abbott, Barbara. (1993) "A Pragmatic Account of the Definiteness Effect in Existential Sentences." *Journal of Pragmatics* 19: 39–55.

Abbott, Barbara. (2006) "Definite and Indefinite." In Keith Brown (ed.), *The Encyclopedia of Language and Linguistics*, 2nd edition vol. 3, 392–399. Oxford: Elsevier.

Aissen, Judith. (1975) "Presentational-*there* Insertion." *Chicago Linguistic Society* 11: 1–14.

Akinnaso, Niyi F. (1982) "On the Differences between Spoken and Written Language." *Language and Speech* 25: 97–125.

Anderwald, Lieselotte. (2001) "*Was/were*-variation in Non-standard British English Today." *English World-Wide* 22(1): 1–21.

Ando, Sadao. (1986) *Studies in Generative Grammar*. Institution for Language and Culture. Yasuda Women's University. (In Japanese)

Ando, Sadao. (1991a) "Sonzaibun Saiko I." *Eigo Seinen* 137(7): 342–344. (In Japanese)

Ando, Sadao. (1991b) "Sonzaibun Saiko II." *Eigo Seinen* 137(8): 396–398. (In Japanese)

Ando, Sadao. (2005) *Gendai Eibunpo Kogi.* (Lectures on Modern English Grammar) Tokyo: Kaitakusya. (In Japanese)

Baker, Carl Lee. (1973) "Definiteness and Indefiniteness in English." *Indiana University Linguistics Club.*

Biber, Douglas. (1988) *Variation across Speech and Writing*. Cambridge: Cambridge University Press.

Biber, Douglas, Stig Johansson, Geoffrey Leech, Susan Conrad & Edward Finegan. (1999) *Longman Grammar of Spoken and Written English*. London: Longman.

Bolinger, Dwight. (1971) *The Phrasal Verb in English*. Cambridge, Mass: Harvard

University Press.

Bolinger, Dwight. (1972) *That's* that. Hague: Mouton.

Bolinger, Dwight. (1977) *Meaning and Form*. London & New York: Longman.

Breivik, Leiv Egil. (1977) "A Note on the Genesis of Existential *there*." *English Studies* 58: 334–348.

Breivik, Leiv Egil. (1981) "On the Interpretation of Existential *there*." *Language* 57: 1–25.

Breivik, Leiv Egil. (1983) *Existential* there: *A Synchronic and Diachronic Study*. Bergen: Department of English, University of Bergen.

Breivik, Leiv Egil. (1989) "On the Causes of Syntactic Change in English." In Leiv Egil Breivik & Ernst Håkon Jahr (eds.), *Language Change*: *Contributions to the Study of its Cause*, 29–70. Berlin: Walter de Gruyter.

Breivik, Leiv Egil. (1990) *Existential* there: *A Synchronic and Diachronic Study*, 2nd edition. Oslo: Novus Press.

Breivik, Leiv Egil. (1991) "On the Typological Status of Old English." In Dieter Kastovsky (ed.), *Historical English Syntax*, 31–50. Berlin: Mouton de Gruyter.

Breivik, Leiv Egil. (1997) "*There* in Space and Time." In Heinrich Ramisch & Kenneth Wynne (eds.), *Language in Time and Space*: *Studiesin Honour of Wolfgang Viereck on the Occasion of his 60th Birthday*, 32–45. Stuttgart: Franz Steiner Verlag.

Breivik, Leiv Egil & Ana E. Martínez-Insua. (2008) "Grammaticalization, Subjectification and Non-concord in English Existential Sentences." *English Studies* 89(3): 351–362.

Breivik, Leiv Egil & Toril Swan. (2000) "The Desemanticisation of Existential *there* in a Synchronic-diachronic Perspective." In Christian Dalton-Puffer & Nikolause Ritt (eds), *Words Structure, Meaning, Function*: *A Festschrift for Dieter Kastovsky*, 19–34. Berlin and New York: Mouton de Gruyter.

Bresnan, Joan. (1994) "Locative Inversion and the Architecture of Universal Grammar." *Language* 70(1): 72–131.

Bybee, Joan L. (2011) "Usage-based Theory and Grammaticalization." In Narrog Heiko & Bernd Heine (eds), *The Oxford Handbook of Grammaticalization*, 69–78. Oxford: Oxford University Press.

Bybee, Joan. (2001) "Main Clauses are Innovative, Subordinate Clauses are Conservative." In Joan Bybee & Michael Noonan (eds.), *Complex Sentences in Grammar and Discourse*, 1–17. John Benjamins: Amsterdam.

Carter, Ronald. (1999) "Standard Grammars, Spoken Grammars: Some Educational Implications." In Tony Bex & Richard Watts (eds.), *Standard English*: *The Widening Debate*, 149–168. London: Longman.

Chametzky, Robert. (1985) "NPs or Argument: Ecocentricity vs. Predication." *Chicago Linguistic Society* 21: 26–39.

Cheshire, Jenny. (1999) "Spoken Standard English." In Tony Bex & Richard Watts (eds.), *Standard English*: *The Widening Debate*, 129–148. London: Longman.

Chomsky, Noam. (1999) "Derivation by Phase." *MIT Occasional Papers in Linguistics* 18: 1–18.

Cole, Peter. (1975) "The Synchronic and Diachronic Status of Conversational Impli-
cature." In Peter Cole & Jerry L. Morgan (eds.), *Syntax and Semantics*, vol. 3:
Speech Acts, 257–88. New York: Academic Press.

Coopmans, Peter. (1989) "Where Stylistic and Syntactic Processes Meet: Locative Inversion in English." *Language* 65(4): 728–751.

Crawford, William. J. (2005) "Verb Agreement and Disagreement: A Corpus Investigation of Concord Variation in Existential *there + be* Constructions." *Journal of
English Linguistics* 33: 35–61.

Crystal, David. (1980) *A First Dictionary of Linguistics and Phonetics*. Boulder:
Westview Press.

Curme, George Olver. (1912) "A History of the English Relative Constructions."
Journal of English and Germanic Philology 11. 10–29; 180–204; 355–380.

Curme, George Olver. (1931) *Syntax: A Grammar of the English Language*, vol. 3.
London and New York: DC Heath & Co.

Denison, David. (1993) *English Historical Syntax*. New York: Longman.

Denison, David. (1998) "Syntax." In Suzanne Romaine (ed.), *The Cambridge History of the English Language*, vol. 4, 92–329. Cambridge: Cambridge University
Press.

DeWolf, Gaelan Dodds. (1992) *Social and Regional Factors in Canadian English*.
Toronto: Canadian Scholar's Press.

Doherty, Cathal. (2000) *Clauses without "that": The Case for Bare Sentential Com-
plementation in English*. New York & London: Garland.

Downing, Angela & Philip Locke. (2002) *A University Course in English Grammar*.
London: Routledge.

Eisikovits, Edina. (1991) "Variation in Subject-verb Agreement in Inner Sydney English." In Jenny Cheshire (ed.), *English around the World*, 235–255. Cambridge:
Cambridge University Press.

Erdmann, Peter. (1976) There: There *Sentences in English: A Relational Study Based
on a Corpus of Written Texts*. München: Tuduv-Verlagsgesellschaft.

Erdmann, Peter. (1980) "On the History of Subject Contact-clauses in English." *Folia
Linguistica Historica* 1: 139–170.

Firbas, Jan. (1966) "Non-thematic Subjects in Contemporary English." *Travaux Lin-
guistiques de Prague* 2: 239–256.

Fischer, Olga. (1989) "The Origin and Spread of the Accusative and Infinitive Construction in English." *Folia Linguistica Historica* 8(1–2): 143–217.

Franz, Wilhelm. (1986) *Die Sprache Shakespeares in Vers und Prosa*, 4th edition.
Tübingen: Max Niemeyer.

Feagin, Crawford. (1979) *Variation and Change in Alabama English: A Sociolinguistic Study of the White Community*. Washington, D.C.: Georgetown University
Press.

Givón, Talmy. (1993) *English Grammar: A Function-based Introduction*, vol. 2. Amsterdam: John Benjamins.

Greenbaum, Sidney & Randolph Quirk. (1990) *A Student's Grammar of the English
Language*. London: Longman.

Haegeman, Liliane M. V. & Jacqueline Guéron. (1999) *English Grammar: A Generative Perspective*. Oxford: Blackwell.

Hannay, Michael. (1985) *English Existentials in Functional Grammar*. Dordrecht-Holland: Foris Publications.

Harris, Martin & Nigel Vincent. (1980) "On Zero Relatives." *Linguistic Inquiry* 11: 805–807.

Hartmann, Jutta M. (2006) "Well, There's the List Reading." In Jakub Dotlacil & Berit Gehrke (eds.), *UiL OTS Working Papers in Linguistics*, 1–15. Utrecht: Utrecht Institute of Linguistics.

Hartmann, Jutta M. (2008) *Expletives in Existentials. English* there *and German* da. (LOT Dissertation Series 181). Utrecht: LOT.

Hay, Jeneffer & Daniel Schreier. (2004) "Reversing the Trajectory of Language Change: Subject-verb Agreement with *be* in New Zealand English." *Language Variation and Change* 16(3): 209–235.

Hoffmann, Sebastian. (2004) "Using the *OED* Quotations Database as a Corpus: A Linguistic Appraisal." *ICAME Journal* 28: 17–30.

Hoffmann, Sebastian. (2005) *Grammaticalization and English Complex Prepositions: A Corpus-based Study*. London and New York: Routledge.

Hopper, Paul J. (1991) "On Some Principles of Grammaticalization." In Elizabeth C. Traugott & Bernd Heine (eds.), *Approaches to Grammaticalization*, vol. 1, 17–35. Amsterdam: John Benjamins.

Hopper, Paul J. & Elizabeth C. Traugott. (2003) *Grammaticalization*, 2nd edition. Cambridge: Cambridge University Press.

Hosaka, Michio. (1999) "On the Development of the Expletive *there* in *there* + *be* Construction." *Studies in Modern English* 15: 1–28.

Huddleston, Rodney & Geoffrey K. Pullum. (2002) *The Cambridge Grammar of the English Language*. Cambridge: Cambridge University Press.

Imamichi, Haruhiko & Shin-ichiro Ishikawa. (2006) "The Semantic and Functional Change in the Contracted Form." *Journal of the School of Language and Communication, Kobe University* 3: 15–36.

Iyeiri, Yoko. (2010) *Verbs of Implicit Negation and their Complements in the History of English*. Amsterdam: John Benjamins; Tokyo: Yushodo Press.

Jaworska, Ewa. (1986) "Prepositional Phrases as Subjects and Objects." *Journal of Linguistics* 22: 355–374.

Jenkins, Lyle. (1975) *The English Existential*. Tübingen: Niemeyer.

Jespersen, Otto. (1927), (1949) *A Modern English Grammar on Historical Principles*, Part III, VII. Copenhagen: Ejnar Munksgaard, London: George Allen & Unwin.

Kathol, Andreas & Robert Levine. (1992) "Inversion as a Linearization Effect." *Proceedings of North East Linguistic Society* 23: 207–221.

Kuno, Susumu. (1971) "The Position of Locatives in Existential Sentences." *Linguistic Inquiry* 2(3): 333–378.

Lakoff, George. (1987) *Women, Fire and Dangerous Things*. Chicago: Chicago University Press.

Lambrecht, Knud. (1988) "*There was a farmer had a dog*: Syntactic Amalgams Revisited." *Proceedings of the Fourteenth Annual Meeting of the Berkeley Linguistic Society*: 319–339.

Levin, Robert. D. (1989) "On Focus Inversion: Syntactic Valence and the Role of a SUBCAT List." *Linguistics* 27(6): 1013–1055.

Lumsden, Michael. (1988) *Existential Sentences*: *Their Structure and Meaning*. London: Croom Helm.

Lyons, John. (1977) *Semantics 2*. Cambridge: Cambridge University Press.

Martinez Insua, Ana E. & Ignacio M. Palacios Martinez. (2003) "A Corpus-Based Approach to Non-Concord in Present-day English Existential *there*-Constructions." *English Studies* 84: 262–283.

Martínez-Insua, Ana E. (2004) *Existential* there-*constructions in Contemporary English*: *A Corpus Driven Analysis of their Use in Speech and Writing*. Munich: Lincoln Europa.

Matsubara, Fuminori. (2000) "*p**P Phases." *Linguistic Analysis* 30: 127–161.

Matsubara, Fuminori. (2009a) "Zenchishi-syugobunn no Ninkajoken nitsuite." *Eigogo-hokenkyu* 16: 35–51. (In Japanese)

Matsubara, Fuminori. (2009b) "Prepositional Phrase Subjects." Ms., Kochi University.

McCawley, James D. (1981) "The Syntax and Semantics of English Relative Clauses." *Lingua* 53: 99–149.

McCawley, James D. (1998) *The Syntactic Phenomena of English*, 2nd edition. Chicago: The University of Chicago Press.

McNally, Louise. (1997) *A Semantics for the English Existential Construction*. New York: Garland.

Meechan, Marjory & Michele Foley. (1994) "On Resolving Disagreement: Linguistic Theory and Variation—*there's* Bridges." *Language Variation and Change* 6(1): 63–85.

Milsark, Gary L. (1974) *Existential Sentences in English*. MIT PhD. dissertation.

Milsark, Gary L. (1977) "Toward an Explanation of Certain Peculiarities of the Existential Construction in English." *Linguistic Analysis* 3: 1–30.

Montgomery, Michael & Curtis Chapman. (1992) "The Pace of Change in Appalachian English." In Matti Rissanen et al. (eds.), *History of Englishes*: *New Methods and Interpretations in Historical Linguistics*, 624–639. Berlin: Mouton de Gruyter.

Montgomery, Michael. (2006) "Notes on the Development of Existential *they*." *American Speech* 81(2): 132–145.

Nagashima, Daisuke. (1992) *A Historical Study of the Introductory there*. Osaka: Intercultural Research Institute, Kansai Gaidai University.

Nagucka, Ruta. (1980) "Grammatical Peculiarities of the Contact-clause in Early Modern English." *Folia Linguistica Historica* 1: 171–184.

Nakajima, Heizo. (1997) "A Generative View of the Cognitive Analysis of Raising." In Masatomo Ukaji, Toshio Nakao, Masaru Kajita, & Shuji Chiba (eds.), *Studies in English Linguistics*: *A Festschrift for Akira Ota on the Occasion of his Eightieth Birthday*, 474–491. Tokyo: Taishukan.

Nakazawa, Noriko. (2006) "*There* Contact Clauses and the Emergence of Relative

Pronouns." *Studies in Modern English* 22: 71–92.

Nishihara, Toshiaki. (1999) "On Locative Inversion and *there* Construction." *English Linguistics* 16: 381–404.

Nishihara, Toshiaki. (2009) "There Jyudotai to Hitaikaku wo Fukumu there Kobun no Hasei nitsuite." *JELS* 26: 209–218. (In Japanese)

Parkes, Malcolm B. (1992) *Pause and Effects: An Introduction to the History of Punctuation in the West.* Berkeley: University of California Press.

Pérez, Guerra, Javier. (1999) *Historical English Syntax: A Statistical Corpus-based Study on the Organisation of Early Modern English Sentences.* München: Lincom Europa.

Pfenninger, Simone E. (2009) *Grammaticalization Path of English and High German Existential Constructions: A Corpus-based Study.* Bern: Peter Lang.

Prince, Ellen F. (1981) "Toward Taxonomy of Given-new Information." In Peter Cole (ed), *Radical Pragmatics*, 223–255. New York: Academic Press.

Prince, Ellen F. (1992) "The ZPG letter: Subjects, Definiteness, and Information Status." In William C. Mann & Sandra A. Thompson (eds.), *Discourse Description: Diverse Linguistic Analyses of a Fund-raising Text*, 295–326. Amsterdam and Philadelphia: John Benjamins.

Quirk, Randolph, Sidney Greenbaum, Geoffrey Leech & Jan Svartvik. (1985) *A Comprehensive Grammar of the English Language.* Harlow: Longman.

Radford, Andrew. (2000) "On Object Displacement in English Passives." *Essex Research Reports in Linguistics* (November 2000) 33: 33–49.

Radford, Andrew. (2004) *English Syntax: An Introduction.* Cambridge: Cambridge University Press.

Rando, Emily & Donna J. Napoli. (1978) "Definiteness in *there*-sentences." *Language* 54(2): 300–313.

Rissanen, Matti. (1999a) "Syntax." In Roger Lass (ed.), *The Cambridge History of the English Language*, vol. 3, 187–331. Cambridge: Cambridge University Press.

Rissanen, Matti. (1999b) "*Isn't it?* or *is it not?* On the Order of Postverbal Subject and Negative Particle in the History of English." In Ingrid Tieken-Boon van Ostade, Gunnel Tottie, & Wim van der Wurff (eds.), *Negation in the History of English*, 189–205. Berlin and New York: Mouton de Gruyter.

Rochemont, Michael S. & Peter W. Culicover. (1990) *English Focus Construction and the Theory of Grammar.* Cambridge: Cambridge University Press.

Ross, John Robert. (1973) "Nouniness." In Osamu Fujimura (ed.), *Three Dimensions of Linguistic Theory*, 70–126. Tokyo: The TEC Corporation. Also reprinted in *Fuzzy Grammar: A Reader* (2004) by Bas Aarts, David Denison, Evelien Keizer, & Gergana Popova (eds.), 351–422. Oxford: Oxford University Press.

Rydén, Mats & Sverker Broström. (1987) *The be/have Variation with Intransitives in English.* Stockholm: Almqvist & Wiksell International.

Schilling-Estes, Natalie & Walt Wolfram. (1995) "Convergent Explanation and Alternative Regularization Patterns: *Were/weren't* Leveling in a Vernacular English Varity." *Language Variation and Change* 6(3): 273–302.

Shibasaki, Reijirou. (2014) "On the Development of *the point is* and Related Issues in the History of American English." *English Linguistics* 31(1): 79–113.

Sinclair, John McH. (1996) "EAGLES. Preliminary Recommendations on Corpus Typology." http://www.ilc.cnr.it/EAGLES/corpustyp/corpustyp.html (Accessed February 2, 2013).

Smith, Jennifer, Mercedes Durham, & Sophie Holmes. (2012) "Bidialectalism or Dialect Death? Explaining Generational Change in the Shetland Islands, Scotland." *American Speech* 87(1): 57–88.

Stowell, Timothy Angus. (1978) "What was There before *there* was There?" *Chicago Linguistic Society* 14: 458–471.

Stowell, Timothy Angus. (1981) *Origins of Phrase Structure.* Doctoral dissertation, MIT.

Svartvik, Jan & Geoffrey Leech. (2006) *English: One Tongue, Many Voices* Macmillan, New York: Palgrave.

Tagliamonte, Sali A. (1997) "Obsolescence in the English Perfect? Evidence from Samaná English." *American Speech* 72(1): 33–68.

Tagliamonte, Sali A. (1998) "*Was/were* Variation across the Generations: View from the City of York." *Language Variation and Change* 10(2): 153–191.

Tagliamonte, Sali A. & Harald R. Baayen. (2012) "Models, Forests, and Trees of York English: *Was/were* Variation as a Case Study for Statistical Practice." *Language Variation and Change* 24(2): 135–178.

Takaki, Isamu. (2010) "*There*-amalgams Revisited: The Possibility of *there be* as a Particle." *English Linguistics* 27: 104–125.

Toyota, Junichi. (2008) *Diachronic Change in the English Passive.* Hampshire, New York: Palgrave Macmillan.

Traugott, Elizabeth Closs & Richard Dasher. (2002) *Regularity in Semantic Change.* Cambridge: Cambridge University Press

Traugott, Elizabeth Closs. (1995) "Subjectification in Grammaticalization." In Dieter Stein & Susan Wright (eds.), *Subjectivity and Subjectivisation*, 31–54. Cambridge: Cambridge University Press.

Ukaji, Masatomo. (1977) "Tag Questions in Shakespeare." *Studies in English Linguistics* 5: 265–280.

Ukaji, Masatomo. (2000) *Eigoshi.* Tokyo: Kaitakusya. (In Japanese)

Ukaji, Masatomo. (2003) "Subject Zero Relatives in Early Modern English." In Masatomo Ukaji, Masayuki Ike-Uchi, & Yoshiki Nishimura (eds.), *Current Issues in English Linguistics*, 248–277. Tokyo: Kaitakusha.

van der Auwera, Johan. (1984) "More on the History of Subject Contact Clauses in English." *Folia Linguistica Historica* 1: 171–184.

Visser, Fredericus Theodorus. (1963) *An Historical Syntax of the English Language*, Part 1: *Syntactic Units with One Verb.* Leiden: E.J. Brill.

Visser, Fredericus Theodorus. (1966) *An Historical Syntax of the English Language*, Part II: *Syntactic Units with One Verb.* Leiden: E.J. Brill.

Visser, Fredericus Theodorus. (1969) *An Historical Syntax of the English Language*, Part III, First Half: *Syntactic Units with Two Verbs.* Leiden: E.J. Brill.

Ward, Gregory & Betty Birner. (1995) "Definiteness and the English Existential."

Language 71(4): 722–742.

Western, August. (1921) *Norsk Riksmåls-grammatikk.* Kristiania [Oslo]: Aschehoug.

Wolfram, Walt & Donna Christian. (1976) "Appalachian Speech." Center for Applied Linguistics, Arlington, VA. http://files.eric.ed.gov/fulltext/ED130511 (Accessed March, 2014)

Woods, Howard B. (1979) *A Socio-dialectology Survey of the English Spoken in Ottawa: A Study of Sociological and Stylistic Variation in Canadian English.* Doctoral dissertation, University of British Columbia.

Wyld, Henry Cecil. (1936) *A History of Modern Colloquial English.* Oxford: Blackwell Publishers.

Yaguchi, Michiko. (2001) "The Function of the Non-deictic *that* in English." *Journal of Pragmatics* 33: 1125–1155.

Yaguchi, Michiko. (2007) "The Diachronic Change of *There* + *be* + S + V Structure. Oral Presentation at Japanese Association for Studies in the History of the English Language, Kyoto University, October 13, 2007. (In Japanese)

Yaguchi, Michiko. (2008) "The Development of the Existential Construction in Contemporary English." Oral Presentation at Japan Association for English Corpus Studies, Tokyo University of Foreign Studies, October 4, 2008. (In Japanese)

Yaguchi, Michiko. (2009) "The Phrase *there's* and Quasi *there* Contact Clauses." *Studies in Modern English* 25: 141–150. (In Japanese)

Yaguchi, Michiko. (2010a) "The Historical Development of the Phrase *there's*: An Analysis of the *Oxford English Dictionary* Data." *English Studies* 91(2): 203–224.

Yaguchi, Michiko. (2010b) "*There* + Singular *be* Construction: Synchronic and Diachronic Perspectives." *English Corpus Studies* 17: 97–113.

Yaguchi, Michiko. (2011) "The Historical Development of *there* Contact Clauses: An Analysis of the *Oxford English Dictionary.*" In Kensei Sugayama (ed.), *Kyoto Working Papers in English and General Linguistics*, vol. 1, 259–273. Tokyo: Kaitakusha.

Yaguchi, Michiko. (2013) "The Diachronic Development of Existential Sentences." In Michiko Yaguchi, Hiroyuki Takagi, Kairi Igarashi, Tsutomu Watanabe, Takafumi Maekawa, & Taiki Yoshimura (eds.), *Kyoto Working Papers in English and General Linguistics* vol. 2, 249–264. Tokyo: Kaitakusha.

Yaguchi, Michiko. (2014) "The Contemporary Change of Existential Sentences in American English and British English." Oral Presentation at 1st International Conference on Language and Linguistics, Davao, August 8, 2014.

Yaguchi, Michiko. (2015) "*There* in *there* Contact Clauses Revisited." *Studies in Modern English* 31: 45–70.

Yaguchi, Michiko. (2016a) "A Thought on the *there's* + NP + *been* Construction." *Setsudai Review of Humanities and Social Sciences* 23: 43–56. (In Japanese)

Yaguchi, Michiko. (2016b) "The Diachronic Development of Subject Raising in Existential Sentences." *Studies in Modern English* 32: 107–115.

Yaguchi, Michiko. (2017) "Notes on the X + *be* + NP + VP, X + *be* + NP + pp, X + *be* + NP + *been* Structures." *Setsudai Review of Humanities and Social Sciences*

24: 45–62. (In Japanese)

Yaguchi, Michiko. (2017) *Existential Sentences from the Diachronic and Synchronic Perspectives: A Descriptive Approach.* Doctoral dissertation, Kobe City University of Foreign Studies.

Yaguchi, Michiko, Yoko Iyeiri, & Yasumasa Baba. (2007) "Number Agreement in *there + be* Sentences and Speech Style in Public Settings: An Analysis of Corpus of Spoken Professional American English." *The Setsudai Review of Humanities and Social Science* 15: 93–105. (In Japanese)

Yanagi, Tomohiro. (2011) "On the Subject Position of Passive Expletive Constructions in Middle English." Oral Presentation at Middle and Modern English Corpus Linguistics Conference 2011, Osaka University, August 28, 2011.

Yasui, Minoru. (1987) *Reikai Gendai Eibunpo Jiten.* (The Encyclopedia of Contemporary English Grammar). Tokyo: Taisyukan. (In Japanese)

Zwicky, Arnold M. & Geoffrey K. Pullum (1983) "Cliticization vs. Inflectiona: English *n't.*" *Language* 59(3): 502–513.

Zwicky, Arnold M. (1985) "Clitics and Particles." *Language* 61(2): 283–305.

Index

Existential Sentences from the Diachronic and Synchronic Perspectives: A Descriptive Approach

著　者　　家口美智子

発行者　　武　村　哲　司

2017年10月28日　第1版第1刷発行©

発行所　　株式会社　開 拓 社

〒113-0023 東京都文京区向丘1-5-2
電話　(03)5842-8900　(代表)
振替　00160-8-39587
http://www.kaitakusha.co.jp

印刷　株式会社 あるむ　　　　　　ISBN978-4-7589-2251-7　C3082